Neal Shine

ON SUNDAY

A collection of columns from Detroit Magazine

Published by the Detroit Free Press
321 W. Lafayette Blvd.
Detroit, Michigan 48231

Neal Shine

ON SUNDAY

A collection of columns from Detroit Magazine

Design and illustration: Dick Mayer
Front cover photography: Tony Spina
Back cover photography: Phyllis Shine (Ireland); Tony Spina (Detroit)
Editor: Jim Cobb
Copy Editing: Pat Dunphy
Proof Editing: Sue Chevalier
Keylining: Terri Sosnowski
Technical Assistance: Brian Bragg, Ann Mieczkowski
Project Co-ordinators: Bill Diem, Michele Kapecky

Manufactured in the United States of America

Library of Congress Cataloging in Publication
Number: 86072034

ISBN 0-937247-03-0

For Phyllis.
Confessor, critic, conscience, helper and sweetheart.

Introduction

Cornelius James Shine joined the Free Press in 1950 as a copyboy, when he still had two years to go at University of Detroit. At the same time, he was working for beer money in the college's sports publicity department and stringing for the Associated Press.

His is a classic newspaper story. His hustle as a copy boy got him a shot at reporting; his reporting won prizes and they made him an editor; his newspaper won prizes, and he became city editor and then managing editor; his life won him respect, and he became the soul of the Free Press.

Now senior managing editor, he is writing again. His columns appear Tuesdays and Thursdays on the Back Page, and in Detroit Magazine on Sunday. No one tells a story better than Neal Shine. Here. Read some.

Contents

1. Growing up

You can tell Depression kids from certain little habits

Aug. 21, 1983

It was in the closing minutes of the annual picnic of the Free Press news department last May when the unthinkable happened.

The barrel set aside for the returnable pop cans was mistaken by some people for a trash barrel.

When it came time to collect the empties, I found that a couple of dozen of them had been buried inadvertently in a soggy mixture of potato salad, baked beans and coleslaw.

It was while I was carefully extracting the cans from this disgusting melange that reporter Ruth Seymour walked up and asked the obvious question. Why was I digging about in that mess?

"Because these cans are worth 10 cents each," I replied, surprised that an explanation was even necessary.

As she knelt down to help me in my unpleasant, but self-assigned, chore, she smiled at me and said, shaking her head: "Boy, you Depression kids."

I have thought a lot about Ruth's comment since that rainy-day picnic last May.

About how those years in the 1930s changed us in such a remarkable way that we are still marked by habits born then.

Marked so clearly that 50 years later we are still dead giveaways as "Depression kids." I suppose the Free Press would not have quarreled with an expense item from me that read: "Returnable pop cans lost. 24 x .10 = $2.40."

But the sad truth is that I would not even consider that as an acceptable option and would have gone to even greater lengths to reclaim those returnables.

My concern for cost containment at the Free Press is overshadowed by a 1930s philosophy that only fools throw away dimes.

If you spend any time at all thinking about it, you can probably trace a number of peculiar behavior patterns to growing up in those hard times.

I know people whose income levels now surpass the gross national product of their old neighborhoods, whose strange habits, products of those times, still control a large part of their lives.

People who wash out plastic bread wrappers so they can be used to wrap leftovers.

9

People with an impressive collection of margarine tubs, used foil and sandwich bags that have seen more than one lunch. Savers of coffee cans, baby food jars and cigar boxes.

People who still wash the light clothes first so they can use the same water for the dark clothes. Who believe that a tea bag is good for more than one cup of tea, even if the second cup is at the next meal.

I am proud to count myself among their number.

I am, for example, a game but inept handyman.

But when it comes to straightening old nails, I am without peer. In fact, I may have Detroit's finest private collection of previously used nails.

I may have some competition from my friend Al Buechel, a school principal in Center Line, who had the good fortune a number of years ago to get the nail reclamation rights on a load of old lumber.

He gave me an impressive selection of these rusted beauties in an old coffee can. I still have most of them, which indicates yet another Depression-era character flaw. The operating philosophy of "don't throw it out, it might come in handy someday."

My mother's garage contains a strange mix of Depression collectibles. Odd-sized pieces of old lumber. A dozen or so used bricks. A wooden ladder repaired by my father in the 1950s that no one has had the nerve to use since its renovation.

Cans and boxes of nails, bolts, hooks and screws and a fascinating assortment of curtain rod hangers and window-shade rollers.

Things kept for years against the day when they might be needed.

In my own basement is at least one legacy from my late father. An old wooden box he gave me, confident in my ability to find some useful purpose for it. It is a most substantial container, with metal hinges and a clasp that allows it to be padlocked.

Technically, according to the information stenciled on it, the box is still the property of the Studebaker Corp. It was built to ship Studebaker transmissions and, in keeping with the printed warning on its top, should have been returned to the company at some point. I have no idea where my father got it.

It is bulky and heavy and always in the way. I keep thinking I should throw it out or give it to somebody who could use it.

But I find it difficult to part with. First off, it was given to me by my father.

And secondly, you never really know when it might come in handy.■

For the young, the river's dangers and delights live on

June 20, 1982

In a time when almost nothing in this town has remained unchanged, there's an almost immutable sameness to that part of the east side we used to call "The Dumps."

That area along the Detroit River from someplace around Harding east to Alter Road, where the old Marine Hospital buffers Detroit's mixed-bag waterfront from the sloping lakeside lawns of the Grosse Pointes.

That area where litter in impressive amounts fights the wild rhubarb and milkweed plants for control of the landscape. Where canals with no names probe into the neighborhoods behind the factories and homes.

A visit back to that part of Detroit in late May was prompted by headlines in the Free Press that told of three little boys who had drowned in those waters along the east side's southern edge.

Three boys on an urban adventure in one of the few places in Detroit where that kind of childhood fantasy is still possible.

The lure of the river is no less magical today than it was 40 years ago when it worked its seductive kind of sorcery on me and on my friends. It was the place where we were forbidden to play. It was always the first place we headed for. For kids from the city, it was high adventure two blocks from home. The lower east side combination of "Life on the Mississippi," "Swiss Family Robinson" and "Treasure Island."

The Detroit River, gateway to the world, with intermediate stops at Belle Isle and Peche Island.

It was not without peril. Not then. Not now. But kids in search of adventure have their minds on other things.

In the fields near the river we built underground "bunks" with roofs of sod supported by poles cut from skunky-smelling trees. Inside we roasted purloined potatoes in smoky wood fires that stung our eyes, and we pretended to be the last people alive in the world, living off the land — at least until suppertime.

We swam in the river and crossed the canals in rowboats in the advanced stages of dry rot, or on rafts made from boards of discarded packing cases.

And we sat quietly on the banks on those occasions when police in boats scraped the bottom looking for a drowning victim, hoping they

11

wouldn't find him while we were there, but still not leaving until we had to.

And there was the time, when I was about nine, that I fell through the ice in the middle of the river while trying to walk across to the east end of Belle Isle. I remember holding onto the edge of the hole and crying while my brother Jim and Ray Mowid pulled me out.

I stood, a few weeks ago, on the spot where we had started our crossing to Belle Isle that day some 40 years ago and was struck by how enticingly close it still looked. And I was struck also by how much adventure was still available in those hidden coves and private places.

Abandoned buildings to rummage through. The old boat house near the ruins of Gar Wood's mansion on Grayhaven. Across the canal, empty boat houses from one of the old estates. The deserted canal-side shops where Gar Wood's mechanics tuned and repaired the great racing boats.

And fields, overgrown with the hardy foliage that flourishes on hard yellow clay amid the litter of a city's industry. Places to climb, places to explore.

Emmit Polk is principal of Keating Elementary School, where two of the boys who drowned in May had been students. The two were brothers. The school, on Dickerson, is close to the river, and Polk understands the lure of the water.

"There's a certain beauty down here, and it's a wonderful world for kids, especially city kids. Why there are even peacocks (on one of the estates) down here, for God's sake! The whole place is a natural attraction for youngsters, and it will never change, and I don't think it should.

"It's not a popular notion to say that these things (drownings) will happen and there's really not a lot we can do about it. But we'll never keep kids away from water or out of trees or from chasing frogs and garter snakes, and we'll never take away their spirit of adventure.

"It doesn't excuse us from taking a hard look at it and attempting to do something about it, but tragedy will still strike from time to time."

On that warm day near the end of May, I looked at a trail at the foot of Kitchener, a few yards from the Stark Elementary School playground. A trail too small for my car.

School was out, and a boy about 10, wearing jeans, sneakers and a red T-shirt, walked along that track, whacking leaves off bushes with the stick he carried.

Heading for the river. ■

War killed the rubber gun
but not fond memories of it

Nov. 21, 1982

If there was any validity to the prevailing theory that a childhood affinity for the weapons of destruction will manifest itself negatively in later life, then I would be among the world's most prolific collectors of things that cut and shoot.

Let me say early that guns make me nervous. That's why I have never owned one and have discharged them only as part of an overall arrangement I had from 1953 to 1955 with the U.S. Army. Wars also make me nervous because they are so dangerous to the people who get caught in them.

Although I do not quarrel with the motives of those thoughtful people who won't buy toy guns for their children, I do have some trouble understanding their ultimate effectiveness.

Just about every kid in my neighborhood carried a replica of some kind of weapon or other. I still attribute that to the direct influence of the movies on local street behavior. And since so many of the movies then involved conflict of one kind or another, it was simply life imitating art, although none of us understood then what that meant.

It was also possible to relate the most recent cinema favorites to the kind of fake weapons in vogue on our block in any given week. Swords, scimitars and stilettos ("The Corsican Brothers," "Son of Monte Cristo"); cutlasses and daggers ("The Sea Hawk," "The Spanish Main"); spears and blowguns (any Tarzan movie); lances, broadswords and shields ("The Man in the Iron Mask," "The Three Musketeers"). Westerns and war films provided the inspiration for a wide variety of firearms from Remingtons to rocket launchers. Sticks and curtain rods doubled as swords and spears of any description, garbage can lids were natural shields, rifles could be carved out of old boards and cap pistols were inexpensive enough so that only our side arms didn't look homemade.

Only one kid in our neighborhood — an only child — owned an air rifle, commonly called a BB gun. It was a single-shot Daisy Red Ryder model, and a BB had to be dropped down the barrel after each shot. It was common practice to carry a few dozen BBs in your mouth, spitting them one at a time into the rifle barrel. The onset of puberty can play havoc with basic co-ordination and it was our modest estimate that he swallowed about three times as much ammunition as he ever fired.

One of my early purchases was a rubber knife that sold for five cents at Kresge's. It had a black handle and a painted silver blade and the paint came off on your lips when you carried the knife in your teeth, which was where you were supposed to carry it if you paid any attention at all to how Jon Hall or Johnny Weissmuller carried their knives.

I ranged the streets and alleys of the east side, knowing that if Maria Montez or Yvonne De Carlo were being held prisoner anywhere in the neighborhood, their captors had better be prepared for the taste of cold steel, which was actually warm, damp rubber. But, I have always maintained, without our fantasies we are hollow.

There was, however, a favorite local weapon which may (or may not) have been indigenous to our neighborhood. The problem with determining that last fact with any kind of accuracy is that I was indigenous to the neighborhood and had absolutely no idea what was going on in other neighborhoods.

This little item was called a rubber gun.

Made of scrap wood, it had a barrel of from 12 to 14 inches. The wooden handle was as crude as the barrel. It fired circular strips of rubber, about a half-inch wide, which had been cut from old inner tubes.

It was a single shot pistol and was loaded by stretching the pieces of inner tube, which looked like industrial-strength rubber bands, from the front of the barrel to a clothespin secured to the handle.

Squeeze the clothespin and the rubber circle went flying toward its target.

The military, I suppose, would categorize the rubber gun as a "close-in weapon," since its maximum effective range was about five feet. Its tactical drawbacks included the fact that you could always hear the projectile coming and it was possible, by ducking, to avoid being hit. If you were hit, it didn't hurt unless you took one in the face from a few feet away, which almost never happened.

The rubber gun, ironically, was killed by war — which almost never happens to any kind of weapon.

But this weapon depended on scrap rubber for its existence, and World War II had priorities that transcended rubber gun production in the neighborhood.

I always thought the rubber gun would make a comeback after the war. It never did. ■

When Mossie got collared, we invoked the saint of torn shirts

Aug. 26, 1984

The discussion with brother Bill, youngest of the Shine boys, turned, as it often does, to the trouble with kids today.

"The trouble with kids today," he said, "is that they're operating on life's high wire without a spiritual safety net."

A product of the same intense Catholic school education as I, Bill pointed out that there was a time when an abundant amount of spiritual insurance was available if you were willing to string an array of religious artifacts around your neck.

A miraculous medal, a St. Christopher medal, an Our Lady of Perpetual Help medal, a scapular medal, a Sacred Heart badge pinned to your underwear and, for the benefit of ambulance attendants, at least one medal or card explaining: "I am a Catholic. In case of accident, please call a priest."

Go to mass and communion on the first Friday of every month for nine months, Bill reminded me, and you could walk straight into heaven on Judgment Day. No questions asked.

Maybe our preoccupation with avoiding hell, Bill suggests, was intensified by the graphic descriptions of the place from people who were responsible for our religious education.

The concept of eternity was described this way: a steel ball the size of the world is brushed by the wing of a sparrow once a year; when the ball is worn away, eternity will just be beginning. It was frightening enough to inspire all of us to take advantage of whatever means necessary to escape a flaming eternity.

I asked the Rev. William Cunningham, pastor of Detroit's Church of the Madonna, if he was as troubled as my little brother is about young people not worrying as much as they should about eternity.

"Maybe they're worrying about something a lot better," he said. "Maybe they're worrying about making an important contribution. Worrying about the concept of building a heaven, versus the concept of going to heaven. I think this is what has torn at the fabric of the so-called 'safety net.'"

"Personally," Father Cunningham continued, "I like the idea of going to heaven. When I was a kid, I used to think that heaven would be like the Riviera Theater on Grand River. All those statues and that beautiful lighting and God sitting up there on the stage."

Brother Bill likes the idea of going to heaven, too, but is bothered more than he can say at the thought of getting there to find his favorite saints sitting around waiting for the earthbound faithful to start making prayerful requests again.

I find myself in at least some measure of agreement with Billy that our young people — and some of our older ones — have failed to take advantage of that important heavenly resource, saints.

As kids, we were so convinced that there were saints who provided against every temporal disaster, we decided we needed to find a saint to keep Mossie Flynn, our fellow fifth-grader, from getting his shirt torn at least once a week by Sister Clarissa.

Mossie (name changed to protect me from the wrath of his family, which can now afford new shirts for everyone) was the youngest of seven Flynn boys, and only the oldest got brand-new shirts.

When the shirts got to Mossie they were seventh-hand, and suffered from what is best described as fabric fatigue.

It should be explained here that the nuns at St. Rose operated in the universal belief that all children, especially boys, suffered from a kind of locomotor deficiency that prevented them from standing or sitting without outside assistance.

We were often pulled to our feet by the hair or the scruff of the neck, but most of time by the most convenient article of clothing. In poor Mossie's case, that was his shirt.

And Mossie's shirts, wearied by years of submersion in hot water and Fels Naphtha, would disintegrate in a tired whisper in Sister Clarissa's hand.

So we decided Mossie needed a patron saint of torn shirts. The closest any of us could come to figuring one out was Joseph, of the wonderful colored coat.

Mossie began to pray regularly to Joseph of the Coat and was still losing three or four shirts a month.

We concluded that Joseph's specialty must be sport coats, and that shirts were covered by another jurisdiction.

Mossie agreed and decided he would just have to find some redemptive value in his suffering. It was the ultimate act of faith for a fifth-grader, and we were properly impressed.

But brother Bill still wants to know that if we had relied more on St. Blase, patron saint of throats, would we have any need for the Heimlich maneuver? ■

Growing up ethnic was no bed of roses

Aug. 18, 1985

We were talking, one recent Monday at lunch, about being different, that painful childhood affliction indigenous to large urban areas like Detroit.

About growing up with one scuffed, tennis-shoed foot in an American schoolyard and the other in some dusty village in a country you knew about only because your parents were born there.

I had one small, unapproved prayer that I uttered in grade school every time it started raining: "Please, God. Don't let my mother come here with my raincoat, rain hat and galoshes." When the knock came on the classroom door, I upgraded the prayer to, "Please, God. Don't let that be my mother." It always was.

I would have to walk to the front of the room while my classmates snickered and take the rubber coat and galoshes from my doting Irish mother, who believed that pneumonia and tuberculosis were the unavoidable penalties for walking in the rain without a raincoat.

But after lunch in Greektown's Pegasus Taverna with Jim Pikulas, Nick Krust and Tom Barbas, I came away thinking how much worse it could have been. I could have been born Greek.

Pikulas is director of administrative services for the Chrysler Corp., Krust is an attorney and president of the Greektown Merchants Association and Barbas is president of Corporate Communications Inc. in Detroit. All are Detroiters whose parents were born in Greece.

"You wanted to be like the rest of the kids," Krust said, "but it was often a losing battle. Take school lunches, for example.

"The other kids had nice, neat, symmetrical sandwiches with ordinary American lunch meat on store-bought white bread. We had three-inch thick roast lamb sandwiches on big, uneven slices of Greek bread and we used to spend most of our time trying to trade with the other kids," he said.

"And they were always larded with garlic," Barbas added, "and you would look for empty bottles to turn in for the deposit so you could throw away your lunch and buy something else."

Krust remembers one painful Saturday when his mother dressed him in the traditional Greek evzone costume and took him downtown to J.L. Hudson's on the streetcar to have his picture taken.

"The streetcar stop was right in front of the Highland Park theater," Krust said, "and all my friends were lined up for the show and here I am in this funny-looking dress and my friends are falling down laughing. It's funny now, but it was very painful then."

Pikulas remembers his first day of school at Crossman Elementary with something less than warm nostalgia.

"I couldn't speak English," he said. "My mother only spoke Greek and my father was working all the time at the restaurant, so I didn't learn any English. I went to school with my cousin that day, and he couldn't speak English, either.

"At some point during school, my cousin told me he had to go to the bathroom. I told him to ask the teacher. He said she couldn't understand him and I knew she couldn't understand me, so eventually he wet his pants. We got kicked out of class and when we got home, we both got walloped."

Krust and Pikulas were altar boys together in St. Nicholas Church at Tuxedo and Hamilton and said that even the church was a childhood problem.

"All the other kids went to real churches," Krust said. "Our church was in an old bank and the big vault was behind the altar."

"And we used to have to bring home a lighted candle every Easter to light the candle in front of the icon we had in the house," Pikulas said. "So at two or three in the morning, after church, we would all be riding home on the streetcar with these lighted candles, afraid they would go out, hot wax burning our hands and my father singeing his clothes trying to protect the flame by holding the candle under his coat."

Krust told of suffering the ultimate ignominy at his 10th birthday party. His mother served cheese and spinach pie, not a local favorite, and then brought out yogurt instead of ice cream. "I can still see those kids poking their spoons in the yogurt trying to figure out what it was," Krust said.

"My mother never went anywhere without a shopping bag," Pikulas said as lunch ended. "It was her trademark."

Then he picked up his shopping bag, which contained two large cans of Greek olive oil, two bunches of oregano, two loaves of Greek bread, a package of figs and some sesame candy.

He smiled and said: "Old habits die hard."　　　■

Can we be held in default
for unpaid spiritual obligations?

May 11, 1986

I seriously considered giving my mother a spiritual bouquet today. It still is, after all, the perfect gift for Mother's Day. Inexpensive but appropriate.

A spiritual promissory note straight from the heart, secured only by good intentions and put together with loving care and a pair of snub-nosed scissors.

The only problem I'm having with the whole thing is determining whether there's a statute of limitations covering spiritual obligations incurred in other years when I recklessly promised more than I could ever possibly have hoped to deliver.

I worry that I might be required to complete all prior spiritual commitments on which I have defaulted before taking on any further devotional burdens.

For those of you not entirely familiar with the sectarian phenomenon of the spiritual bouquet, it involved a process in which you pledged, in writing, to say prayers, recite rosaries, attend mass and receive communion for the intention of a specific person. Usually your mother. Usually on Mother's Day.

The specific numbers you attached to these various offerings were entirely up to you, and largely depended on how much you wanted to impress the object of your spiritual beneficence, and how much of your future you were willing to spend whispering prayers or reciting the rosary.

The routine was always the same. A week or so before Mother's Day the nuns at St. Rose School would pass out a small piece of paper on which had been mimeographed a number of spiritual selections — masses, rosaries, holy communions, visits to the blessed sacrament and ejaculations.

Opposite each item was a line in which you wrote a number, pledging to fulfill every promised prayer, mass or rosary in the name of the person for whom the bouquet was intended.

The piece of paper was then enhanced by a little creativity, some construction paper and artificial lace, and put together with mucilage that smelled like dead fish.

The aforementioned ejaculations were short, prayerful utterances such as "My Lord and my God," or "Jesus, Mary and Joseph," dozens of which could be recited in minutes.

This, of course, led to an overloading of that category since it was a relatively easy commitment to fulfill.

You could do maybe 100 or 200 on the way to school every morning, carefully counting ("My Lord and My God 21, My Lord and My God 22"), making sure not to exceed the amount pledged.

Since it probably took 15 or 20 minutes to say one rosary, the advantage of the ejaculation was obvious.

It is safe to assume that in the week after Mother's Day, heaven was immersed in a virtual tidal wave of prayer, the result of a sudden burst of religious fervor from kids delivering on recently presented spiritual bouquets.

I am equally convinced that within a week the pious offerings diminished sharply as nicer weather gave way to more temporal pursuits, baseball being chief among them.

Since the process was unencumbered by deadlines or cutoff dates, promised prayers not payable on demand carried little moral pressure. "As long as I do them all before I die" seemed a sufficient response to the persistent whisperings of the conscience.

But I still worried enough about what I owe to ask my mother to find any old spiritual bouquets she might have kept.

The oldest one she found was dated May 12, 1940, Mother's Day. The verse read: "May the Mother of Christ, from her throne high above, Shower blessings this day on the mother I love."

On the card, my brother Jim and I pledged five masses, seven holy communions, four rosaries, seven visits to the blessed sacrament and one ejaculation. I'm sure I meant to write in 100, but probably forgot to put down the zeroes in the rush to get it finished on time.

So I think I'll try to fulfill those prayers already promised, just in case I failed to do so in 1940, but I have decided not to commit further prayerful pledges to paper.

What I will do is say a prayer for my mother every time I think of her. Which is often. ∎

Mess with the Mummy, Indiana, and you'll wear bandages, too

Sept. 9, 1984

I was thinking about the time Lon Chaney Jr., known to the cinema sophisticates who patronized the Plaza Theater as The Wolf Man, jumped out of the fog and tried to choke Evelyn Ankers to death.

And how Claude Rains, who was his father, had to kill his own son by running him through with a silver-tipped cane with a wolf's head handle and some weird kind of star design on it, which we all knew was vital to effective werewolf-killing.

I was thinking, too, about how the Mummy, fueled by a steady diet of tanna leaves (which we all knew was what mummies ate), came back after 3,000 years to kill Dick Foran but instead fell in love with Elyse Knox, but could not pursue the relationship because the townsfolk set him on fire along with his conniving master, Turhan Bey, leaving Ms. Knox free to eventually marry Tom Harmon.

What I was really thinking about was that if PG-13 was an operative code 40 years ago, I probably would have missed a lot of good movies.

There has been a surprisingly contentious exchange of late over movie violence and just how much of it — if any — kids should be exposed to.

Most of the discussion is a direct result of the carryings-on of one Mr. Indiana Jones and has led to the institution of the PG-13 rating, a device to help parents protect their pre-teen kids from excessive violence in movies that are rated PG.

It should be recorded early in this exercise that I have nothing against ratings for the movies. I'm just glad I never had to contend with them as a kid. Dealing with my mother and the Catholic Legion of Decency was difficult enough.

The Legion of Decency had its own rating system. Class A-1, unobjectionable for general patronage; Class A-2, unobjectionable for adults; Class B, objectionable in part; Class C, condemned.

The first category always had a definite Western tilt, approving without reservation such celluloid favorites as "Pals of the Pecos," "Santa Fe Scouts," "Days of Old Cheyenne," "Frontier Fury" and "Riders of the Rio Grande."

You could always be reasonably sure that you were not risking salvation by seeing any movie with Lash Larue, Johnny Mack Brown,

Ken Maynard, Smiley Burnette or Al (Fuzzy) St. John.

The list of approved and disapproved movies was published in the Michigan Catholic, which my mother clipped and posted.

To tell the truth, it was hardly ever a problem. The movies in the B classification never sounded very good, and none of the neighborhood theaters showed C movies.

There was hardly a stir on the block when the Legion of Decency condemned Greta Garbo's "Two-Faced Woman." It sounded like a dumb movie, and Greta Garbo sounded like a boring actress.

But every now and then the people in charge of the ratings would rank a movie like "The Mummy's Curse" as an A-2, and it would require considerable conversation at home to convince the keeper of the list that murderous mummies belonged right up there in A-1 with Hoppy and Wild Bill Elliott.

In fact, mummy movies were hands-down neighborhood favorites: "The Mummy," "The Mummy's Hand," "The Mummy's Curse," "The Mummy's Tomb."

Violent? Maybe not in a league with this Indiana Jones guy, but enough to send you hustling to the back of the theater a few times to replenish your supply of Jujubes.

Catharine Rambeau, who writes about movies in another part of the Free Press, discussed the violence in "Indiana Jones and the Temple of Doom": "Every major phobia and a few minor ones are here to churn your guts — fear of heights and falling, claustrophobia, death by impalement, drowning, crushing, entombment and fire . . . snakes . . . and carnivorous crocodiles. . . ."

Now, I would hate to reduce all this to a point-by-point comparison of the "Temple of Doom" with movies I have known and loved. But every cowboy worth his spurs has jumped from at least one cliff in his career, most of the time with his horse.

And what's more claustrophobic than being buried alive for 3,000 years? They did that to the Mummy, and even tore out his tongue before the burial.

Jon Hall wrestled at least one python per film to impress Maria Montez, and whenever a canoe overturned in a Buster Crabbe movie, everybody in the theater knew what was coming next: Cut to the crocs slipping into the water, heading for the swimmers.

What I'd like to see, actually, is Indiana Jones going one-on-one with the Mummy.

My money would be on the quiet guy with the moldy bandages. ∎

Just keep your chin up, Tarzan, when you get that sinking feeling

June 30, 1985

A couple of weeks ago I was walking alone on a deserted stretch of beach on Lake St. Clair near Stoney Point, Ontario, when one foot disappeared suddenly in a patch of soft, wet sand.

A single thought flashed through my mind: "Quicksand!"

I pulled my foot from the ooze and quickly headed for higher ground, pleased that after more than 40 years I had not lost my ability to react instinctively to the threat of quicksand.

I submit that if you had childhood access to a neighborhood theater, dozens of jungle movies left some basic impressions that have not faded even though a few years have intervened.

I don't necessarily dwell on it, but I still have a quiet concern for such equatorial dangers as boa constrictors, poison-tipped darts fired from blowguns, unfriendly crocodiles, killer ants, large, hairy spiders with deadly poison in their stings, and hidden mantraps, their bottoms lined with sharpened bamboo stakes.

But quicksand always represented a special terror. Maybe it was because things like blowguns always did their deadly work quickly and efficiently. One dart in the neck and it was over in seconds.

The quicksand scenes were never rushed. The screaming victim struggled against the pulling, sucking sand as would-be rescuers vainly tried to reach their disappearing colleague with sticks that were always too short or vines that never stretched quite far enough.

Finally, the realization dawned that all was lost and the victim stopped struggling. As the ooze closed in, so did the camera.

The victim had a few final moments to contemplate his fate, then disappeared quietly into the slime.

The surface bubbled heavily once or twice and then all was calm. The final shot was of a floating pith helmet.

After a few quiet minutes one of the rescuers said something like, "Poor devil," and then the survivors pushed on into the jungle to face the next danger.

We were constantly on the alert for quicksand on the banks of the Detroit River and its adjacent canals.

There were, from time to time, intermittent reports from my friends of narrow escapes from local quicksand, but I never witnessed one, which did nothing to reduce my concern that these deadly traps were real.

On our regular treks to that adventureland along the banks of the river, we usually walked in single file, led by a trusted pal who carried a long stick, poking the soggy ground in front on him as we proceeded.

When the ground yielded suspiciously to his probings, he would call out, "Quicksand," which we would repeat in turn to those behind us, as we made our way cautiously around the treacherous area.

Shortly after my recent personal encounter on the shores of Lake St. Clair, I came across an article in Science Digest that suggested, to my astonishment, that quicksand represents no real danger to people.

The article explained that quicksand is sand so thoroughly saturated with water that it forms a suspension — a mixture in which solid particles float temporarily in a liquid. Until the particles in it settle, a suspension flows just like a thick fluid. It's possible to drown in quicksand, but you have to work at it.

"The reason it's hard to drown even in a deep pool of quicksand," the piece continues, "is that water alone is denser than the human body (that's why people float), and sand is denser still. The combination makes a body more buoyant in quicksand than in a swimming pool. Surviving an encounter with quicksand is just a matter of floating and gently swimming to safety."

I ask you, as reasonable human beings, if it was all this easy wouldn't it have been figured out years ago by Jon Hall, Buster Crabbe, Maria Montez, Johnny Weissmuller or Sabu? These were not dumb people.

Think for a minute of all those frantic rescue attempts they were involved in without one of them ever saying: "Just float and gently swim to safety."

It all supports my strong feeling that there are some things in which science should not be nosing around.

The next thing they'll be telling us is that the only threat posed by those deadly blowguns is the danger of infection from dirty darts.

Unwilling as I am to fly in the face of contemporary scientific thought, I am going to offer you this bit of advice:

If, God forbid, you ever get caught in quicksand, call for help but do not struggle. Because the harder you struggle, the faster you disappear. Everybody knows that. ■

It's about time to set
this record straight

March 21, 1982

The specifics of the dispute that was at issue then are no longer clear to me.

It had something to do with a rule interpretation in a game of alley football — traditionally a game with few rules, and those that existed usually were indigenous to the alley in which the contest took place.

Rules like "Anything kicked into Conover's yard is two points against the kicking team" or "Passes that bounce on a garage roof more than once before being caught are incomplete." It was during one of those games that some point of conflict arose that could not be resolved by shouting or shoving. So we turned to Bill Stern for help.

It was 1940 or 1941 and Bill Stern was the NBC radio sports commentator and such a fount of fascinating sports lore that we almost never missed his weekly "Sports Newsreel" program.

So a detailed letter was drafted and sent to Mr. Stern, asking him for a ruling. In a couple of weeks, we had a detailed reply. The argument was settled. Nobody protested. Bill Stern had spoken.

Afterward, everybody involved was allowed to keep the letter for a week.

But what we most liked about Bill Stern, who died in 1971, was his program and his stories. We felt we weren't just getting sports lore, we were getting history lessons.

We learned such fascinating things as the *real* reason Thomas Edison was deaf. He lost his hearing, according to Bill Stern, after being beaned in a baseball game by the pitcher Jesse James.

As Abraham Lincoln lay mortally wounded, Stern told us, he opened his eyes and looked at Col. Abner Doubleday and urged him — with his dying breath — not to let the great game of baseball die.

The stories were endless and remarkable. It never entered our minds that they might not be true. They wouldn't let them put stuff over the radio that wasn't true, would they? Of course not.

So it was back to the radio every Friday night, waiting for the musical theme, sung to the tune of "Mademoiselle from Armentieres":

"Bill Stern, the Colgate Shave Cream Man is on the air

"Bill Stern, the Colgate Shave Cream Man with stories rare ... "

Exactly how rare I learned one fateful day not long ago when Bill Davidson came to town to do research for a magazine story.

Davidson is an author, magazine writer and a contributing editor of TV Guide magazine who works out of Los Angeles. A mutual friend suggested we have lunch. We did. It was going beautifully until Davidson mentioned that one of his first jobs was writing for Bill Stern's "Sports Newsreel" in 1939.

"You wrote all those great sports vignettes for him?" I asked excitedly. "Sure did," he replied. "Where did you get all those wonderful stories," I pushed. "Made 'em up," he said.

It was probably my imagination, but it seemed that as he uttered those words a stillness fell over the dining room of the Pontchartrain Wine Cellars. An imagined moment of silence for one more shattered childhood memory.

"Made 'em up?" I repeated weakly. "Honest Abe and Abner Doubleday?" He nodded. "Tom Edison and Jesse James?" Another nod.

"You see," he explained as gently as he could, "I was just out of New York University, writing sports for space rates for the New York World-Telegram, when Bill Stern offered me $25 a week to write this stuff.

"I started out with the orthodox type of sports stories, but Stern said they weren't dramatic enough. That's when we started writing all the lies," he said.

"Some of them had some basis in fact," he added, "but not many and not much. For example, Cardinal Spellman really did play third base for Fordham. But he was pretty ordinary, and we made him sound like Pie Traynor. Do you remember the Finnish javelin thrower?"

Did I ever. The brave young Olympian serving his country in the Russo-Finnish war. Tying hand grenades to javelins and hurling them with deadly precision into the Russian lines as tiny Finland stood courageously in the face of Soviet might. How much of that was made up?

"All of it. We figured we wouldn't be getting any complaints from Helsinki with the war and all."

Davidson said he did all of Stern's writing in those days, even his assignments for Liberty magazine. "You have to understand that he wasn't very literate," he said.

But, I protested, we got this nice letter from him one time about our football game.

"I wrote all his letters, too," Davidson said. "All he ever did was sign them."

I look at it this way. The less time spent brooding about little disappointments like this, the better. Besides, I could have spent the rest of my life blaming Jesse James for Thomas Edison's hearing difficulties. ■

Knots stumped Troop 20, but reform came anyway

June 13, 1982

It was not the kind of Boy Scout troop Lord Baden-Powell had in mind when he originated the idea of scouting in 1908.

Troop 20, Detroit Area Council, Boy Scouts of America, where a recommendation from a judge or a juvenile officer was often essential to membership.

It operated out of the old Fifth Precinct, also known as McClellan Station, on McClellan just north of Kercheval. The scoutmaster, Roy Prince, was a policeman and so were his assistants.

The membership included a number of walk-ins who thought it would be nice to be in scouting and a number who were told that the next meeting was at 7 p.m. Friday and to be there — or else.

Unspoken in that warning was the specter of swift and sure punishment in juvenile court for any one of a number of high crimes available to Detroit kids in the 1940s.

Swimming naked in the canals at the foot of Beniteau; running the hoist after hours at the Hi-Speed gas station; swinging on the fire escape at the Michigan Bell office on Kercheval; playing hardball on the Lillibridge School playground under the sign that said "No Hardball Playing." An endless list of opportunities for delinquency.

It was while taking advantage of one of those opportunities that I first came into contact with Troop 20.

Along with a couple of friends, I was collared while hopping slow-moving freight cars on the Detroit Terminal Railroad tracks near the Chrysler Jefferson plant.

We were taken in a police car to McClellan Station to answer for our violation of the railroad's property rights.

In all honesty, we did not consider it as big a deal as the police apparently did. It seemed the trains in that area never went faster than five miles an hour and we did not feel as though we had somehow had a part in disrupting America's transportation lifeline.

At the station we were taken before the juvenile officer who, by everything we could figure out, hated kids. He referred to us in terms that lead me now to believe that he did not have his master's degree in social work. One of the appellations I still remember — and the most printable — was "candidates for electrocution."

27

He then enrolled us in Troop 20, effective the following Friday, 7 p.m. It was the beginning of a series of beautiful friendships, memories of which still linger.

A few weeks ago I sat down to lunch with a couple of veterans of Troop 20, Bill Vasilides and Peter Bakalis. Both of them insisted that their membership was entirely voluntary and not mandated by any segment of the criminal justice system. I print that disclaimer here to protect their reputations with the Corps of Engineers, where Vasilides is a civil engineer, and Ford Motor Co., where Bakalis is a purchasing executive.

We dredged up as many memories as we could, filling in for each other the empty spaces created by the passage of years.

We talked of the time we were all awarded the Gen. Eisenhower medal for our contributions to the war effort for collecting old newspapers. Actually, we collected newspapers and sold them to salvage companies as a means of raising money.

We also buried most of the troop under the papers in the back of the truck when it was being weighed at the wastepaper yard in order to enhance the ultimate payoff. There was some feeling that we had tricked Ike into sending us the medal, but he was winning the war and we were contributing some wastepaper to the cause, just not as much as Ike or the guy who owned the wastepaper company thought.

We talked of the way the lives of those old Boy Scouts turned out. One was an architect, another a lawyer, one a city assessor in a Detroit suburb. There was a gas station owner, a tool and die maker, a commercial artist, a couple of policemen, a fire department lieutenant. None, as far as we knew, ended up in jail.

We talked of Roy Prince, who died in 1971, and wondered why he bothered with a bunch of kids who never learned to tie the knots, the points of the compass or the Morse Code. Who embarrassed him regularly at every scouting event by finishing last in whatever we competed in. Who demonstrated their competitive spirit at these events by trying to start fights with other troops, knowing that their scouting talents had limits but that they could probably finish first in fighting.

We decided, after a while, that maybe he did it because he saw something in us that we didn't see in ourselves. And we decided that we kind of liked that. ■

Let me be the first to leak my employment history

Aug. 8, 1982

There are times when I feel that there are demonstrable drawbacks to working for the Free Press for more than 30 years.

It has nothing to do with the quality of the work situation here or the character of the people I have worked with over the years. The work has never involved any activity that would hurt your back, and my colleagues have been, with a few magnificent exceptions, nice people to be around.

Still I feel unfulfilled when I am completing the personal history portion of any kind of official document or loan application and I am required to list my "employment history" in the 10 or 12 spaces allotted for that information. I am troubled because the phrase "Detroit Free Press, 1950-present," conveys so little sense of history — and uses up only one space.

I have had other jobs, heaven knows, but never listed them even though I always felt the document would look ever so much better with all those spaces filled.

So it is time I filled those gaps in my life as an employe.

1942. Several weeks. Sadler's Drugs, E. Jefferson and Hillger. Salary: 12.5 cents an hour (an inducement to work an even number of hours each day since Mr. Sadler always resolved the .5 cents difference in favor of the company). Duties: General cleanup and pest control. Reason for leaving: Mrs. Sadler didn't think I worked very hard. Allowed to resign. Comments: Lost enthusiasm for position when it became clear that security on the soda fountain was impossible to breach.

1944. February to May. Sullivan's Meat Market, E. Jefferson near Gray. Salary: 35 cents an hour. Duties: Egg-washing and product quality control, hot dog division. Eliminated hen-house residue from eggs and removed from hot dogs any colors not indigenous to that product and which might impact negatively on consumer confidence in frankfurters. Reason for leaving: Accumulated more than $7 in savings, enough for the fielder's glove, Bruce Campbell autograph model, on sale at Tool Shop Sporting Goods. Told Mr. Sullivan job was interfering with my ability to make good grades. Small lie. Actually, job was interfering with baseball, which, in turn, was interfering with my school work, which was never all that terrific anyway.

1945. Some summer Saturdays. Independent ice distributor whose name I can't remember. Salary: Worked free. Duties: Delivered ice in 25- and 50-pound chunks to east side neighborhoods where electric refrigeration had not yet made significant inroads. Comments: My first high-glamor job. Got to wear heavy leather belt, which held two pairs of ice tongs (which jangled nicely when you walked) and a scabbard with an ice pick, and a worn leather flap over one shoulder on which to hoist the blocks of ice. Talked into the job by schoolmate Royal Wilson, a paid helper on the truck, who billed it as not so much a non-paying job as it was an opportunity to meet girls my age who found icemen irresistible. Reason for leaving: Earnings potential seemed limited, as did future of the ice-delivery business. Also, never met any girls.

1948. June-September. LKR Chemical Products. Charlotte and Park. Salary: 75 cents an hour. Duties: Mixed black house paint with asbestos fibers in an old bathtub using a garden hoe. Mixture was then sold in gallon cans as "Formula LKR," and billed as a marvelous caulking compound that would not "crack, chip, peel or blister," which it never did, because it never got hard enough to do any of those things. Comments: Was promoted to roofer at $1.10 an hour. Hardest job I ever had. Smell of tar cooking still makes my muscles ache. Reason for leaving: Decided to go to college to learn an easier trade, which I did.

Dec. 1955-Jan. 1956. Detroit Parks and Recreation Dept. Salary: $1.50 an hour. Duties: Guard at the Civic Center Ice Skating Rink, foot of Woodward. Responsible for maintaining a reasonable semblance of order on the ice, including the rule that all skaters circle the rink in the same direction. Comments: Took the job during Detroit's first newspaper strike. Since I was unable to skate, recruited a group of regular skaters at the rink, kids from the Lebanese-American community around Congress and Orleans, to assist me. In my behalf, they enforced the rules against speed skating, cracking the whip and indiscriminate horseplay while I stood by on shaky ankles. Kids thought my name was "Shaheen," which helped. Reason for leaving: Strike ended and kids were starting to suspect that maybe I was not Lebanese after all.

Not enough there, perhaps, to convince a loan officer to turn loose some money, but, all in all, not an unimpressive work record.   ■

A.C. is right; there'll never be a number like old No. 1

April 3, 1983

One of the minor inconveniences in preparing material for Detroit magazine is an advance deadline requirement that makes timely comment on the news of the day a bit difficult.

So, for that reason, the contention between Anthony Carter and the United States Football League over which number will grace his jersey is probably settled by now.

But the principle that prompted the disagreement remains and certainly deserves attention from someone who understands the problem.

Mr. Carter is a talented pass-catcher from the University of Michigan who signed a contract with the Michigan Panthers.

At U-M his jersey was No. 1. On the Michigan Panthers his jersey was No. 1. Then someone in the USFL decided that Mr. Carter should have a number in the 80s, the series of numbers designated by the league for wide receivers.

Anthony Carter was more than a trifle upset by the ruling and vowed to fight to keep his number. It is a reaction that has my fullest sympathy.

There is a symbiosis between an athlete and the numbers on his shirt that sort of defies good sense. So there's really no reason to try to explain it here except to say that if there's one thing in the world I understand it's any kind of passion for the unimportant issues in life.

The first numbered jersey I ever wore in a serious athletic encounter was a faded yellow football jersey with a narrow, blue No. 1 on the front and back. No similarity exists between my performance under that numerical designation and that of any other person who ever claimed the number, up to and especially, Anthony Carter.

Kids need to succeed at things to establish contact with those first, early feelings of self-worth. And even though making the team depended as much on a willingness to come to practice and show up for the games as it did on athletic talent, getting a jersey represented a personal victory.

If you wanted to make the team, you could. Just show up. No cuts. No drops. No sense of having failed.

And the jersey was the tangible symbol of your accomplishment. It belonged to you alone and the number affixed to it was your number.

I had long coveted the jersey with No. 1. When its previous owner,

Wally Keeler, graduated, I took advantage of the lack of a formal process for assigning numbers. I dug that jersey out of the laundry pile in the locker room after the last game and took it home and kept it there until next season.

Every other piece of equipment was utilitarian. When it came to helmets, pads and pants, all that mattered was serviceability and, to a lesser degree, fit.

It was not unusual to wear different equipment in different games, but nobody ever traded jerseys. It was a time, too, before tear-away jerseys were an accepted part of the game. In the event of a jersey being torn away it was the responsibility of the player from whom it was torn to have it repaired in time for the next game.

So tattered jerseys would be carefully folded and carried home for the kind of attention only a mother could provide.

I can't help but think that Anthony Carter's mother missed out on something very special by never having had the opportunity to sew up the rips in her son's No. 1 jersey.

On the St. Rose Golden Bears, a non-fierce competitor in the Catholic League's Second Division on the east side, I was an interior lineman.

It was a position for which I was unsuited in terms of talent, temperament and enthusiasm, not to mention physique.

There was a mean-spirited attitude on the line that ran counter to my own natural willingness to make friends in any circumstance. Soft answers, I found, may indeed turn away wrath, but on a football line they simply generated more wrath.

But I was part of a team. I had my own jersey with my own number, and nothing would change that. Not even mean-spirited opponents.

I don't know what ever happened to yellow jersey No. 1. It probably ended up in the rag bag Mrs. Matte kept in the church basement for cleaning purposes. A less than ignominious end, I might add, since few football jerseys end their days in the service of God.

One fragment, however, survives. A torn piece of old yellow fabric pasted on the black page of a photo album. It was pasted there by a girl who picked it up on the field one Sunday after a game. She was a sophomore then and liked me a lot.

In fact, she still likes me a lot. We keep the album on a shelf in our closet. ∎

I'll finally make the championship game — 39 years later

June 8, 1986

In 1947, at the top of summer, when shoes stuck to the tar strips in the street and the bricks in every building collected the heat of the day and carried it, sticky and unpleasant, into the evening, we decided that this was going to be the year.

Forget about last year and what might have been. That was gone. This was going to be the season to remember.

Then somebody got out the football so we'd all be ready this time.

All through July and August we threw it, kicked it and caught it. On the sand at Olsen's Beach, on the grass at Waterworks Park or on the hard, gravel playground behind Lillibridge School. September couldn't come too soon.

There had been, of course, that brief flirtation with greatness a few years earlier. St. Rose won two east side championships in two years, both of which ended badly when we were bused to the west side to play St. Alphonsus for the city title.

But we were on the sidelines then, not really a part of it. The winning or the losing not in our control.

So we sat on the hot afternoon sidewalk in front of the candy store and, one more time, put the names down on a lined sheet of paper.

Bill Aubin, Larry Keegan, Chuck Perucca, Jack Brosnan, Frank Willard, Joe Callahan, Neal Shine, Joe Schulte, Larry Ranger, Jack Kenny, Joe Coach, Paul Bosen, Rich Brennan, Richard Conover, Pat Kane and Bill Burke. It was perfect. How could anything possibly go wrong?

Even Sophie, who owned the candy store then and whose last name I no longer remember, was caught up in the excitement.

When we won the city championship, she said, she would give a party for us in the store. Everything free.

In addition to the personal distinction, for which we all hungered, we also felt in some strange way that the championship would finally vindicate Gallagher Field.

Gallagher Field was ugly. No blade of grass ever grew there.

It had always been a storage yard for streetcars. Its conversion to a playground was an uncomplicated process. The city brought in trucks that dumped mountains of yellow clay on top of the iron tracks and a bulldozer pushed it around until the tracks were covered.

After the first rain the sun baked it to a hardness roughly comparable to the main runway at City Airport.

The players from the other schools hated to play there. Home field pride being what it was, we pretended to love it, even though our relationship with that piece of ground was uneven, at best.

The opening game that year — our first step on the path to glory — was with St. Martin's. That parish was sometimes called St. Martin's on the Lake, even though it was closer to a canal than to the lake. As far as I know, nobody ever suggested that it be called St. Martin's on the Canal.

We lost that opening Sunday, 6-0.

But to me, the most monumental tragedy of that whole season was not losing the opening game, but the fact that I was not there.

I was in Cottage Hospital, sick with something the doctors finally decided was food poisoning, although I have always believed they were never really sure.

I lost 20 pounds, missed a few more games, and when I came back I was never able to win back my spot in the starting lineup.

We won the rest of our games that season, but so did St. Martin's, and they got to go to the west side for the championship.

Although I think about that year often, it was brought to mind this time by an invitation from Walt Bazylewicz, of the Archdiocese of Detroit. He asked me if I would serve, along with WJR's J.P. McCarthy, as co-chairman of the Catholic League football championship game this year.

I accepted without telling him I had seriously planned to be there 39 years ago, but something happened.

I still drive past Gallagher Field every day, and its appearance has not improved with time. I keep wishing we could have done more for it that year.

Maybe I'll ask Walt to let me say a few words about it at the championship game. ■

While son flirted with the GOP, father toed the party line

Dec. 16, 1984

With the election safely behind us, I feel free now to discuss an important subject without fear of impeding the efficient conduct of the political process that allows us, every four years, to pick a president.

I have always been fascinated by the factors that impel us to cast our precious vote for one candidate or another.

There is always the chance, albeit a small one, that voters will make their decision strictly on the issues.

But after these issues have been refined and reconditioned on the basis of the voter's family history, tax bracket, social, cultural, religious and ethnic background, they are no longer recognizable as issues.

So when we are alone in the voting booth without an unadorned issue to help us, we simply fall back on what I call the "Emotional Imprint" factor.

Somewhere, in the recesses of our inner selves, is something that has marked us so deeply that it often controls how we vote.

There is no valid political reason, for example, why Dorothy Comstock Riley, a successful candidate this year for the Michigan Supreme Court, should have garnered even a single vote because the Southeastern High School basketball team won the city championship in 1945.

But at a neighborhood reunion a few weeks ago, I was part of a conversation in which a Southeastern graduate talked in glowing detail about being at the championship game that year at Olympia Stadium when Southeastern beat Mackenzie 29-28.

"Wally Riley was the captain of the team," the man said, "and his wife just ran for the Supreme Court, so I voted for her."

"Just because her husband was on that championship team 40 years ago?" he was asked. "You know of a better reason?" was the reply.

Wallace D. Riley, now a Detroit attorney, had little notion back then that more was at stake that day than basketball.

My own involvement with partisan politics began in 1940, when I was 10.

Wendell Willkie was running against Franklin D. Roosevelt and word among the neighborhood kids that year was that if Willkie won, he was going to paint the White House black.

Despite that, I took advantage of an offer one Sunday morning to pass out several dozen "Win With Willkie" broadsides to the houses on my block.

The offer was made by a kid who was passing the leaflets out in front of church after mass. He told me he'd give me a dime if I would distribute them on Lycaste between Jefferson and Kercheval.

Ten cents was nothing to be ignored then and I accepted the offer, even though I knew loyalty to FDR ran deep in the neighborhood and even deeper in the Shine household.

My father, it seemed, changed newspapers weekly based on whichever one committed the most recent editorial outrage against the president.

And there wasn't a store on E. Jefferson that didn't have a picture of President Roosevelt in the window or behind the counter.

One store window had a wonderful picture that showed, depending on where you stood when you looked at it, either the American flag, the Statue of Liberty or FDR.

When I was finished delivering the leaflets, I made the mistake of bringing the leftovers home.

My father asked me what I was doing with them. I told him.

He looked at me with that look all fathers have when they're trying to decide whether or not to smack you. He didn't. Instead he calmly told me to go to every house where I had left a leaflet and retrieve it.

If it was not still on the porch, he said, then ring the doorbell and get it back.

I collected all of them, including the one from Mr. Anderson who was reading it when I asked for it back.

My father then escorted me to the basement and I watched while he pitched Mr. Willkie's campaign material into the furnace.

I was then instructed to take the 10 cents back to church and drop it in the poor box. Which I did, and which caused my father to comment that it was the first thing the Republicans had ever done for poor people in Detroit.

The impression that episode left with me was that a political party that inspired that kind of loyalty should be taken seriously.

Politically, I will go only as far as to say that I have never passed out literature for Thomas E. Dewey, Dwight Eisenhower, Barry Goldwater, Richard Nixon, Gerald Ford or Ronald Reagan.

Old emotional imprints die hard.   ■

The Goodfellows bring to mind a sad-eyed girl and her thanks

Dec. 9, 1984

In other years, they had arranged it so you would not have to work in your own neighborhood.

Somebody with some sensitivity for what could happen had made sure of that.

So when we gathered that morning during Christmas week, 1944, in the basement of the Knights of Columbus Hall on Amity and Parkview, across the alley from the McClellan police station, it was with the same warm feelings as in previous years.

The policemen and the volunteers would feed us a light breakfast and then we would sort the boxes by street address and stack them to be loaded on the trucks.

It was the day the Goodfellows distributed their packages, and we would be helping them again this Christmas. To us, it was the most important thing we would do all year.

Our Boy Scout troop — a police troop from McClellan station — was responsible for helping with deliveries in that precinct.

Although they were packed when they got to our basement distribution center, we knew what was in the packages.

With the kind of curiosity peculiar to children, we had peeked inside some of them.

The package for the girls contained a doll, a dress, some sensible underwear that buttoned up the front, a certificate for a pair of shoes and some hard candy.

The boys got a small toy — an airplane or a truck — shirt and pants, the same kind of serviceable underwear and a slip for the shoes and the same small box of candy.

We were loading the truck when I realized the addresses on the boxes were from my own neighborhood. I knew I would be uncomfortable if I had to deliver a package to a family I knew.

There was no real stigma attached to being poor in that neighborhood in those years. It was a neighborhood where poverty was relative. Nobody ever had much. People who had even less than that were the poor.

I thought I could avoid any problems by volunteering to work on the truck. The thing was, everybody wanted to work on the truck. It was easi-

37

er — and warmer. I was told I would be delivering the packages that day.

Before the truck left, I climbed in back and sorted through all the boxes, looking for names I recognized. I knew a few families, but none well. And they probably wouldn't know me. It was some comfort.

Toward the end of the afternoon, I was handed a package from the back of the truck. I ran up the front steps of the house whose number was on the box and rang the bell.

I looked again at the label and my heart froze. It was the home of a girl in my ninth-grade class. I didn't know her well. She was a quiet, pretty, dark-haired girl who had come from another school the previous year. I had apparently not noticed the name when I had looked through the packages earlier.

At the bottom of the label, under her name and the names and ages of her brothers and sisters, was the typewritten notation: "Father in prison."

At that point, I seriously considered running away, but someone was coming to answer the door.

"Please, God," I prayed, "don't let it be her." It was.

She opened the door part-way and looked at me in surprise. Before she could say anything, I pushed the package into her hands, wished her Merry Christmas from the Goodfellows, turned around and walked back to the truck.

We never spoke about that brief encounter until one night about 10 years ago, at a school reunion.

After some small talk, she finally said: "You're still bothered about the day you brought the package to our house, aren't you?" I told her I was.

She told me she was bothered that day, too. That she ran back in the house and cried. Cried for being poor. For having a father in jail. And for being ashamed of it.

Then she told me that what I had done that day was a good thing and to please stop being bothered by it. She said for three years there would have been no Christmas for them without the Goodfellows. Then she thanked me for that painful day in 1944 and kissed me on the cheek.

The Goodfellows will be out tomorrow. They will march from the News and Free Press behind the mounted police and the Cody High School band to their appointed corners where they will sell papers to raise $585,000 for the 42,500 packages they will deliver this year.

I will give my check to one of them, remembering too clearly a sad-eyed girl in 1944 and a kiss on the cheek 30 years later. ∎

You'd exchange longing glances, then check her phone exchange

Oct. 14, 1984

Chances were, back in those glorious golden days of the '40s, that you would have less trouble getting a phone number from a girl of recent acquaintance than you would have getting her address.

There seemed to be some operative principle at work then that girls would rather hear from you by phone than have you show up at their house, where their father could object in person to your attention to his daughter.

There were lots of places around Detroit where the opportunities to meet attractive new friends were virtually limitless — Eastwood Park, Jefferson Beach, Belle Isle and the skating rink on Boblo.

But if the friendships established on summer evenings at those places were to have any continuity, it was probably going to be — at least at the start — by phone.

That's why I was hopelessly in love with IVanhoe 3306 long before I knew that the object of my connection lived at 5911 St. Clair.

It's only fair to add that to her I was, for a substantial period of time, simply DRexel 6371, not 1532 Lycaste. My mother had little appetite for the spiritual snares that she believed lurked in teenage romantic relationships. Girls on the porch were one of the danger signs she watched for.

What brought a lot of this to mind was seeing a delivery truck out Grand River near St. Mary of Redford Church a few weeks back with a phone number on the side still using the old TUxedo exchange.

I found myself asking why this truck from Grosse Pointe was making deliveries way out in VErmont territory.

It occurred to me that not only were phone numbers easier to remember in the days before all-number calling, telephone exchanges were also invaluable indicators of a full array of geographic and demographic information about the person who belonged to the phone number.

But our main interest in the information a phone exchange provided tended more toward geography than to social or class distinction. The unspoken rule was: If you had to transfer streetcars more than once, it probably wasn't going to work out.

This was generally not a problem at Eastwood, Belle Isle or Olsen's

Beach. The girls you met there were most likely of MUrray, TWinbrook, DRexel, LEnox, PRospect, PIngree, OLive or PLaza, with maybe a NIagara or TUxedo or two, but we always suspected that those two exchanges had better places to swim.

But all were exchanges whose locations were within an acceptable walk or streetcar ride in the event that the relationship progressed to the point of: "Would you like to come over to my house someday?"

Boblo was a different story. It was a magnet for girls of every exotic telephone exchange imaginable.

On any given night at the Boblo roller rink, you could find an amazing collection of REdfords, TYlers, HOgarths, VInewoods, UNiversitys, LAfayettes, DAvisons, EVergreens, ARlingtons, GLendales, CEdars, ORegons, TErraces, REdfords, TEnnysons and MElroses.

On the boat ride back, conversations would often go like this:

"Can I call you?"

"OK. It's FItzroy 1234."

The next consideration was whether you wanted to get involved with a girl who lived near Belle Isle and might be dating a member of the Field and Jefferson gang or a football player from St. Charles.

Woodward was almost always an absolute barrier to even casual romance, even though we knew that TYlers were good dancers and VInewoods and UNiversitys were good skaters. And if you told them you'd like to learn to polka, GLendale and TRinity girls would always offer to teach you.

The system worked most of the time, but it was not foolproof.

There was the time one of my youthful colleagues returned from Boblo smitten with a TOwnsend beauty.

One in the group said he had pursued a TOwnsend earlier in the summer who went to Central High.

When she discovered that he was Catholic and told him she was Jewish, they decided that young love was complicated enough without religion being a factor, and said goodby.

"Make the call," said another. "I met a wonderful TOwnsend last year on Belle Isle and she was from Visitation."

So whatever happened to the love affair between IVanhoe and DRexel?

Well, nearly 40 years later we share an 885 with a call-waiting option. Efficient, to be sure.

But not nearly as romantic. ∎

Saying the blind date was
a nice Catholic girl was no help

April 24, 1983

Almost everybody I know has a story about a blind date.

Some of them are lovely tales. Of love discovered. Of matches that have withstood the years. Of one blissful encounter whose memory has remained as clear and as true as the moment it happened.

But a lot of them are horror stories. Stories of incredible mismatches. Painful, seemingly endless evenings. A good idea at seven that turns to disaster by eleven.

Dating, blind or otherwise, was not a large part of my social life during my formative years. The big reasons were the regular reminders, in school and in church, of the ultimate and eternal penalty extracted for anything less than rigorous and unwavering adherence to the code. And the code always seemed to involve "keeping company." And we all knew what that meant.

I dated some in high school. More in college, on the ground that the day I would be forced to face up to the question of eternal damnation was such a long way off that perhaps the code might get changed along the way. It seemed worth the risk.

But if I was willing to risk the level of my participation in eternity on a few dates, I certainly was not going to risk it with anybody I had not met in advance. Hence, the absence in my life of the blind date. Or, the almost absence.

Like I said earlier, almost everybody has a story about a blind date. I had one blind date in my life. As a result, I have one blind date story and I'm willing to share it with you.

The redundant ritual which takes place on the beaches of southern Florida each year during college spring break has not changed measurably since I first saw it close up in 1952. Which is no tribute to the imaginations of the generations of its young participants, most of whom have since become full partners in the American system. Also a frightening thought.

So with my brother Jim and a U-D classmate, Jerry Kowalczyk, I joined the faithful on the sands of Ft. Lauderdale, unaware that fate was flinging me swiftly toward my first blind date.

The party was the party of the year at the University of Miami. Some Detroit friends who attended Miami got us tickets.

41

Now, they said, all we needed were dates.

Back in Detroit I had an unofficial (no ring) fiancee. Would she mind if I went on one innocent date with another girl to a college party? You bet she would. What were the chances of her ever finding out? Very slim.

All that resolved, my concern turned to the question at hand. My blind date.

"Let's call Marion," one of my friends said. "Neal's tall enough for her." Danger signal.

"It's the day of the party, won't she already have a date?" asked another. "Not yet," said friend No. 1. Another danger signal. I started to get nervous.

"How tall is she?" I asked. "Just right for you," was the answer. "But don't worry, she's always running for queen of something." I was suddenly feeling less nervous.

"Only she never wins," piped up another voice. I was getting nervous again.

The arrangement was made and I met Marion Ettie. She was a lovely young woman from Miami and a junior at the university.

She had, indeed, run for a few queenships. Finished second in the school's Miss Tempo contest. Was a Sweetheart of Sigma Chi and had been elected University of Miami Calendar Girl.

We went to dinner, to the party and to Sunday mass the next morning. It was all very nice.

When I got back to Detroit I found that word of the blind date had preceded me. My local love was talking about making the relationship even less official than it was. She was not buying the "she was a nice Catholic girl" argument.

The ice was just beginning to warm when complications set in. Marion Ettie's picture started showing up in all the Detroit papers and in the newsreels.

She had been named the 1953 Orange Bowl Queen. And she did not look like the convent-approved version of a nice Catholic girl.

I was able to patch things up with my friend and we got married a year later. I have not seen Marion Ettie since.

The Orange Bowl Committee doesn't know where she is. The last clipping about her in the Miami Herald reports that she married an Air Force officer and moved away from Florida.

The story, written in 1963, also reported that she and her husband had five children.

Like I have been telling you all along, a nice Catholic girl. ■

Basic training memories
of a night in the doghouse

July 27, 1986

Al Kauffman wants to save Ft. Custer.

Kauffman, who lives in Royal Oak, was mustered out of the Army at Ft. Custer in 1952 and went back for the first time a year ago. He recently wrote me about it.

"I was surprised to find that most of the post was long gone," he said, "with only a small area used for reserve training still there. What is left is rapidly disappearing and I'm afraid it will be totally gone in a short time."

Kauffman believes some official agency should take steps to preserve some of the old barracks buildings, or at least erect historical markers to remind future generations of what had been there.

I told Kauffman that although I admired his concern for historic preservation, I could not, for the life of me, understand why anybody would want to save an Army training camp.

When I was drafted in 1953, I bypassed Ft. Custer and was sent for basic training to a place called Camp Pickett, an unimposing garrison located on several thousand uninviting acres of scrub land near Blackstone, Va., 60 miles south of Richmond.

It had been built in 1942 to train soldiers in World War II, was closed after the war and reopened in 1950 when the Korean war started.

It might be that my negative recollection of the geography has been conditioned by the unpleasantness of my stay there, but I vividly remember it as uncommonly hot, unbearably humid and unbelievably dusty.

Add to this a collection of training officers and non-coms who made the Marquis de Sade look like Mother Teresa, and the result was, undeniably, the worst eight weeks of my life.

The truth is, I was not altogether enthusiastic about leaving a pregnant wife and an entry-level position in my chosen profession — copyboy at the Free Press — for the questionable rewards of military life, so I suspected that some attitude adjustment would be required.

What I did not suspect was a training regimen whose intensity could have been interpreted as a sign that North Koreans were on the highway heading for Blackstone.

The training I could understand. If I was going to have to fight in Korea, it was probably a good idea to know some of this stuff. But I had difficulty seeing the military value in being rousted out of bed at 2 a.m. by a drunken platoon sergeant and being forced to run several miles while singing the sergeant's favorite songs.

Then there was the time the company commander decided that the best way to replace body salts was not to rely on generally unreliable recruits to take their salt tablets, but to put salt in the drinking water.

So before every road march, a salt tablet was dropped in each canteen and 10 pounds of salt poured into the mobile water tank that accompanied us.

After several days of watching the salt water make soldiers sick, I decided that it was time to explain to the company commander that it was not possible to drink salt water without getting ill.

He may be a captain, I told myself, but he is a reasonable man. After all, this is America.

After I explained in detail my theory about the negative properties of brine when ingested by humans, the captain thanked me. Then he told me to get my full field pack, rifle and steel helmet and march around the company area for five hours.

After that, he had me scrub the inside of the doghouse of our mascot, an obese boxer named Cap. He suggested that I do a good job because that's where I would be sleeping that night.

I spent much of the night repelling the overweight boxer, who was as troubled about being dispossessed as I was about sleeping in his undersized quarters, which smelled equally of fat dog and Fels Naphtha.

Camp Pickett is now Ft. Pickett, and the folks there tell me they have no plans to close it.

I told them that if there is ever a drive to turn the place into a military monument, I would be pleased if they didn't call me for a contribution. ■

2. My mother came from Ireland

At last, the goods on Mom
— 35 years too late

Jan. 10, 1982

There was a time in my life when it would have been advantageous to have had a little good stuff on my mother.

Some point after the onset of puberty and before my freshman year in college.

Not blackmail stuff, heaven forbid. Just something to provide a little leverage.

A couple of weeks ago, I got it. It came in the mail from a small town in Middlesex, England. A place called Edgeware. Unfortunately, the information is about 35 years too late to do me any good. Instead of leverage, what I've got now is nostalgia.

The letter is from a nice Irish gentleman named Tommy Doyle, who somehow got hold of a copy of Detroit Magazine in Edgeware. But I've learned not to question the wondrous reaching power of the Free Press.

In that issue of the magazine was a story I had done on being Irish. It contained a picture of Tommy Doyle's mother along with my own grandmother in Carrick-on-Shannon, the town where my mother lived until she left, at age 18, for the United States. It was also the town where Tommy Doyle lived and, apparently, paid close attention to what was going on.

In his letter to me, the opening reference to my mother was, "that young, very beautiful, kind and gentle lady." I knew it was going to be good stuff.

For as long as I can remember, my mother has always been my mother. Our relationship was strictly mother and son. I got bopped for not moving quickly enough when called, whacked for bad marks in school, chastised for a lack of enthusiasm in keeping the house clean, cuffed for fighting with my brothers and otherwise harassed, justifiably, for a host of childhood transgressions.

When I discovered that girls were more fun to be around than I had ever imagined they would be, the maternal heat got turned up.

Interrogations began in earnest right after dinner.

"Where are you going tonight?"

"To the candy store."

"To do what?"

"Hang around."

47

"With whom?"

"With the guys."

"Hmmph!"

Inside me a nagging stool pigeon of a conscience was shouting: "He's going to kiss girls on the lawn in front of Lillibridge School and hold hands with them down at the river! That's what he's going to do!"

That's what I was going to do.

But it wasn't easy. Mary Ellen Conlon Shine was a one-woman moral majority. She could spot a fleck of lipstick at 50 paces in unacceptable light. She went to bed only after I had returned from the Lillibridge lawn and only after I had been thoroughly debriefed on the evening's activities and after she had repeated the previous night's warning on the occasion of sin.

The fact was I had already faced up to the occasion of sin and found it less disagreeable than I had fancied.

The problem was I lacked a viable defense. When the prosecution had rested, the defense usually went to bed.

Mothers were mothers. Period. What did they know about the lure of things like the Lillibridge lawn?

Tommy Doyle settled all of that in two pages of block printing.

"When your mother left Carrick," he wrote, "I saw grown men and boys cry. The boys went to the station and hid behind the hedge. . . . When the train pulled out, they bawled their eyes out. All have been called home now. Matt Jack, Jim Feely, John Dolan, Harry McGowan, John Gavin, Johnnie Gill, Paddy Hart, J.P. Murry, old John Lavin, the blacksmith. They were all in love with your mother. If she smiled at them, it made their day. God rest their souls."

There are nine names. Not bad for an 18-year-old Irish girl in a small town and with a strict father.

Tommy spoke only in passing of his own affection for Mary Ellen, the temptress of Carrick-on-Shannon. He did mention, however, that after she sailed for the New World, he went off and joined the Foreign Legion. He didn't say why.

When I showed the letter to my mother, she allowed as how there was some bit of exaggeration involved. The intervening years, she concluded, had played tricks with poor Tommy's memory. After a few smiles and a tear or two, she allowed that perhaps it was closer to the mark than she first thought.

He forgot to mention, she pointed out, that when she got on the boat for America that day in 1927, she was engaged to one of the Carrick boys, but took his ring off shortly after departure so as not to interfere with her efforts to make shipboard friends.

Tommy Doyle, where were you when I needed you? ■

Evidence that our ancestors were boat people themselves

June 29, 1986

I don't know how old I was before I figured out that most of the parents in my neighborhood did not come from the same place — a mysterious land across the ocean called "The Old Country."

It was, actually, a reasonable theory for a child to embrace.

Neither I nor most of the kids I grew up with had ever seen our grandparents. That was because our grandparents were in "The Old Country." It was also where our parents lived before they came here.

And in the evening, on the front porches, they would talk about the place they called "The Old Country."

Sometimes they called it "home," and often, in the middle of a story, their eyes would get wet and they would stop and stare off beyond the other side of the porch railing, and nobody would say anything until they started talking again.

So it was always a real place to me. The place they left for a better life. A place that would always be part of them.

Adding to the evidence that supported this one-world theory were the boat pictures.

Most of the families had them, and they hung in gilt dime store frames on the front room wall, next to the posed, formal portraits of the old people who still lived in "The Old Country."

The shipboard pictures indicated a universal lack of photographic creativity.

People shoulder-to-shoulder on an open deck, staring at the camera, pushing to get in position so at least their faces would appear in the picture.

The men wore caps and had big mustaches, and the women wore old-fashioned hats or head scarves and carried babies or large bundles, or both.

My mother never put her boat picture on the wall. I think she decided at some point over the years that it was not a particularly flattering likeness.

She keeps it, with other bits of another lifetime, in an old, tin orange-and-blue cigar box with "Humo" scrolled on the lid, along with the suggested counter price of two for 25 cents.

The picture was taken in 1927 on the Republic, a United States Lines ship, a few hours away from New York harbor.

It is true to its genre. A crowd of people on the deck peering anxiously in the direction of the camera, and in the background, the sky and the sea an unfocused gray.

In the middle of the crowd is Mary Ellen Conlon, her small face looking out from under a hat pulled down tightly on her head. She is not smiling.

She was 18, the oldest in her family, on her way to a job as a housekeeper for a family in Duluth, wondering already if it had been a horrible mistake to ever have left Carrick-on-Shannon.

It was not surprising, after she and my father were married in 1929, that the neighborhood in which they chose to live was a neighborhood of people who had come from some other place and had a picture of themselves on the boat to prove it.

A Free Press reporter — a Texan whose family went back several generations in the Southwest — once asked me what it was like growing up in a neighborhood where most of the kids were first-generation Americans. What kind of lessons had I learned there?

I don't recall what I told him — something that touched on the interesting sociology of the immigrant experience, I suppose.

But what I should have told him was that I learned about Irish ghosts and tasted homemade Italian wine and got oplatki from Polish neighbors at Christmas; that I learned how to say my name in Greek and knew why the Orthodox Christians celebrated Easter on a different Sunday.

That I listened to accordion music in backyard grape arbors and cried at sad songs about other places, even though I couldn't understand the words.

I learned that you couldn't play boccie properly unless you could talk to the ball in Italian. And that Mr. Magri was the best at it, because after he rolled the ball he froze in his follow-through, not moving, like a statue, until the ball stopped rolling.

And I learned how much this new country still owes to "The Old Country."

Wherever that might be. ∎

A Good Housekeeping seal
and a religious education

Feb. 2, 1986

"It was the part of town they called St. George's Terrace," she told me. "I suppose today you'd call it the high-rent district. All the leading citizens of the town lived there. Protestants, mostly."

We were talking about the sometimes unappreciated profession of cleaning other people's houses, my mother and I. We were discussing a story on the subject that had appeared in the Free Press, a story that dealt with whether or not it was universally accepted as honorable work.

Mary Ellen Conlon Shine felt compelled to discuss in some detail her own impressive work history in that area, which began when she went to work at 14 as a live-in housekeeper for Dr. Bradshaw in St. George's Terrace in her hometown, Carrick-on-Shannon, Ireland.

"I left school when I was 12," she said. "I came down one morning ready to go to school and my mother said, 'There'll be no more school. I need you here.'"

The decision didn't surprise her. There were eight children then (there would eventually be 13) and she was the oldest. She was, indeed, needed at home.

Taking care of other people's houses seemed a natural enough pursuit, she said, "because that's what young girls did then."

She worked for Miss Skinner for a while and then moved into the Bradshaws' to take care of their house.

"I cleaned, cooked, answered the door, ran errands, and every afternoon put on a white apron and served tea."

She left Ireland in 1927, when she was 18, for Duluth, Minn., where she got a job as a housekeeper. "It was the kind of work I knew how to do," she said.

"Were you any good at it?" I asked.

She hesitated a moment, smiled and said: "Not especially. But I was good enough at it to keep a job."

She left Duluth after less than a year and came to Detroit after a younger brother, Mike, came here to work in the automobile industry.

"I got a job as a housekeeper with a family around Gratiot and Fischer," she said. "They were Jewish and kept a kosher household.

"They were very patient with me in explaining things like separate dishes for milk and meat and how they even had to be washed separately."

She said it took her longer than it should have to understand that the process involved religious observance and was not designed specifically to create extra work for her.

This family's patience apparently extended to her limited expertise as a practitioner of the art of food preparation.

"One day they brought home some liverwurst and told me to serve it for lunch. I had never seen liverwurst before and didn't know what to do with it, so I put it in a pan of water and boiled it."

How did it turn out? I asked.

"It melted," she said. "When I lifted the lid, it looked like soup."

She had one more job in Detroit before she married Patrick J. Shine, whom she had met while riding his streetcar on the way to work for the family for whom she had boiled the liverwurst.

"I got a housekeeping job with a family named Fleischer who lived on Philip, south of Jefferson. They owned a department store."

The Fleischers were also Jewish, but my mother's education in the rubric of Judaism that had begun with the family in the Gratiot-Fischer area still contained some significant gaps.

"I was still very young and very green," she explained, "but it never occurred to me that everybody didn't celebrate Christmas."

So one December day in 1928, she took the Fleischer children out and bought a Christmas tree.

"When the parents got home that night we had the tree up and decorated. They had brought company home with them. When they saw the tree, they just stood there in the doorway and stared at it. The kids were delighted. Their parents were stunned."

While the children cried, the tree was removed and Mary Ellen Conlon's education in comparative religions was advanced one more degree.

I asked her if those years of cleaning for other people had any impact on her own housekeeping.

"Not at all," she said. "I keep a pretty clean house, but I'm not a fanatic about it. If I don't feel like cleaning house one day, I'll wait till the next. And if I miss a few spots, I don't lose any sleep over it.

"Nobody ever died from a little bit of dust." ∎

When Mom went shopping, the salespeople hid

Sept. 22, 1985

Whenever I hear merchants talking about "walk-in business," I know they are talking about my mother. She never saw a store she didn't like.

I had mostly forgotten about her lifelong involvement as a serious participant in the Detroit area's retailing industry until I was driving her through downtown Detroit one morning.

"How I used to love coming down here," she sighed. "If your father had the day off, I'd leave you kids with him, take the streetcar downtown and spend the whole day. Shop all morning, have lunch at Sanders, shop all afternoon." The merchants who took comfort in caveat emptor soon learned that my mother had reversed that maxim. With her, it was caveat venditor — let the seller beware.

Kids have an unusually high embarrassment level, but mine was always more acute than the norm. I could sense it whenever my mother was on a confrontation course with a salesperson, and I would head for the door and wait for her outside.

The disputes involved such basics as price, quality, freshness and, very often, size. At the shoe store, the conversation often went like this:

My mother (squeezing the new oxford I was wearing): "They're too tight."

The salesman: "They'll stretch."

My mother: "You'll stretch. Get him the next size."

The salesman: "They're too big."

My mother: "He'll grow into them."

My mother never lost a fight with a merchant. One memorable triumph involved a pair of gray flannel trousers she had bought for me at J.L. Hudson's.

They were wonderfully soft slacks, the height of campus style, and I wore them to class at the University of Detroit every day for a year. When the material in the crotch disintegrated to the point they could no longer be worn without causing talk, my mother took them back to Hudson's and demanded a refund, using her time-tested claim of shoddy goods.

The Hudson's people countered with the fair wear-and-tear defense, but had no defense against an irate woman holding up a pair of pants in the middle of a crowded department, one hand thrust through the worn fabric of the crotch, loudly demanding to know if this was what Hudson's called quality workmanship.

She got a refund and I got a new pair of gray flannels.

She considered her children absolute extensions of her dedication, surrogates obliged to maintain the same standards in the marketplace as she did.

She operated from the personal belief that shopkeepers, especially grocers, would palm off on children what they could not sell to discerning adults.

I still find it painful to recall the days I lurked outside neighborhood markets until the place was empty of customers so I could return lettuce with too many brown leaves, dented cans, limp stalks of celery, bruised fruit, hot dogs with suspicious green flecks and hamburger that looked "tainted."

A couple of weeks ago Jim Monnig, a bookseller whose shop is in Grosse Pointe Park, sent me an interesting piece of out-of-date literature.

It is a 1953 promotion piece for the Detroit News, listing the effectiveness of News advertising in the Detroit area's "29 major shopping centers."

What's interesting is that the 29 areas are intersections, pre-dating the shopping malls.

Places like Jefferson and Chalmers, Mack and Chalmers, Harper and Chalmers, Houston and Hayes, Gratiot and Seven Mile, Jos. Campau and Holbrook, McNichols and San Juan, Livernois and Fenkell, Grand River and Oakman.

It also has photographs showing stores like Neisner's, Kresge's, Woolworth's, Federal's, Fintex, Richman's, Linda Lee, Kinsel's, Cunningham's, Sanders, Awrey's, Willens.

I have given the book to my mother who will, I am sure, recall a shopping adventure to match every single storefront. ■

For Mom's kids, no fare was always fare enough

Jan. 8, 1984

We were sitting around the table in the basement of the Amalgamated Transit Union hall over on Lothrop and the conversation turned to the question of whether or not to pay the full fare.

James Jenkins, Ernest Bledsoe and Frank Perdue are retired now, but between them they have given nearly 100 years of service to the old Department of Street Railways (DSR).

The morning we met they talked about the notch on the pole on streetcars and buses. It measured 44 inches from the floor and separated the full fares from the free rides.

Strict enforcement of the rule of the notch, these gentlemen pointed out, was a sometimes thing.

"Sure, we watched for the people who were taller than the mark and should be paying," Perdue said, "but we used a little judgment, too." Perdue, 64, drove a DSR bus for 33 years.

"I'd say we were fairly liberal in the way we looked at it," Jenkins said. "The fare was six cents, and even though that doesn't sound like much today, money was pretty scarce then and every nickel was looked after."

Jenkins, 67, was a streetcar conductor and worked out of the Jefferson Car Barns on St. Jean, where the 5th Precinct police station is now.

"If a mother got on with four or five kids and dropped 12 or 18 cents in the fare box, we'd just flip the lid and let it go."

Bledsoe, 69, is also a former conductor. He remembers the direct appeal from some of the kids who rode his streetcar.

"They'd come through and say to me: 'Conductor, I haven't got enough money for lunch and car fare both.' Well, you can't tell a kid no in a case like that, and I figured lunch was more important so I'd let 'em ride for nothing."

Some of those youngsters, Bledsoe said, would repay the fare when they had the money, often the next day.

Jenkins, Bledsoe and Perdue spoke in detail of the lengths to which people went to avoid paying the fare. How half the city mastered the use of the transfer to enable them to make a round trip on one fare. How the people with expired transfers would wait for their stop, hand the conductor an expired transfer folded in quarters and rush out the open doors.

Jenkins even recalls people using old betting slips from a policy house called "Yellow Dog," because the slips resembled DSR transfers.

But none of the three remembered encountering my mother. I assured them that if they ever had, they would remember.

My mother's aversion to paying in full for her children was obviously prompted by the economic realities of the time, but I have since come to suspect that she was intrigued by the challenge.

I was nearly out of high school before I paid the grown-up price at Nick and Mack's barber shop. Nick would try, subtly, to determine my age.

"Why, you must be in high school by now," he would say politely.

"Eighth grade," I would reply tersely, having been coached carefully before leaving home on acceptable responses.

On the D & C boats, the Pennsylvania Railroad and at the neighborhood theaters, the standing rule was always, "Quit standing up so straight." It was the antithesis of the world's most basic maternal instruction to children.

I was brought up to consider ticket takers, railroad conductors and bus drivers as natural enemies and developed an automatic slouch in their presence.

But I always suspected that my mother considered the DSR her greatest challenge.

Riding the bus or streetcar with her was an adventure in the politics of confrontation.

There were rules about riding public transportation. Never be the first or the last past the fare box. Always get in the middle of the crowd. Move briskly past the driver or conductor; lingering in the area of the 44-inch notch can be risky.

Move quickly to the rear of the bus or streetcar and do not present yourself as an exhibit if a dispute arises over your height.

When disputes did arise, my mother inevitably won simply because she was prepared to argue, however illogically, until the driver got tired of it and gave in.

One time — the only time I recall — she ran up against a bus driver as tenacious as she.

They argued back and forth for several miles until my mother finally said to him: "I am tired of arguing with you. Open the doors and let us off right here."

The bus stopped, and, as my mother marched off, her frown turned into a sly, victorious smile. It was our stop. ■

We sit on it, sleep on it, and store our memories in it

Nov. 24, 1985

What is this thing we have about furniture?

We seem to cherish it far beyond its useful years, pass it back and forth within the family and keep track of its movement from one place to another as if we fully expected Sotheby's to contact us one day about offering it at auction.

One of my early jobs involved helping the owner of a small cartage business move furniture out of houses under the watchful eye of a court bailiff.

Those situations usually involved divorce settlements and a court-mandated division of household goods. The bailiff had a list of what furniture stayed and what was to be put on the truck. The parties to the action invariably disputed the removal of each piece — often at the top of their lungs — as it was carried away.

There were often tearful negotiations over certain items, to which the party from which these pieces were being separated professed a profound attachment.

Then we would carry something back inside while both parties initialed the list on the bailiff's clipboard indicating that this departure from the earlier agreement was satisfactory to both sides.

Although I could not imagine how people could ever become that passionate about their beds and dressers, the experience left its mark on me.

Several years ago, I bought a couch from a Free Press reporter who, at the age of 40, was packing it all in to spend the rest of his days sailing in the Caribbean. He was selling his house and all he owned.

He was helping me put the couch in the back of my station wagon when I saw the look on his wife's face. I felt as if I was making off with one of their children.

All the years we kept that couch I never felt right about having it in the house. I never felt it was really mine.

It made one move with us and eventually ended up in a series of University of Michigan dormitory rooms. Every time I saw it there, the old feeling returned.

When our son Tom graduated and told me that he had sold the old red couch, I was secretly relieved.

But every now and then I still wonder, uneasily, whatever became of it and find myself, on a football Saturday, looking at the old furniture that always seems to be piled at Ann Arbor curbs, to see if someone has finally consigned that couch to the trash.

We were talking about home furnishings at dinner one recent evening when my mother recalled the day during the Depression that Crowley's sent a truck around to repossess our furniture.

The move to Beniteau from a rented, furnished apartment on St. Jean involved a major purchase of furniture.

We got it all from Crowley's. From the kitchen to the dining room to the living room to the bedrooms. And we got it the old-fashioned way. On credit.

It wasn't long before we fell behind in the payments. Some time later, two men — an older man and his younger helper — showed up on the porch and said they were there to pick up the furniture.

My mother swung the door open and declared: "Take it! Take it all! We paid too much for it in the first place and I can buy more with what we still owe on this."

Then she directed the attention of the stunned men to the three small children standing inside the door.

"While you're at it, take them, too," she said. "If you're taking their beds, you might as well take them."

Show me the man who can carry on in the face of all that and I'll show you a man devoid of even the most basic human emotions.

The young helper looked at the older man who, my mother remembers, shrugged and said, "To hell with it. We're not taking this furniture."

My father later worked out a $5-a-month repayment program with Crowley's and we got to keep the furniture — and the kids.

The fact is that 50 years later much of that furniture is still in my mother's house or in the family. She still has a bed, the dining room table and chairs and a buffet. The kitchen table is at our cottage in Canada and our son Jim has the china cabinet in his dining room in Bradenton, Fla.

So maybe I know more than I realized I knew about why we care so much about our furniture. At any rate, I'm glad Crowley's did not repossess my two brothers and me. They probably would have moved us to the west side, where we would never have been heard of again. ■

Stars in 'Upstairs, Downstairs,' but not born to play the part

March 17, 1985

If there was one thing all of us understood in the beginning it was that exotic adventures almost never live up to the extravagant expectations we attach to them.

So we were emotionally prepared for whatever letdown there might be and determined to enjoy our two weeks in an Irish castle regardless. But it was a letdown that never came.

We had rented the castle through an agency in New York that represented the owner. It sounded like a wonderful family vacation.

It's not that I have any pretensions to royalty, mind you. It's just that I have always admired, maybe even envied, the life-style of people born to the purple, a style not readily available to most of us born to the green.

The group of vacationers included my two brothers and their wives, my wife, myself, two of our children, my mother and two close friends.

The place is called Glin Castle and it stands on a beautiful rise of land overlooking the Shannon River where it meets the Atlantic. It is at the edge of the village of Glin, in County Limerick.

The castle, which is more than 200 years old, is the ancestral home of the FitzGerald family. It has been continuously occupied by the FitzGeralds, whose male descendants carry the title Knight of Glin.

When people heard we were renting a castle in Ireland, the first question always seemed to be: "Are you going there to find your roots?" The answer was that we knew about our roots in Ireland, and none of them was in a castle. We were going there, we replied, to enjoy somebody else's roots.

The Shine farm, where my father was born and reared and which is now owned by my first cousin, is only a few miles from the castle, but as far as I know none of the Shines ever took high tea there with the knight or any of his predecessors.

But in the second week of August, here we were, passing through the big gate, up the long drive to the castle.

We were greeted by Nancy Ellis, one of the housekeepers, who opened the door and welcomed us. We walked into the entrance hall and behind me I heard my wife whisper, "Oh, my God!" Which translates: "Here we are again, in over our heads."

The huge hall was imposing, even intimidating. Battle flags, a great stone fireplace, heroic portraits of FitzGeralds of other centuries, a golden harp on the staircase. This was going to be our house for two weeks? It was all a bit overwhelming — and this was only the front hall.

Nancy Ellis broke the awkward silence by asking: "Are you friends of Willie Nolan's?" Indeed. Willie is the brother of Margaret Shine, wife of my cousin Con. Suddenly it was all a little less overpowering.

The problem with living out of your element by more than a few degrees is the nagging realization that you know it's all a charade. And you wonder who else knows.

The knight, his wife and children were out of the country when we arrived, but were expected back by the following weekend. I was convinced he would walk in one afternoon in his riding togs and ascot and say in his clipped Anglo-Irish accent: "Shine. You aren't by any chance the same Shines who used to live in the upper flat on Lycaste, next to the alley, are you?"

It took us a few days to become accustomed enough to our elegant surroundings to stop whispering. We were convinced that someone would walk in as we had coffee in the sitting room or tea in the drawing room and demand to know what we were doing in this house.

My mother, who is 76, did better than the rest of us right from the start.

She spent much of her time in the kitchen with the cook and three housekeepers, and we could tell from the noisy laughter that drifted up from behind the stairs that all was well with Mary Ellen Shine and her new friends.

At one point during our stay I said to her — in jest, you understand — "Why don't you spend less time in the kitchen and more time acting like you belong here?"

She gave me one of her patented mother looks. "I know where I belong and I know where you belong, and it's not here." And with that she went back to the kitchen and the laughing started again.

It was two storybook weeks, and my strongest memory of our departure was my mother tearfully embracing the ladies from the kitchen and promising to find all of them husbands in America.

I will probably never go back to Glin Castle, but if I do, I promise to spend more time in the kitchen.

Mother was right. There are some things about being Irish that are impossible to deny. ■

So tongues wouldn't wag, Annie never went to Paris

Dec. 15, 1985

James Conlon's responsibility for supervising the operation of the Arthur Guinness & Sons brewery warehouse made him a citizen of substance in Carrick-on-Shannon.

On the streets of that small Irish town, the women called him Mr. Conlon and the men tipped their hats to him or would tug on the bill of their caps when he passed and say, "Fine day, James." And he would respond, "Grand day, indeed, thank God."

If any of this was a burden to him, it was one he accepted seriously and with good grace.

Station was important to him, and if being a leading citizen of the town required that he be an upright example to every soul in Carrick, then he was prepared to undertake that responsibility.

Appearances were as important to him as anything in his life, and he feared scandal above all other earthly torments.

People speak out loud about public transgressions, he once told me, but scandal is something they whisper about.

The very thought of them whispering about him was frightening to consider.

When his daughter, who was destined in 1930 to become my mother, was walking out with young Beresford, the son of the town's Protestant minister, she was convinced that her life was more at risk than her eternal soul if this was ever discovered by her father.

Murder was one thing, scandal something else entirely.

All of which may help to explain why he wouldn't let Annie go to Paris.

Annie was the youngest of his 13 children. She was the only one of the Conlon offspring still living at home when I visited Ireland for the first time in 1954. I was stationed with the Army in Austria when I made the visit.

She was 23 then, a few months younger than I. She was a happy young woman who laughed a lot and was as amused at having a nephew older than she as I was at having a younger aunt.

She became my personal guide to the wonders of Carrick-on-Shannon, but warned me on our first outing that if I continued taking such big strides, there would be nothing of the town left for us to see for the rest of my stay. She told me all she could about this place where my mother had been born and reared and about the people who lived there.

Since she worked for some of the families in the town, she was a keeper of their secrets, which she freely shared with me, something she felt comfortable with because I was only passing through.

Some of the people, she confided to me one day, wouldn't buy milk from Mrs. McGreevy because she let her cows eat the grass in the town cemetery.

Not that it hurt the milk or anything, Annie said, but some people just didn't feel comfortable about it.

When it was close to the time for me to leave, I mentioned to the family that I was stopping in Paris for a weekend on my way back to my post in Austria.

Later that day, Annie asked me what Paris was like. I told her it was not like Carrick. She asked if I thought she'd ever get to see it. I told her that all things were possible. Then I said if she really wanted to see Paris, I would take her with me.

Since she showed me Carrick-on-Shannon, I said, the least I could do would be to show her Paris.

I told my grandfather that I wanted to take Annie to Paris for a weekend. It wouldn't cost much, I told him, and I'd send her back to Dublin and she could take the train home. He looked at me for a moment without speaking. Then he told me he couldn't let her go.

I asked him why. "You have a wife and a baby in America," he said, surprised that I even had to ask.

I offered to call my wife and have her tell him that she didn't object. He said that wasn't the point. It was the appearance of it all, he said. It just wouldn't look right, Annie going off to France with a married man, even if he was her nephew. People would talk.

He could live with a lot of things. People talking was not among them.

Annie cried, and I assured her that she'd see Paris someday.

She has four children now and lives near London, and her marriage has not been the most pleasant circumstance in her life.

I see her from time to time, but we never talk about the decision James Conlon made one fall day in 1954.

And I never ask her if she's been to Paris yet, because I know the answer. ■

Friends in high places
and fairies under the bed

March 13, 1983

There's really no overwhelming reason to be writing about John Sheehan today, unless it's the fact that St. Patrick's Day is near upon us and requires at least some sort of acknowledgement here.

My Irish background notwithstanding, St. Patrick's Day was never a substantial event in our house. My parents, both from Ireland, were more intent on all of us being part of the country they had chosen than they were in singing mournful songs about the place they had left behind.

But there was always a sense of Irishness in our lives, and nobody personified it more for me than John Sheehan.

He was married to my father's sister, Kate, and they lived with their daughter, Helen, on the side of a hill in the Hazelwood district of Pittsburgh. The street was called Gladstone. The next street was Parnell, and the one up the hill was Home Rule, which gives you some hint of the ethnic makeup of the neighborhood.

At the bottom of the hill, the Jones & Laughlin steel mill ranged along the banks of the Monongahela River, just over the tracks of the Monongahela Connecting Railroad, which everybody called the "Mon-Con."

My two brothers and I were sent to Pennsylvania every summer in the late 1930s to stay with our Aunt Mary, my father's other sister, who owned a small roadside restaurant, a Sunoco station and one tourist cabin in the hills of western Pennsylvania. The collective medical wisdom of the day allowed that it was impossible for infantile paralysis, the crippler of city kids, to flourish in any healthy, pastoral setting. Hence, our journey east each year.

Kate and Mary were wonderfully gentle women whose soft West Kerry brogues still drift quietly to mind whenever I think of them. I vividly remember how close Aunt Mary came to maiming herself each time she sliced fresh bread.

She hugged the loaf to a bosom of prodigious proportions with one arm and sliced with the other, pulling the sharp knife ever closer to her torso with each stroke, while I sat at the table, my eyes squeezed shut, waiting for disaster.

She was still intact when she died, which I always considered the ultimate salute to her precision.

But Uncle John was, in a word, different.

My father delighted in recalling the day in 1932 when John Sheehan climbed to the roof of his house to announce loudly, lest there be any doubt in the neighborhood, that he favored Jack Sharkey in his heavyweight championship fight with Max Schmeling, because Sharkey was a "good Catholic boy."

We would always spend some weeks with Aunt Kate and Uncle John before leaving for the country, and in the bedroom I shared with my brothers, it was possible to hear John Sheehan conduct his nightly conversations with God. Not prayers, exactly, but plain talk in which God obviously participated, even though we could never hear Him.

Uncle John would also tell us of the fairies — the little people — and how sometimes at night they would pluck bright little tunes on the springs of his bed.

It might be the selective recollection of childhood, but I can remember lying in bed in that house, walls glowing orange from the fires of the men making steel down the hill at J & L, and hearing the soft sound of music through the bedroom wall.

Aunt Kate died in the early 1950s, and my last clear memory of Uncle John is from her funeral.

The wake was at the O'Toole and O'Connor funeral home in Hazelwood, across from St. Stephen's Church.

The night before the funeral, Uncle John and either O'Toole or O'Connor, I was never really sure which one, had some contentious words about the casket.

With the funeral director at his side, Uncle John walked up to the casket and rapped loudly on it with his knuckles. He had ordered oak, he told the director, and said that not only did the wood look like hemlock, it sounded like hemlock. He pronounced it "himlock."

The dispute was settled later to Uncle John's satisfaction after an original invoice was produced.

John Sheehan died a few years later, and I remember how sad I felt. I had no grandparents in this country, and he and Aunt Kate and Aunt Mary were as close as I ever got to having them.

I think of John Sheehan now and then, most often on nights when I can't sleep. And, if I let my imagination have its way, it seems sometimes that I can hear the soft tinkle of Irish music coming from somewhere beyond the bedroom wall. ■

The little man stepped out of the Irish twilight

March 14, 1982

There is a small town in County Sligo, Ireland, called Dromahair, which means "ridge of the two demons." That translation isn't terribly important to this story except where it might provide some basis of explanation for what happened there one quiet May evening in 1978.

Night comes slowly to Ireland. A kind of soft twilight clings to the countryside for hours, as if reluctant to surrender another day to the darkness. And when night comes, it does so slowly and deliberately, almost in keeping with the character of the Irish themselves.

It is probably a consequence of Irish twilight that so many things in that enchanted country aren't what they seem to be. The half-light of an Irish evening has done more for fable and legend than all of the writers who ever dealt with the phenomena of the unexplained.

It was the twilight of a spring day four years ago when I drove to the ruins of a Franciscan abbey near Dromahair. My uncle, who was a schoolmaster nearby, had taken me there in 1954, and I remember how fond he was of the place and how he talked about its serenity and how he liked to go there because he could almost feel the gentle presence of St. Francis.

I wanted to go there again, mostly because I wanted my wife to see it, and not because of any residual feelings of mysticism from my first visit.

We were still miles from the place when I began worrying that it might be too dark to see the abbey by the time we got there.

But there was still enough light as we drew close enough to see the ruins of the abbey against the pale yellow of the sky.

We drove a narrow track up the hill, stopped next to a low stone wall and decided that our stay would be brief.

I didn't see where he came from. Over the small stone fence, my wife said, briskly and sprightly, until he stood in front of us, smiling. He was perhaps 5½ feet tall, maybe a bit shorter. The only thing distinctive about his dress was the old vest he wore and a felt hat that had seen better days. He carried a short stick, something that looked more like a crooked swagger stick than a walking stick.

"Welcome to Dromahair abbey," he said. "Would you like to see it? I can tell you a lot about it."

We had driven a long way to see it, I told him, and we'd appreciate anything he could tell us about it.

We followed him through the ruins as he described every room with a familiarity that was unsettling. This was the cloister, he said. Over here was the bake house. This stone was a mill where the flour was ground. This room was for the choir. There were windows here, he explained, pointing to the lancet openings in the ruined wall, so that the monks could have light to read their hymnals.

He led us through the nave and the transept, the buttery and the kitchen, stepping quickly over the stones as he explained what life was like in these rooms more than 400 years ago. This is the refectory, he said, and walked to a spot and said it was the place where one of the monks read to the others at every meal. There was nothing there to indicate that a lectern or anything else had ever stood there. But he seemed to know that was the spot.

All the while, he spoke of the inhabitants of this ancient place as "the little brothers." In the cloister, he pointed to a sculptured relief, in a crumbling column, of St. Francis of Assisi preaching to the birds and said: "That's what he called them, you know. Little brothers."

I remembered then. The Franciscans. The order of friars minor. Little brothers.

He said the abbey had been built in 1508. When the King of England disbanded the monasteries after the Reformation, the little brothers left. They returned, but only for a while, "after Cromwell," he said.

It was almost dark, and the tour was ending. In the classic gesture of the tourist, I offered him some money for his services. He waved his hand. "No need for that," he said. "Just remember that this place is more than just a lot of old stones."

He touched the crooked stick to the brim of his hat, said, "Safe home," and stepped over the wall.

I walked to the wall to see where he had gone, so I might have some idea of where he had come from. But in the time it had taken me to walk three feet, he was not to be seen.

My wife walked to the wall and looked over the meadow that sloped away from the abbey. There were no houses, no trees, no bicycle being pedaled away.

I will make no judgments here as to the mysterious arrival and departure of a little man who knew a lot about an old abbey. My wife, who can claim only a fractional Celtic heritage, is convinced he was a local farmer who walked off into the quickening darkness.

Maybe it was the twilight. I'm not entirely convinced. ■

On a dark night, at the gates
of a forgotten graveyard . . .

March 11, 1984

In Gaelic, the phrase "Cloon na Morav" translates as "Meadow of the Dead."

In more basic terms, which the Irish avoid whenever possible, it means a graveyard.

I found myself wishing, the other day, for an opportunity that is unlikely to present itself. For the chance to stand at the gates of one of these meadows of the dead. To be there with Jeremiah Curtin and Jeremiah King.

In the heart of an Irish night, black as a rook's wing. In the shadow of the huge stone slabs. The only earthly sound, the soft whisper of wind in the bracken.

But I know Mr. Curtin is dead and I suspect that the same circumstance has befallen Mr. King. Pity.

You see, Jeremiah King put together a book in 1931 called "County Kerry Past and Present. A Handbook to the Local and Family History of the County." A book with little more to recommend it than a cumbersome title and a list of families from that Irish county. King also included his personal reflections on the validity of certain Irish folkways.

Jeremiah Curtin, who was born in Detroit in 1835 and died in 1906, was also an author. A remarkable linguist and folklorist, he wrote a number of books including one called "Tales of the Fairies and of the Ghost World," stories Curtin collected from the oral tradition in southwest Munster, a province in Ireland that includes County Kerry.

In his book, King deals perfunctorily with the subject that Curtin spent his life studying. "There are no fairies or ghosts or pookas or leprechauns or banshees now in Kerry, up the airy mountain or down the rushy glen, no good folk or little men in green jackets and red caps," King wrote.

He calls them things "no longer believed in . . . illusory creations of the imagination."

On the other hand, there's more than a hint of his own Celtic mysticism and romanticism in Jeremiah Curtin's stories, an ingredient that helps overcome any temptation to confuse ghost stories with social science.

Curtin made several trips to Ireland and visited people in their cottages and huts to collect the stories and mythology still preserved in the oral tradition of 19th-Century Ireland.

His efforts were not without the drawbacks indigenous to rural Irish life in those days.

"He could not quite get used to the practice of sharing the house with the pigs," D.L. Olmsted wrote in 1975 in the International Journal for the History of Linguistics. "Several times, when he arrived to collect myths, the swine were ejected from the peasant cottage, but, since they squealed so much, they were let back in, making work impossible."

Curtin's stories are simple and straightforward. The matter-of-fact recitations of the people he talked to. Words put down as they were spoken. Stories that reflect an almost benign acceptance of the unexplained rather than a fear of the supernatural.

Ghost stories, fairy stories. Stories of the dead come back to life.

Like one he called "The Dead Mother."

It is a story about a young widow from Cloghane, Mary Shea, who takes her two daughters to America, leaving her young son in the care of her brother-in-law. After a year in America, the woman "took a fever and died."

About the time of Mary Shea's death, a young girl walking on the beach near Cloghane meets a woman who says she is Mary Shea.

"I died two weeks ago," she tells the girl, "but don't be in dread of me for I'll do you no harm. When you go home tomorrow, go to my mother and tell her that I died in America, and that you saw me on this strand, that I am walking back and forth perishing with the cold. Tell her to buy a pair of shoes and stockings and give them to some poor person in my name, for God's sake."

The dead Mary Shea, the story relates, had been to her house in Cloghane the night before and found that her little boy was being mistreated by his uncle. She went to the child's room, took him in her arms and told him that soon all would be right, that he would be with his sisters in America. That he would never see his mother again.

Mary Shea's mother bought the shoes and stockings and gave them to a poor woman "for God's sake and the good of Mary's soul, and Mary was seen no more on the strand after that."

So it would please me, in this octave of the feast of St. Patrick, to stand at the rusting gates of an Irish cemetery with the two Jeremiahs on the odd chance that, in the quiet of an Irish night, we might bump into Mary Shea.

Illusory creations, indeed, Mr. King.   ∎

All the Shines drank a toast to old Patrick — whoever he was

Sept. 30, 1984

According to the old Tenants Ledger in Ireland's Glin Castle, the first Shine to pay rent to the owners of the castle and its surrounding lands was one Patrick Shine.

Beginning in 1857, Patrick Shine, a farmer from the village of Glin, paid the Knight of Glin one pound, 10 shillings a year to be allowed to till a small piece of land. Fifteen shillings to be paid every six months.

In a neat Spencerian hand, some long-forgotten clerk scrupulously recorded each payment, noting how much was paid in cash and subtracting the two shillings and sixpence which was paid in Mr. Shine's behalf by what was called the "poor rate."

Those were not good times in Ireland, but Patrick Shine made his payments on time, and the clerk entered each shilling, each penny in the big book which today rests, with other rent ledgers, on a table in the castle's library.

There is no explanation why, on Nov. 13, 1876, a line was struck through Patrick Shine's name with a notation showing that the rent had been raised to three pounds a year and that the parcel of land had been "leased to M. White for 31 years."

On other pages of the ledger, there are places where the keeper of the accounts noted that various tenants had failed to pay the rent in a timely fashion and had been evicted and the lands "surrendered to the knight."

But there's nothing in the ledger to indicate that Patrick Shine had died or had been evicted for failing to pay his rent, or that he was unable to pay the new, higher rent and had simply walked away from the piece of land he had worked for nearly 20 years.

Last month, 108 years after the name of Patrick Shine was stricken from the official records of the Tenants Ledger, the Shines from America went back to Glin Castle — through the massive stone entrance, up the great sweeping drive and inside the 200-year-old ancestral home of the Knights of Glin — through the front door.

It is a wonderful place, a massive Georgian-style house to which battlements were added in 1812, giving it a Gothic look.

It stands on the estuary of the Shannon River, in County Limerick, at the edge of the pleasant and friendly village of Glin.

We had read in the New York Times that the present Knight of Glin, whose family traces its heritage in Ireland to the 13th Century, had made the castle available for rentals. We decided that would be a magnificent way to enjoy a vacation in Ireland.

After all, it was less than 10 miles from the old Shine family farm at Kilbaha, which is being worked by cousins Con and Margaret. Cousins Jack and Bridey have a shop in Moyvane, which is the next town over from Glin.

Cousins Ned and Sheila live across the street from the shop, and cousins Eileen and Tom have a farm not far away.

In fact, that whole corner of southwest Ireland is rich with first and second cousins, not to mention Aunt Nora, 88, my father's youngest sister.

Arrangements were made through the rental agent, and the Shines from America moved into Glin Castle for two weeks. There were nine of us. My wife and I, my two brothers and their wives, my mother and two of my children. Two family friends also accompanied us.

We discovered Patrick Shine's name in the old ledger the first day there. None of the local Shines was quite sure who he was or how he fit in the family line. But there was agreement that if he was a Shine, he was probably one of us.

At night, over coffee, we would talk about him. About who he might have been. About the kind of life he had, about what might have become of him. There was talk that if he had been evicted for non-payment of rent that we should settle up with the present knight in behalf of old Patrick and clear his name.

A priest from Armagh, in Northern Ireland, a friend who came to visit us at the castle, suggested that a better course might be to demand repayment of all the rents Patrick Shine had ever paid.

We never really decided the issue, but on Aug. 26 we invited all the Shines we could find to a party at the castle. They came, nearly 50 of them, to a great castle they had seen all their lives — but always from outside the gates.

We had a fiddler on the terrace, sandwiches and pastries in the grand entrance hall, punch in the drawing room.

And later in the day, when the sun had turned the haze on the hills of Clare across the Shannon to a soft blue, we offered a quiet toast to the memory of Patrick Shine, whoever he was. ■

3. The old neighborhood

A sanctuary and a refuge whose days are numbered

Feb. 26, 1984

There was a name and a phone number on the pad, and a brief message.

"Wants you to call. Says they are going to tear down the church."

The moment I read it I knew the caller was talking about St. Rose.

I knew because of all the churches in all the times of our lives, there is usually one that always remains part of you.

The place where you began your first cautious relationship with God. The place where the rites of passage were first identified. Where the requiem mass was the logical extension of baptism, and all the things in the middle were simply stops on the way to *dies irae*.

After a couple of calls, I learned the information was substantially correct. The church was old. It was too expensive to heat and maintain for a parish of only 150 families.

The parishioners were allowed to vote after mass on the last Sunday in January. Merge with neighboring St. Bernard's or build a chapel in the basement of the old school to maintain the parish community. They chose the chapel.

The Rev. Joe Connelly is pastor — and the only priest — at St. Rose. He is 37 and has been there since last May 1.

"There was a beautiful culture that developed around these parishes in other years," he says, "but much of that has changed."

Of the decision to tear down the church: "It's not something you like to do in your first year in a parish."

"It doesn't seem as though a lot of thought has gone into this decision," one parishioner, Marie Oresti, said. "I realize that the church is not just a building, but the building represents a heritage and that should not be forgotten.

"We tried to buy some time, but I think we've run out of time," she said. "Twenty years from now people will look around and wonder whatever happened to those beautiful churches we used to have."

I have spent a lot of time in the past few days thinking all the good thoughts I can about St. Rose Church. I am surprised at the number of memories of that fine place that have very little to do with God.

Of course, it was where I made my first communion and my confirmation. Where I attended mass every school-day morning for 12 years. It was where I squirmed through endless droning verses of "By the Cross Her Station Keeping" every Friday of every Lent of my young life.

From the promise of glory of Forty Hours Devotion to the threat of everlasting fire of the weekend retreats with the Passionist Fathers.

But the recurring thought of that wonderful old building on Kercheval and Beniteau is that whatever it represented as a house of worship, it was always sanctuary from those who would blacken your eye, split your lip or bloody your nose.

Pursuit inside its hallowed precincts was permitted, but violence was not.

It was not out of character to see two out-of-breath boys walking briskly up the aisle, one obviously tracking the other. There had been a fight outside and the one getting the worst of it had reached the safety of the church.

Crossing in front of the sanctuary, executing a skidding genuflection, they would slide into a pew to see who could outwait the other.

I remember at least one personal, heart-thumping, terror-filled escape into church.

Earlier in the day the word circulated in school that a kid from Foch Intermediate with a reputation for battering others had announced that he would batter me. He caught me after school outside the candy store, across from the church.

My characteristic stance when faced with conflict certain not to go my way was to survey the situation carefully and then beg for my life.

It was in the middle of my begging mode, which he was enjoying, that I was overcome with the temptation to punch him as hard as I could in the nose.

Which is what I did, and in the same motion headed full speed for church.

I said a prayer of thanksgiving that he was not a Catholic and did not follow me into church, and for the fact that he was not able to watch all eight doors, allowing me to dash to the freedom of home.

I will miss St. Rose Church for all the reasons we miss the things that were part of our lives.

If some of the former parishioners would like to help with the costs of building the new chapel, Father Connelly says it would be a nice gesture.

The way I look at it, I think I probably owe something for the afternoon St. Rose Church saved my life. ∎

For Billy it was just a yawn — snoozing with the dead

Feb. 21, 1982

The Doherty Funeral Home opened in 1926 in the big old house on E. Jefferson near Harding. A year later, Billy Doherty was born there in an upstairs bedroom.

For the next 22 years the place was home to Billy. For a large part of that time, Billy Doherty was a minor legend with the other kids in the neighborhood.

He was the guy who lived in the funeral home. All the time. After everybody went home. After the lights were turned off. He slept upstairs when there were dead people downstairs.

We were certainly familiar with funeral homes. In neighborhoods as ethnic as ours, wakes and funerals were part of the culture. There was no point at which parents decided children were "mature enough" to go to the funeral home. If you were old enough to be taken along without being a nuisance, you were allowed to go. The mixed smells of flowers and candle wax and the soft sound of organ music being piped in through scratchy sound systems are among my early memories of places like Doherty's.

If the open approach to the inevitability of death is a good thing, then we got a lot of a good thing. We understood that people died. Not just old people, but sometimes kids our own age or the brothers of our friends who got killed in the war. The process seemed more natural than mysterious.

But if we were able to deal with the reality of death, we never came close to understanding how Billy Doherty could ever get a good night's sleep in his upstairs bedroom knowing full well what was downstairs. Going to a funeral home on official business was one thing. Living there was yet another.

In deference to the nature of his family's business, we never stood on Billy's front porch and called him to come out and play. We knocked softly on the back door and then always politely declined his mother's offer to come inside and wait for him there. "That's OK, Mrs. Doherty, we'll wait out here. It really isn't raining all that hard."

I don't know if anybody ever asked him how he managed to maintain what appeared to the rest of us to be a normal existence while living full-time in a funeral home. I never did. Until a few weeks ago.

I decided that enough time had gone by for us to be able to have a straightforward talk about those times. We could call it something like: "Recollections of a Kid Who Grew Up Living in a Funeral Home."

Billy is 55 now and the office manager of the St. Clair Shores branch of Graham Mortgage Corp., where I'm sure nobody calls him Billy.

He said the room in which he was born was his bedroom all the years he lived there.

Was his life any different because his house was also a funeral home?

"No. Not really. Since I was born there and grew up there, it was a very natural thing."

How about noises and bumps in the night? Strange footsteps on the stairs in the dark?

"Nope. Nothing like that."

Voices, then? Howls, moans? That kind of stuff."

"No. None of that kind of stuff."

It was, with the exception of getting to talk with Billy after all these years, a disappointing and non-productive interview.

It was an interview that could have been turned around if only Billy Doherty had started a single sentence with: "Well, I remember this one night. It was dark and cold, the wind outside was howling and I heard this sound coming from downstairs. . . ." No such luck.

There were some drawbacks, he admitted. "We had to be quiet a lot of the time. No running around. No loud music on the radio. Things like that. Sometimes it was sort of like living in a church."

Billy served a hitch in the Navy and then moved out of the home in 1949 and got married. He stayed in the funeral business with his family until 1968, when he went into real estate full-time.

With room for only two funerals at once (three in a pinch), Billy said it was difficult to make a living in such a small operation, and he decided that real estate provided a better opportunity. In 1969, his family sold the business to another funeral director.

My friend Terry Gibney, an embalmer, knew the Dohertys well and provided his services for their business successors. He recalled the time, post-Doherty, that he came in the back door of the funeral home to do his work, peeked into one of the parlors and saw the mourners stretched out on the floor. Some bizarre religious practice, he assumed. Actually, it was a holdup.

The point of all this is that I sort of wish it had happened when Billy Doherty was a kid so we could have at least started this interview with: "Well, there was this one night when these guys came in with guns. . . ."

But, what the heck. It was good talking with you again, Billy. ■

Commer Cleaners was more than just a business

Aug. 22, 1982

The old neon sign in the window reads "Commer Cleaners Since 1916."

Last month a new sign went up under the old one telling all who might be interested that the cleaning shop was closing Aug. 1 and reopening Aug. 16 "for pickup only."

With a little basic deduction it was possible to figure out that another neighborhood institution was about to bite the dust and that after the picking up would come the locking up.

Commer Cleaners is on the corner of E. Jefferson and Hart, across the street from the Dixieland pool room and the Engine 32 fire station. Next door to the vacant lot where Mr. Causley used to run the trailer rental and a few blocks east of the Jefferson Precinct police station.

When Morris and Louis Commer opened the place in 1916, there were three other stores on Jefferson between Hart and Grosse Pointe. The brothers, who had opened their first tailor shop in Kansas City in 1912, liked that spot on Jefferson and built a more substantial structure there in 1921, the place where the business has operated ever since.

My earliest recollection of Commer Cleaners is from 1939 or 1940 when I was an "unofficial" employe of the Detroit News. If you think this is an admission that trips easily off the typewriter, think of how you'd feel telling dinner guests over dessert that you think the canned beans might have had a touch of botulism.

By unofficial I mean that I was too young for the route I was carrying but worked on the side for a kid named Roger Callahan. Roger subcontracted parts of his route, for less than the going rate, to underage kids who were referred to by the overage kids as "stooges."

On Sunday mornings, on my way to my unofficial route, I would look through the Commer Cleaners window and see Louis Commer in his undershirt, pants rolled up to his knees, mopping the floor with steady, even strokes.

He always looked up and smiled at me, oblivious to or in spite of my status as a stooge. I never spoke to him in my life, but I knew I liked him.

We didn't have a lot of clothes around the house in those days that needed professional dry cleaning and the things that did looked almost professionally done after a few applications of Energine and a couple of passes with a hot iron over a damp dish towel.

Commer Cleaners is being run now by Roy Commer, Morris' son, who has been running or helping run the place since the early 1950s. Roy, 62, has spent most of his life in or over the shop. His parents lived above it when he was born and he and Carol, his wife of 40 years, live there now.

The unhappy task of closing it has fallen to him. Talking in the shop a few days before his Aug. 1 deadline, Roy had trouble saying words like closing or shutting down.

"We really don't have customers here, we have friends," he said. He pointed to the open area at the counters and said: "No bars, no walls, no plastic partitions. And we never had a problem."

He said the cleaning shop wasn't really a neighborhood business anymore, since there was less of the neighborhood than there had been in previous years. "The customers came from all over," Roy said. "Trenton, Port Huron. Not just from around here. Lots of people who live in the Jeffersonian, lawyers and judges. But it just wasn't enough anymore. We had a lot of clothes come in but not enough going out. People just didn't come back and get them."

While we talked , Bill Fitzgerald, running hard in the final days of the primary as a Democratic candidate for governor, came in.

"I've lost track of two suits," Fitz explained. "I'm not sure, but I think they might be here." Only one of them was.

As Fitzgerald was leaving with 50 percent of his missing wardrobe, he turned to me and said: "You should really do a column about this place. It's an institution around here."

It was the first time Bill Fitzgerald had ever suggested I do a column about anybody else but him, and I took it as the ultimate tribute to Roy and Carol Commer and their cleaning establishment.

Roy is not sure what he'll do after he closes. He's not going to retire, he says, because he doesn't want to. He said he'll have time, at least, to give it a lot of thought. But he and Carol say they'll miss it terribly.

I keep thinking that what I'd like to do is get up some Sunday morning before it gets light and trudge past that window again and look for an old man inside mopping the floor. Maybe he's still got a smile for the stooge who's still fooling around with newspapers 40 years later. ■

Nick Bakalis was like
a dean among grocers

April 4, 1982

Parental expectations being what they were then, it is not surprising that Peter Bakalis decided not to make the grocery business his life's work.

But before he decided to sell the store, known officially as Nick's Friendly Market, Nick Bakalis offered his son one more chance at running his own business. One more chance at the 14-hour day and the seven-day week.

"He wanted to make sure that I didn't want the business before he started looking for a buyer," Peter says. "I told him that I knew how important the grocery business had been to our family, but that I was going to find a job in industry. He wasn't disappointed. He just wanted me to know that the store was there if I wanted it."

The store was on the corner of E. Vernor and Lillibridge, and every day of the week Nick Bakalis opened it at 9 a.m. and closed it at 10 p.m. He wanted Peter, his only son, to go to college, and he wanted him to have at least the option of using his master's of business administration to make a successful life for himself selling groceries.

Peter was known generally by the neighborhood kids as "Tucky," a corruption of "Taki," which is what his parents called him. Which was, in turn, a shortened version of "Panayoitaki," which is the nickname for "Panayoitis," which Peter discovered when he registered for the draft was his real first name. We didn't know any of that at the time, which is probably just as well.

And while we're at it, "Bakalis" itself means "grocer" in Greek. "My father's last name was Alexander," Peter says, "and he didn't know how to spell it for the immigration officials when he came to this country in 1917. So when they asked him his name, he gave them one he could spell, Bakalis, because he and his father had both been grocers in Greece."

Tucky is now an executive at Ford Motor Co. where, corporate decorum being what it is, he is known as "Peter N. Bakalis, Procurement Manager, Stamped Parts Department, Body and Assembly Purchasing, Ford North American Automotive Operations." Bakalis still means grocer, and there is no Greek diminutive for his title at Ford.

He was one of a handful of kids we knew who had the misfortune of having a family grocery store to occupy their after-school hours. I wouldn't say that those kids — the Bogoses and the Zogbys, among them — were turned into drudges by the responsibility of their family enterprises, but the rest of us felt that their flexibility to do things like hang around playgrounds was severely reduced.

As far as I know, none of these kids ever stayed in the grocery business, although I confess to having lost track of the Zogbys. But two of the Bogos boys, Paul and Larry, are partners in their own law firm in Detroit, where I'm sure they extend credit to their clients as readily as their father did to his customers.

Peter Bakalis, on the other hand, figured that he could make some contribution to the family business based on what he was learning in the business school at Wayne.

"I remember trying to give my father some advice on his pricing policies, and he told me he didn't have one," Peter says. "When I told him about inventory turn rates and what he should stock and how much he should buy, he said he had already figured that out.

"When I tried explaining pricing elasticity to him, he told me that if he could sell day-old donuts at a price of two for five cents or three for a dime and get most of his customers to take advantage of the 10-cent offer, he didn't need any more pricing elasticity than that.

"He finally told me: 'You go to school and listen to the professors and do what they tell you, and I'll run the store.' " Peter's father sold his store in the early 1960s to a buyer who ran the business into the ground in about three years.

"My father took the business over again in about 1966, when he was 72," Peter recalls. "It was a mess, and it took him three years to get it back to where it had been. When he was satisfied that it was in good shape, he sold it again. It's still there. Still serving the neighborhood."

Nick Bakalis died in 1976, when he was 82. Peter remembers what may have been one of the proudest days in his father's life.

"The dean of the business school at Wayne, Walter Folley, came by to meet my family, and my father baked strawberry cream pies for the occasion. So we took the pies to where we lived up over the store, and my father sat down with the dean to talk about business."

A nice memory of a nice man. Nick Bakalis, the grocer, explaining his version of pricing policy and inventory turn rates to the dean of the business school. ■

Something dies when a library closes its doors to the world

May 8, 1983

It was a walk of something under two miles, depending on route and diversions.

From the house by the alley at Lycaste and Jefferson to the low, salmon-colored brick building at Mack and Montclair.

It was never a terribly inspiring walk. Down Kercheval to Fairview. Look in the window of Saylor's drugstore to see if Helen Arnold was running the soda fountain. (If she was, stop in and buy something from her.) Up Fairview, past Foch Intermediate and Southeastern High. Across Goethe (pronounced go-thee) to Montclair to Mack.

Then through the front door of that building, under the stone lintel in which was carved the legend: "Detroit Public Library, The C. I. Walker Branch."

And into another world.

Passage out of that east-side Detroit neighborhood to places limited only by the quality of your fantasy life and the contents of the Walker Branch card catalog file. All you had to do was pick a destination. The words in the books did the rest.

To Camelot with Tennyson: "But who hath seen her wave her hand? Or at the casement seen her stand? Or is she known in all the land, the Lady of Shalott?"

To the Orient with Kipling: "By the old Moulmein Pagoda, lookin' lazy at the sea, There's a Burma girl a-settin', and I know she thinks o' me; For the wind is in the palm trees, and the temple bells they say: 'Come you back, you British soldier; come you back to Mandalay!' "

Down to the sea with John Masefield: "I must go down to the seas again, to the vagrant gypsy life, To the gull's way and the whale's way where the wind's like a whetted knife ... "

Or drifting on a muddy river with Huckleberry Finn: "We catched fish and talked and we took a swim now and then to keep off sleepiness. It was kind of solemn drifting down the big, still river, laying on our backs and looking up at the stars, and we didn't even feel like talking loud. ..."

It was so easy. Take a book from the shelf and let the words on the pages take you where they would.

Wonderful words which fired the imagination, gave substance to dreams and threw open the gates to a world filled with wonders that defied even the most creative of my daydreams.

The Walker Branch represented nearly as important a part of my childhood as did home and school. I knew the maximum number of allowable withdrawals and never took any less. But I preferred reading in the busy silence of the library to the ritual of selecting and checking out the books and taking them home.

There was a comfort among the volumes in that old library that is hard to describe. So I spent as many hours as I could there. Left only when supper beckoned or when the doors were about to be closed for the night.

One of the librarians, a woman whose name I never knew, represents very special memories of those times.

Her hair was beginning to gray and she favored print dresses of what I thought at the time was silk, but probably wasn't. When she walked through the library she trailed a hint of a perfume which I learned in subsequent years was called Yankee Clover.

She would have books saved for me when I arrived at the library and would slide them across the desk with a smile. "I think you will like these," she would say.

She gave me a book by Sholem Asch, an author I had never heard of. It was called "East River" and was about Jewish immigrants in New York in the early part of the century.

When I returned it she asked me if I liked it. I told her I did, which was true. I did not tell her it made me cry or that I was ashamed of the way the Irish treated the Jews in the book.

One day she gave me a book titled: "Bob Gordon, Cub Reporter." It was about a college student who worked on his uncle's newspaper for a summer which was filled with adventure and excitement.

The book raised the first thoughts in my mind about journalism, and they never diminished.

Cities close more libraries than they open these days, a tragedy too immense to be measured. They closed the Walker Branch one Monday in June 1975. Took down the flag, moved the books and locked up the doors to the world.

The words in stone still say it's a library, but a bigger sign says it's a church now.

I stood outside the building a few weeks ago thinking about Camelot and Mandalay and salt spray — and the lingering scent of Yankee Clover. ∎

Matinees down at the Jefferson:
Double features, little creatures

Feb. 17, 1985

The reason I remember where I was on Dec. 7, 1941, doesn't have a lot to do with Pearl Harbor.

It's just that Dec. 7 was a Sunday and I knew where I was every Sunday in 1941. The same place I had been every Sunday in 1940 — at the movies.

I don't remember what pictures I saw that day, but then the featured attractions were never the overwhelming reason for going to the show. You went because it was part of your life.

It was what kids did on Saturdays and Sundays.

A check of old movie listings for that date shows that the Plaza Theater, E. Jefferson and Lycaste, was featuring Anita Louise and Russell Hayden in "Two in a Taxi"; Michael Whalen in "Sign of the Wolf," and a third feature, "King of the Texas Rangers," the dramatis personae for that one blessedly unlisted.

There was nothing in that Sunday lineup that anyone — now or then — would ever mistake for a cinema classic, but the quality of the films had no bearing whatever on the decision to patronize. Prudent purchasers we were not. But the price was right and there were always enough ancillary inducements from the theater managers to make us feel wanted.

If the East End, across the street and down the block from the Plaza, was featuring some hotshot on stage doing incredible things with a Duncan yo-yo, the Plaza would fight back with a free candy bar, a comic book and two serials instead of one.

The most remarkable thing was the number of movie houses within walking distance.

Within easy reach of everyone in our east side neighborhood, in addition to the East End and Plaza, were the Admiral, the Deluxe, the Lakewood, the Booth, the President, the Cinderella and the Jefferson. The Jefferson was also known locally as "The Bug," testimony to the presence there of hundreds of little creatures who appeared when the lights went out and apparently existed on popcorn droppings and black Jujubes.

In a pinch, the Vogue, the Uptown or the Whittier were available, but they required some involvement with public transit, which was never built into our entertainment budget.

The Free Press movie guide for those years lists some 110 theaters in the area, the majority of them in the neighborhoods.

Going through those old listings, I was reminded again of what always seemed to be the case in the 1930s and 1940s. That the good movies were playing in another theater in a part of town as alien to us as Persia. That if we wanted to see "Sergeant York" it would be playing at the Beverly, and we would end up in a local theater with one of Guy Kibbee's "Scattergood Baines" features.

I wonder now if the kids who lived near the Lasky, the Iris, the Home, the Irving, the Farnum, the Linwood-LaSalle, the Crystal or the Tuxedo had the same problem.

Another interesting aspect of those old movie listings was the absence of the precise time each feature would begin. Probably because it never was important to see the last part of the movie first, especially if you were going to sit through it three more times anyway.

One of the people we took for granted then was the person who ran the place, the theater manager.

Mel Tork is 78 and retired. From 1925 to 1955 he was a theater manager. At the Jefferson when it had silent movies and stage acts, later at the Ideal on Mack at Montclair, and at the Booth, on the west edge of Water Works Park.

"Our Saturday matinee at the Ideal was the big day," he recalls. "For five cents you got a free candy bar, a double feature, cartoons, serials. It got so crowded most Saturdays we'd give an extra candy bar to kids who'd sit two to a seat."

During the week, Tork says, it was an adult crowd. "Couples would come regularly twice a week, when the features changed. It was their night out and they'd dress up for it. Coats, ties. Dresses for the ladies. None of this blue jean stuff."

He talked, too, of that great American institution, Dish Night.

"We had it two nights a week, and we'd give away more dishes in a week than Hudson's would sell. About 800 or 900 dishes.

"But by the end of the 1940s," Tork says, "movie theaters were going out of business right and left. TV. People stayed home and watched it and it didn't cost anything."

I suppose it was not much of a tradeoff. Milton Berle in place of such celluloid wonders as "Enemy Agents Meet Ellery Queen" or "Calling Dr. Gillespie."

But I, for one, would have felt more at home with the "Texaco Star Theater" if they had shown it at the Jefferson, insects and all. ∎

Lay down your video fears, parents, the galaxy is safe

July 11, 1982

It could be that today's video arcades will eventually occupy the same questionable place in the social history of Detroit that was once the unchallenged province of that misunderstood institution, the poolroom. But I don't really think so.

Poolrooms, sometimes called pool halls or billiard parlors, had unenviable reputations as places where all manner of nefarious activity thrived.

They were characterized as venal places harboring the city's misfits. Idlers who lay in wait for unsuspecting youth in order to turn them from productive pursuits into the kind of persons universally scorned by society. Loafers. And therein lies the difference.

Places where the air is split with the piercing and undulating sounds of electronic conflict will never produce any really effective loafers. People locked to the controls of a machine, eyes frozen to exploding images on a screen, trying to repel the invaders of the evil Gorfian robot empire, do not have the stuff of which great loungers are made.

Creative loafing requires, most of all, atmosphere. Restful, almost somnolent surroundings, which video arcades will never provide.

These arcades are being opened at virtually the same rate as the inflatable tennis houses a few years back. Parents are mobilizing against what they see as a threat to the behavioral well-being of their children. As one who survived the marshaled temptations of the poolroom, I would like to allay as many parental fears as possible. In other words, stop worrying. It's no big deal.

In 1926, in a Page One headline, the Free Press warned of the dangers lurking within the smoky confines of the billiard parlor.

POOLROOMS — 'CRIME NESTS'
Vice Experts Declare They Lure Boys
to Lives of Banditry and Viciousness

One of the experts called poolrooms "cesspools of crime" and "a meeting place of loafers and young rascals, experimentalists in petty crime. ..." Another characterized these establishments as "convenient places for habitual loafers to do nothing, a place for meeting and plotting ... and deciding on a little sortie into crime."

Though I will concede that a decided lack of productive activity transpired within those walls, I feel compelled to come to the defense of the place where I learned a lot about life.

Despite the seediness of its surroundings — and many of its occupants — the poolroom had its own quiet dignity and a standard of etiquette that went quite beyond the posted prohibitions against gambling, loitering, swearing, roughhousing and spitting anywhere except in vessels provided for that purpose.

For example, there was never loud talking when someone was lining up a shot. No noisy chalking of cue tips. No coughs or throat-clearing. Some quiet observations were allowed, however, but were generally limited to such undisputed statements of fact as, "That's a lot of green, Eddie."

The lighting was always, in a word, subdued. Green-shaded lights hung low over each pool table and enabled you to identify the person you were playing either by the color of his trousers or recognition of a disembodied voice that would say quietly from beyond the light, "Didn't leave you much."

The poolroom responsible for at least part of my character formation was known alternately through the years as Tiny's, Harp's and Fleming's, the names of its owners. It was on Kercheval near Fairview, but exists now only in neighborhood lore. It was replaced by a VFW post, and later by the New Greater Whole Truth Temple, proving that it is possible to superimpose sanctity on premises where it had previously been in terribly short supply.

I spent time recently in a video arcade watching intent teenagers using laser cannons to scatter electronic fragments of make-believe villains across glass galaxies. At the controls of Space Invader, Armor Attack, Berzerk, Spectar, Gorf, Pac-Man, Space Zap, Star Castle and Galaxian, they disintegrated little green blips at 25 cents per space war.

It's good for them, I reasoned after leaving the place. It's a computer world, and it gives them a head start in that kind of technology. It's also good, they say, for hand-eye co-ordination. What good, I asked myself, has my ability to sink a straight-rail shot ever been to me in my life?

I found myself wishing I could have convinced my mother then that snooker improved hand-eye co-ordination. I wouldn't have had to waste all that time brushing cue chalk off my clothes. ■

Carrying out wasn't in
at the Chinese Teapot

Nov. 7, 1982

Most of us measure the elegance in our lives on different scales.

Flashy cars, exotic vacations, fine clothes, impressive jewelry, magnificent houses.

I had a neighbor who measured his ambitious passage through the various economic levels in his life by the quality of his lawn. Rye, Kentucky blue, Fylking, Adelphi, Merion blue and finally, Washington bent.

It was possible to accurately track his corporate progress over the years by watching him rip out his lawn to replace it with something better.

Personally, I have a thing for restaurants.

Perhaps it's because that from a very early age I associated restaurant eating with easy living.

Any place where the tables were already set, where the choices were listed in writing and where, when the meal was finished, the dishes were left on the table for somebody else to wash, was a place where I wanted to spend a lot of mealtimes.

As a result, my mind is cluttered with memories of meals not prepared by my mother and not eaten in a house. Memories that start with dinner in a forgotten restaurant on E. Jefferson when I was in the first or second grade. It was an outing made memorable when Tom McKenna, who roomed in our home most of his life, drank the water from his finger bowl. An event that delighted my father and embarrassed my mother so totally that, 45 years later, it's still known in family lore as "the night Mc-Kenna drank the finger bowl."

At our house, eating out was not high on the agenda of things to do. Economics had something to do with it. Actually, economics had everything to do with it.

So, with the exception of the night McKenna made famous, my early restaurant experiences didn't gather any significant momentum until high school, when such things as proms and seasonal dances required a late dinner to make the evening a social success.

I will confess the prospect of dining out appealed to me a lot more than the dancing ever did, and almost as much as the time spent parked in the lot at Detroit City Airport for post-dinner conversation. The intervening years have not substantially altered my priorities, although I gave up the airport parking lot long before they paved it, lighted it and began charging by the hour.

Now comes that venerable east side institution, the Chinese Teapot Cafe, E. Jefferson and Lemay. An Oriental outpost in a neighborhood that has slipped some since the place was opened in 1934 or 1935. Fortunately, it's a neighborhood where people still understand more about survival than they do about urban demographics.

The Chinese Teapot still stands and, sadly, so do the customers. It's a carryout restaurant now where, according to the sign in the window, a paper plate runs you a nickel extra and chopsticks are 40 cents a pair, but the plastic forks are free.

Time was, when the Chinese Teapot represented the ultimate in elegant dining on that strip of E. Jefferson.

Admittedly, the local competition was not formidable. The S & C Coffee Car, Carden's and a few dinettes and lunchrooms where food was available, but not always advisable.

But the Chinese Teapot would have held its own, regardless. It was the first restaurant I had ever been in where the floor covering was carpeting and not linoleum. Cloth napkins may not have been marked a social breakthrough in your life, but it was worth the price of the chow mein just to have one of that brigade of Chinese waiters drape that crisp linen square on your lap, place the menu on the table and disappear silently into the kitchen while you and your date decided what you could afford.

As I have said before, memories are best left intact and going back looking to reinforce them will only disappoint you.

I went back to the Chinese Teapot a couple of nights ago. What was the entrance lobby is now the place where people order through the slit in the thick plastic shield.

Beyond the plastic, the old restaurant remains virtually unchanged. The tables with their red cloths, the booths with their high partitions of dark wood are still there. A heroic Chinese tapestry still covers the top of the back wall. The lady behind the shield, Mee Lee, says the Chinese Teapot converted to carryout two years ago when the owner's illness made it impossible to run the restaurant as it always had been.

"But it was better," Mrs. Lee said, looking back at the empty tables, "when people were in here."

But what the Chinese Teapot is today will never damage the memory of what it used to be. And the egg rolls are still very tasty.   ■

Come back to the five-and-dime and back to Maybelline

April 29, 1984

In 1936 Sigmund Littman decided to go head-to-head with Kresge's on the same small block of E. Jefferson.

The day he opened his store on the corner of Beniteau, one of his first visitors was the manager of the S.S. Kresge store down the street, on the corner of Engle.

He dropped in to make sure that Littman understood the realities of doing business on that block.

"He looked around the store," Walter Littman says, "and then told my father: 'You'll never last.' "

It's been about 15 years now since Kresge's sold its store to Littman's and moved off the block.

"We operated both stores for a while," says Walter Littman, who has been running the business since the death of his father 10 years ago. "Then we decided to move everything and run it all out of here, the old Kresge store."

On the list of venerable neighborhood institutions, the five-and-10-cent store should rank somewhere in the top 10. Right after church, school, grocery and library. Ahead of funeral home, poolroom and bar.

In that east side neighborhood, when both stores were operating, the distinction between them was largely in the way they were identified.

Kresge's was simply "the dime store." Littman's was always "Littman's."

Littman's got the more personal designation because Mr. Littman was always there. None of us recalls ever being waited on in the dime store by S.S. Kresge.

And the Littmans lived with their four children in an apartment over the store. Nobody lived over the Kresge store. When they closed up every night, that was it.

Littman's, too, had a sense of family about it. Those were people from the neighborhood working there.

Winifred Weaver and Beatrice Carey, whose husband became a City Council member. There was Harry Bassett. And Harry's wife. And Harry's sister-in-law. And Harry's brother-in-law.

So it shouldn't have surprised me to find Harry still working there when I dropped by the store a few weeks ago. So is his sister-in-law, Mildred Lipke. Harry is 68 now. He started working for Mr. Littman in 1933.

Mildred is 76 and started working for Mr. Littman 56 years ago, long before he bought the Jefferson store.

She was in the basement this day, in a blue smock, putting together Easter baskets. Filling them and wrapping them and listening to me talk about memorable shopping events in my life at Littman's.

Like the time I bought a 10-cent bottle of Radio Girl perfume for Mother's Day.

"Never a big seller," she said. "Not like Blue Waltz, or Evening in Paris," which she said was a particular favorite in the neighborhood. It made me regret, after all these years, that I did not go with my alternate choices that day, the Maybelline lipstick or the stationery in the small cedar box.

Walter Littman is 53. His wife, Dolores, works with him now. Their two children reared, educated and leading their own lives.

He says they decided to stay in the neighborhood, even when Kresge's moved, because it seemed like the right thing to do.

"We bought the store from Kresge's because we believed it was still a viable neighborhood to do business in."

Business isn't as good as it once was. The people just aren't there anymore, and neither are a lot of the houses.

So Walter has started a wholesale business, imprinting T-shirts, team jackets, warm-ups, caps and sweats, to keep the store paying.

But business was brisk in the store the day we spoke. Conversation was interrupted by a man looking for a flashlight, a kid who needed oil for his bike, a woman with two little boys looking for brown paint for her walls, a young man who needed a tumbler for his lock and an old man who needed a collar for his dog.

But I kept drifting back to other major purchases. Lead soldiers, paper Halloween masks, rubber daggers, goldfish, cap pistols, yo-yos, candy orange slices, mucilage guaranteed to bleed through the paper and mess up your social studies project, chunks of chocolate from the world's biggest Hershey bar and turtles with a name written on their shell.

I asked Walter if he still sold marbles. He said he did.

I told him I wanted to buy a bag.

"Where are the marbles?" he shouted across the store to his wife.

"We don't carry them anymore," she shouted back.

Probably just as well.

Who shoots marbles anymore, anyway?   ■

Memories of an urban oasis and an extraordinary park

Aug. 17, 1986

In the beginning, they called it Water Works Park.

A practical enough name, since the park land surrounded the pumps and buildings that supplied water to a growing city.

But in 1910 the Board of Water Commissioners thought the place should have a real name, so they got together and voted to call it Gladwin Park, in honor of the major who commanded Ft. Detroit during the siege of Pontiac.

As far as I have been able to determine, the new name never caught on.

In the heart of every person who ever sat in the shade of its elms or watched the great wheels turn in the pump house or climbed the 202 steps to the top of the old tower or splashed in the dormant waters of the wading pool, it was then, and always would be, Water Works Park.

A hundred acres or so of urban respite behind an overdone Victorian monument built in 1893 to the memory of a man who guaranteed his place in Detroit history by leaving the city enough money to pay for it.

Parks, for all their beauty, can sometimes be unimaginative places. There's just so much you can do with trees and flowers.

There was never anything ordinary about Water Works Park. When Chauncey Hurlbut died in 1885 he left $200,000 to beautify the park. He had been president of the Detroit Board of Water Commissioners.

The first thing they did was build a monument to Hurlbut, a great memorial gate at the park entrance. A tribute in stone with arches and stairways and a grand dome topped by a gray eagle.

But the grand attraction always was the old pump house. A twin-domed building with soaring ceilings and high windows, a place that always smelled of oil and steam. Where you could stand behind the polished brass railings and watch wheels bigger than a house turning the pumps that brought the water from the mouth of Lake St. Clair to every home in the city, even the ones on the west side.

Dominating the park was a 185-foot tower that enclosed the old standpipe, and near the front gate there was a clock made of flowers, its hands powered by — what else — flowing water.

Close by were flowers planted in the shape of an American flag and a floral calendar that required the replanting every day of one group of flowers to coincide with the date.

And there was the Hurlbut Branch of the library, where a woman everyone called Miss Hannah would disappear behind the shelves and return with exactly what you had requested and a couple of books you hadn't asked for but she knew you would like.

The wading pool was like a large saucer, no deeper than a kid's bottom. In the middle, aimed at the sky, was a thin pipe that sent a continuous spray of water into the air.

If you tired of the park, a ferry at the river's edge would whisk you to Belle Isle for a dime.

In front of an ancient pear tree, a bronze marker on a large granite stone told that this was the last of the pear trees planted along the river in the late 1700s by the French settlers. On our trips to the park my father would always read the words aloud and then have us do the same.

If being part of a city utility made the park attractive, it was also its undoing.

Fear of sabotage led to the park's closing in World War II. It reopened in 1945, but closed again during the Korean war. Only a small corner was ever reopened.

But by that time the flower clock had been sent to Greenfield Village, the library, the tower and the old pump house had been torn down and long grass grew where the flag and calendar had blossomed every spring.

The wading pool was condemned as unhealthy, and somebody stole the bronze bust of Chauncey Hurlbut from its pedestal in the memorial gate.

Today Hurlbut's gate is fenced to keep people out. There are stands for swings inside the park, but there are no swings and the grass needs cutting.

The stone that stood in front of the old pear tree is still there, but somebody has taken the plaque.

Which is only a symbolic loss for me. I still remember most of what it said. ■

Nothing much is cooking at 'The Apartments' anymore

June 15, 1986

If there was a formal name for them, nobody ever used it. We just called them "The Apartments."

Nothing terribly fancy about them. Square, unadorned, three-story red brick buildings. No decorative scrollwork, fluted concrete columns or iron grilles. Not even a girl's named chiseled in the stone lintels over the doors, like so many other apartments on our side of town.

The Apartments were on Kercheval between Defer and St. Jean.

Pat Murphy lived there. So did Stewart Matte, Fred Cox, Harold Schubert, the Banfield twins, Dolores Murtaugh and Jack Hackett. And others whose names I don't remember.

At night, after school, the dark, narrow hallways steamed with the marshaled aromas of dinners on the stove. The muffled noise of children and radios drifted from behind the dark, lacquered doors.

On summer evenings, you could stand on Kercheval and hear Harold Schubert practicing on his drums.

But you had to stand quietly outside the door of Pat Murphy's apartment to hear him playing his violin, the soft pizzicato of "Two Guitars" drifting through the halls and disappearing in the sharp smell of cooked cabbage.

My friend Billy Cook lived there, too. The middle door on the St. Jean side. First floor. Apt. 22.

"It's the little things you remember," Cook said recently. "Like how hard it was to find a place to park here, right by the front door."

We were sitting in a car a few weeks ago, at the curb in front of the middle door on the St. Jean side. Billy was talking about another time at The Apartments.

"The Clairmount streetcar ran right past my bedroom window, and the car barns were right across the street," he said, pointing to the place where St. Maron Church now sits behind a low brick wall.

"In the middle of the night, the drunks would get into the wrong building. They'd bang at our door until my father got up and chased them away.

"It was our whole world, right here," he said. "In the courtyard out back, we built a kind of miniature golf course, four or five holes, and we'd play and the fathers would bet pennies on us."

The courtyard wasn't much more than a narrow airspace between the buildings. A spot where the sun never shone and grass never grew.

"Our whole world was here. In the buildings, in the yard, in the alleys out back. Even the roof was a playground."

The Cooks — Billy, his younger sister, Joan, and their parents — moved into The Apartments when Billy was four. It's where he lived until he left home to get married, 16 years later. His parents, both dead now, moved to Roseville in 1952.

"But this was always where I lived," he said. "This was home."

Cook will be 56 this year. His wife died three years ago and his four children are married.

He has been a Detroit policeman for 32 years. He is a sergeant assigned to the extradition unit dealing with crimes against property.

There are no crimes left to be committed against The Apartments. When the last tenants left several months ago, the unofficial salvage crews moved in and took what they could, and the vandals have just about finished the job.

The windows are broken, the doors kicked in, and whatever was not worth removing has been broken and left on the floor.

The front door to Apt. 22 — Billy Cook's apartment — has been ripped from the hinges and thrown on the floor of the front room. In the small kitchen, an old wringer washer lay on its side next to broken parts of a toilet bowl. A Murphy bed, its springs rusted, is still bolted to a wall.

"Our first TV was an Admiral," Cook said. He walked to a corner of the littered front room and pointed to a spot near the windows. "We put it right here."

Chunks of plaster and pieces of broken furniture block the hallway, and water from rain and leaking pipes gives the whole place a damp, musty smell.

It was probably my imagination; as we left I thought I detected the lingering smell of cabbage cooking. ∎

Memories that stand
in the way of progress

Aug. 24, 1986

In many ways, the Chrysler Jefferson plant was one of the reasons the neighborhood was there in the first place. So I guess it should not be too surprising that the company would end up one day being the instrument of its passing.

It made sense to live near the factory, to be able to walk to work. Save the carfare, get a little extra sleep in the morning and get home early enough to read the afternoon paper before dinner.

In the morning darkness they would pass through the alley next to our house on Lycaste on the way to work, an uneven gray line, caps pulled low, hands in their pockets, their arms pressing black lunch buckets tightly against their sides.

Through Mr. Causley's trailer lot, past the big Frankenmuth beer sign, across the railroad tracks and through the front gate to spend the day doing what they had done yesterday and would be doing again tomorrow — building cars.

It was an ideal arrangement. The neighborhood needed Chrysler. Chrysler needed the neighborhood. Nobody talked about it ever being any different.

Now Chrysler and the city will finish off what's left of the neighborhood and turn an aging factory and an aging residential area into something better. It's an idea that's difficult to quarrel with.

But even when the inevitability of some kind of change was obvious, we took what comfort there was in knowing that, even in its decline, it was still there. Still the neighborhood. The place where our lives were shaped.

In cities like Detroit the only real durability neighborhoods have is whatever permanence we give them in our recollections.

They will be, in our memories, whatever we want them to be. Even a touch better than they ever were, if that's how we prefer to remember them. The important thing is that we not forget what they once meant to us.

I drive through that east side neighborhood nearly every day, always alert for signs of recent or pending demolition, ready to assign to each new pile of rubble the memories that were part of whatever it was that no longer exists.

A grocery store, the home of a friend, the Chinese laundry, a movie theater, the church. No longer tangible reminders of another time.

But as long as the house at 1532 Lycaste stood, I reasoned, part of me would still be there, in that small upstairs flat.

It wasn't the best house on the street. Flats never were.

Something about renters and their perceived lack of enthusiasm for improving property they didn't own.

Mr. Bailer's house was always one of the nicest.

He had been in the Spanish-American War and lived with Mrs. Bailer in the neat, brick bungalow with a big porch and wicker furniture where he and his wife would sit on summer evenings to make sure the neighborhood kids didn't walk on their lawn. They tore that house down a few years ago.

And Mr. Conover's. His flowers and shrubs were the best on the block. In his backyard he built a rock garden, and he stocked a large pond with fish, including a gar pike that looked enough like a swordfish for us to assume that's what it was. But the Conover house is gone, too.

But 1532 is still there, hanging on like O. Henry's last leaf, one of a dozen remaining houses where there once were three times that many. Saved by whatever arbitrary process it is that decides which houses will stand and which will fall.

I knocked on the door of that upper flat a few weeks ago, not sure of what I would say to whoever answered. Nobody did.

Through an open front-room window I could hear music playing, so I called out. No answer.

A man across the street, Walter Williams, who rents the house Mrs. Coates used to own, said he didn't think anybody was home. Probably just as well. No use confusing strangers with old ghosts.

I will probably wait until after the last tenants have departed and before the wreckers arrive before I go back and stand in those empty rooms again.

I need a little time with whatever memories still cling to those walls to make sure they never fade. ■

4. The family Shine

hair today,

gone tomorrow

Thanks to a petty burglar, the Shine boys were a cut above

Jan. 20, 1985

One night in the late 1930s, a burglar entered our house on Beniteau and made off with a case of empty E & B beer bottles, two dimes from the kitchen cupboard and a pair of manual hair clippers.

It was not what you would call the heist of the decade, even for that neighborhood. But for my brothers and me, it was a major turning point in our lives. It marked the end of the homemade haircut.

Absent the clippers, we were suddenly introduced to the wonderful world of the barber shop. Talcum and brilliantine and a dazzling line of sweet-smelling emollients. And a legitimate haircut.

One questionable felony and there we were, literally a cut above our grade-school peers who showed up regularly looking like sheep that wiggled too much during the shearing. Gouges showed white every place the clippers dug too deep.

The tonsorial fashion of the day, at least on our side of town, was close to the skin on the sides as high as possible, while still leaving enough on top to stick up wildly whenever you took off your Ace cap.

The mother-as-barber syndrome was less a reflection of reduced circumstances than it was a tangible protest of the high cost of haircuts. Why spend good money in a barber shop, the reasoning went, when you can do just as good a job at home?

An operating philosophy, I might add, that came from people who did not have to go to school with their heads looking like quilts.

More specifically, from mothers who did not worry about their sons looking like Alfalfa Switzer when the boy wanted to look like Freddie Bartholomew.

So, imagine my surprise when, one day in the closing years of the 1950s, my wife came home with a complete barber kit and told me she was enrolling in an adult education course in home barbering.

"Why spend good money in a barber shop. . . ." she began. I told her I knew the rest of the quote.

Once a week, she would go off to night school with her clippers in a cigar box, usually with one of the Kelly boys in tow to use as a "model." Actually, it was somebody to practice on.

The Kellys lived down the street and had enough boys for the eight-week course.

They have all gone on to make their way in life, but I'm afraid I will always remember them sitting on the couch in our front room waiting quietly to be led off to the class, wondering what kind of homemade haircut the night held in store for them.

As far as I was ever able to determine, barber school was not, for my wife, a multi-dimensional educational experience.

She learned one basic hair style. Close.

It became known to the two oldest Shine boys, Jim and Tom, as a "buzz job."

It was not a complicated procedure. Just attach the plastic rake-like device to the front of the clippers and glide it over the head until all that separated the skin from the clippers was an eighth of an inch of hair.

The close crop was not in style, I am happy to say, in my childhood. That kind of haircut usually indicated some infectious disorder of the scalp and was most often worn with a tarry salve that smelled like camphor, the end of an old silk stocking with a knot on top pulled over the head to keep dangerous microbes from leaping about the classroom.

I have since adopted, involuntarily, a hair style that approximates the ones my kids had in the '50s and '60s, but I don't often talk about it.

At some point, Jim and Tom became too old for the buzz jobs and insisted on their rights to proper barbering.

I recall arranging for Jim to get a haircut at the barber shop I used downtown.

I made an appointment for him with Jimmy Vento, whose shop was then in the Sheraton Cadillac. Just tell them your name, I told him. It's all set.

Jim walked into the shop. When they said, "Can we help you?" he said "Shine."

He was escorted to the back of the shop where he was given a shoe shine.

He thought it went with the haircut. They thought it an absolute waste of money to put polish on shoes that looked that bad.

It all worked out eventually. Jim got his haircut and his shoes have never looked that good since.

But what worried me then was the thought that I was raising boys unprepared to deal with the complexities of good grooming.

At his age, I had years of barber shop experience behind me.

Maybe I had failed them in not letting them experience earlier the invigorating splash of Lucky Tiger. ∎

A little bag of souvenirs unspoiled by war or fire

Dec. 25, 1983

Our house on Beniteau burned down one night in 1937.

Whenever I think of that fire, I think of Christmas.

Not because the fire was during the Christmas holiday season. In fact, it happened in the fall and I was standing in my pajamas on Mrs. Johnson's porch next door listening to the sound of the fire and wondering if my bed was burning.

I was standing there holding a grapefruit that Frankie McPharlin had handed me. He lived down the street and it was the only gesture he could come up with on short notice to let me know that he was sorry my house was burning down.

And I remember the small khaki bag with the words "Merry Christmas" stitched in red on the side.

The bag was piled on Mrs. Johnson's porch with other things we had managed to save that night. It was the bag a Salvation Army worker had given my father when he was recovering from scarlet fever in a military hospital in France on Christmas Day 1918, a little more than a month after the end of World War I.

Then it had contained nuts and fruit and cigarets, a razor and a couple of packages of Gillette blades.

In the intervening years it had become the repository for an unrelated collection of odds and ends, all dating to the war years. Letters, postcards, photographs, official papers. Tattered reminders of his first great adventure as an American.

After the fire, the little bag was all that was left of his memories of the Great War.

Infrequently, but with great ceremony, my father would take the bag down from its shelf in the front hall closet, open it and remove the contents.

Each item had its own story.

The railroad tickets from Chaumont to Paris. The order of induction from J.E.W. Lumley, representing draft board No. 19 in Detroit. The letter from Gen. John J. Pershing thanking my father — and every other American soldier — for participating in the defeat of the "forces of autocracy."

The "Soldiers' French Course," a little blue book with enough French phrases to help any soldier get by in town or in the trenches.

A guide to the Riviera complete with maps and information for the area from the assistant U.S. provost marshal, information on tipping, suggestions for side trips and, almost as an afterthought, a warning about the need "to be careful and not divulge military secrets to civilians in Nice."

There was mail from friends wishing him well in the service, including a letter from a Mr. and Mrs. John Doyle, who lived on Dragoon.

Dated March 14, 1918, it dealt directly with the real possibility that war can be lethal. It read, in part: "Please accept this rosary and Happy Death cross as a token of remembrance . . . and may God bless and keep you and bring you safely back to your friends."

But there were some letters in the bag that my father never read aloud.

He would carefully unfold the brittle pages with the neat script in ink turned brown by time and read them silently before putting them them back in the bag.

Years later I would read those letters, most of them from his mother in Ireland, and understand why he was moved by them.

They spoke of unimaginable hardships at home and of an unyielding faith that things would get better.

At the end of the war, she learned for the first time that my father and his brother had been sent to France.

"My Dear and My Darling Pat,

"Once more a few lines to the land of liberty. How proud we are to know that you and my poor Mick are back to Detroit. How can I ever return the thanks to the good God that saved ye.

"If I knew you were in France it would have killed me. I thought I had all the trouble in the world in my mind for fear you would have to go. Many a mass I got said for both of you, but thank God they were not without the desired effect.

"All I want now is for you and Mike to come home. I would rather see one sight of ye than all the money in America.

"I remain, as ever, your fond mother."

Neither my father nor his brother ever returned to Ireland.

I took the bag off the closet shelf a couple of weeks ago and put it under the Christmas tree so my children and their children can look at the postcards and read the letters.

It will remind me of a fire in 1937. And of how happy I am that my father had no need in 1918 of the Happy Death cross.

And the day will be, as Christmas should be, a holiday for remembering. ∎

Selling was one thing,
but it took Jimmy to collect

Dec. 18, 1983

The Old Newsboys marched past my office window a couple of Mondays ago. They were on the way to their appointed intersections to sell newspapers at inflated rates to make sure that Christmas joy gets the broadest application possible.

It was with the same sense of regret this year that I watched them march away again — without me.

It's not that I consider this fine group closed to my participation. A large number of them are old and good friends and would at least tolerate my presence among them.

And I am a bona fide old newsboy by way of my years of service as carrier of the Detroit Times in the early 1940s.

But my uneven tenure as a carrier-businessman remains the principal reason for my reluctance to march off each Christmas season with my aging colleagues to do good works. Also, I will never sell another paper in my life without the help and encouragement of Jimmy the Collector.

My performance as a carrier can be honestly described as adequate. But as a businessman, I was painfully inept. My route was, at all times, alarmingly close to insolvency. Only Jimmy kept us afloat.

The Times took its money off the top each week, and profits had to be squeezed from our abundance of slow-pay subscribers.

The route was on Pennsylvania, some 110 customers between Jefferson and Kercheval. Jimmy was my younger brother by two years and a full partner in the route.

That block of Pennsylvania was a neighborhood of substantial homes. But it also contained a number of apartment buildings that contained a number of customers whose roots were not, it is safe to say, deep in the soil of Detroit.

Those were the war years, remember, and there was a certain amount of transience in the neighborhood, mostly among people who had come here from other places to work. This necessitated frequent trips during the week to that block of Pennsylvania to see who might be moving out.

Our interest in the migratory patterns of our customers was limited to those who owed us money, which was at any given time an alarmingly large percentage of our clientele.

And that's where Jimmy came in.

I was, and still am, reluctant to ask people for things. When customers told me they'd pay next week (even though that's what they said last week) I never objected.

Jimmy's responsibility was collecting the uncollectibles. And he was masterful at it.

A redhead with a face splashed with freckles, he would not be denied our due.

As I stood in the background in embarrassed silence, he demanded payment from our worst payers, standing in the doorway so that it was impossible for them to close the door without first pushing him out of the way.

When one woman insisted that she had no money in the house and told him repeatedly to come back on Saturday, he pointed to a table in her dining room and said: "There's some money."

The woman, angry now, told him the money was for the insurance man. Jimmy told her: "Well, pay me with it and tell the insurance man to come back Saturday." She paid him.

Another time, we saw a family loading a rented trailer with household goods, a reasonably dependable indicator that a serious relocation was taking place.

The woman helping load the trailer was one of our major delinquent accounts. Four weeks' worth of the daily and Sunday Times. Total indebtedness: $1.80.

They were not moving out, she said, just taking some things to the west side. Come back next week and I'll pay you, she said.

Jimmy believed there would be no next week. He also knew that if she ever reached the safety of the west side, we could forget the $1.80.

As I watched from the other side of the street, Jimmy took a floor lamp from the trailer and told the woman he would bring the lamp back next week when he came to collect.

She threatened to call the police. He offered to wait. He told her that if she thought the cops were going to stand by and let her beat an 11-year-old out of a buck-eighty by moving to the west side, she did not fully understand the quality of law enforcement in Detroit. She paid, scattering the change on the street.

Jimmy did not let go of the lamp until I had retrieved the money and he had counted it.

Jimmy is a lawyer in Boston now, doing well, as I always knew he would.

Maybe next December I'll ask him to come home for a few days so we can get out and sell some papers with the Old Newsboys.

I'll sell. He can collect. ∎

A mistress' rumpled fenders and fiancee's ruffled feathers

Feb. 24, 1985

In a conversation the other day with my friend Bob Saylor, I told him he shares equally with the Jesuits the responsibility for arming me with a college degree and then turning me loose on an unsuspecting world.

The Society of Jesus and the University of Detroit educated me — or came as close to doing that as was possible — but Bob Saylor is the guy who got me to school every day.

It was possible to get from the lower east side to U-D on public transportation, if standing in bus stops in the dark twice a day was something you liked.

An option was to buy a car — which was not an option at our house — or find a classmate from your side of town who had a car but not enough friends at U-D to fill it every day.

It is stretching it some to call what Bob Saylor had a car. It was a 1937 Plymouth with a rumble seat and enough safety defects for a Ralph Nader documentary.

I got to ride in the rumble seat, where I wrapped myself in a smelly canvas tarpaulin as a protection against bad weather. The only advantage in riding outside was that you did not have to deal firsthand with the car's mechanical shortcomings.

"It had a few things wrong with it," Saylor admits. "There was no first gear and no reverse. The ignition was busted and you had to use a penny to start it. The brakes weren't very good, either."

The rear license plate was mounted on the taillight assembly, which eventually rusted through and fell off one day in front of Saylor's house on Chalmers.

The absence of light and license resulted in his arrest one morning while driving on Freud en route to U-D.

"It cost me $25 to get it out of police custody," Saylor says. Then, with a catch in his voice, he adds: "I finally paid some guy over on Continental $25 to take it off my hands. I still miss it."

Most of us understand that kind of misdirected tenderness for the first car in our lives.

Shortly before I finished U-D in 1952, I took $721 to Buchanan Chevrolet in Highland Park and bought a 1947, faded-green Chevrolet Club Coupe with Vacumatic Shift. It quickly became an object of my immoderate affection.

Of course I loved my girlfriend, who was by that time my unofficial (no ring) fiancee. But the Chevy inspired a different kind of love.

Both loves were put to the test one night in 1952 when my girlfriend borrowed my car and on her way home hurled it into the rear of an auto being driven by a Mr. Cornwallis, who had stopped unexpectedly on Kercheval in front of the Sheridan Theater. My Irish father, incidentally, believed that anyone named after an English general was probably at fault.

My friend brought my horribly damaged car back the next morning. She had not been at all pleased with my response the previous evening when she called from the accident scene. Convinced I could not deal with the trauma of seeing my car broken and bleeding on that stretch of Kercheval, I told her to call her father.

In the morning, she came into my house, dropped my keys on the table and said icily: "I will have it repaired." A response I equated with a person returning your thoroughbred with a broken leg and offering to pay for the plaster cast.

Even though I was not entirely pleased with her cavalier approach to this tragedy or the level of her remorse, I did not suggest we call off the wedding. In fact, I took her along on the honeymoon in the redone Chevy just to show that I was a person capable of forgiving even the most flagrant outrage.

While I was in the Army, she sold the car for $100 to help finance the purchase of a later-model Chevy. The newer car was nice, but I have never felt the same about any car since the Club Coupe.

Mr. Saylor has long since gone to work in Detroit for Petersen Publishing Co., which produces such prestigious automotive publications as "Motor Trend," "Hot Rod," "Car Craft," "Sports Car Graphic" and a bunch of others, none of which has ever featured stories like "Driving With Only Two Gears" or "Starting Your Car With Coins."

I consider it living testimony to God's sense of humor that Bob Saylor of the '37 Plymouth is even remotely connected with people who each year name a "Motor Trend Car of the Year."

But it has occurred to me that I should talk with Bob to see if he can use his considerable influence at Petersen to get Car of the Year designations for the 1937 Plymouth and the 1947 Chevrolet Club Coupe.

Posthumously, of course. ■

How I spent my honeymoon
... avoiding Benson Ford

Jan. 23, 1983

Tomorrow marks the 30th year of my marriage and it is probably time I discussed the considerable effort I expended on my honeymoon avoiding Benson Ford.

Thirty years married may not be an entirely remarkable tenure, but it is a milestone that pleases me since I have always felt strongly about the importance of seniority.

And if you can acquire that kind of longevity with someone you like more than anyone else, it makes things ever so much better.

But back to Benson Ford.

I have always believed that a good honeymoon is an important prelude to a good marriage.

So, despite a fiscal condition that bordered on insolvency, my new bride and I decided that we would expend our cash reserve on a honeymoon to be remembered at a spot we couldn't afford.

We picked a place called the Ponte Vedra Club, near Jacksonville, Fla., because we had seen it mentioned in the society pages and decided that if it was good enough for society, it was good enough for us.

We had the 1947 Chevrolet Club Coupe, with Vacumatic Shift and a 1948 grille, painted dark blue as our concession to the bloodlines of the Ponte Vedra clientele.

On Jan. 28, 1953, we drove up to the main building of the club, pledging to each other that we would never disclose, not by word, deed or facial expression, what we knew to be the cold truth. That the only thing which would qualify us as part of the "in crowd" at the Ponte Vedra Club was the reality that we were "in" over our heads.

If anybody at the club figured that out, they made a successful effort to conceal it. The service was exquisite. The staff wonderful. The food better than anything we ever had at the Hart Grill or even the Chinese Teapot.

Then we found out about Benson Ford.

There was a notice on the club bulletin board indicating that he was a member of the Ponte Vedra Club and staying there at the time.

My new wife and I conjured up a frightening scenario which went something like this: "Hello, I'm Benson Ford. I understand you two are from Detroit?"

"That's right, Benson. I'm Neal Shine. I'm in publishing. This is my wife, Phyllis. She's connected with the aircraft industry. Happy to meet you."

The frightening part involved any expansion of the conversation which would reveal that I was a copyboy at the Detroit Free Press and my wife was a secretary at Continental Aviation.

So we kept an eye out for Benson. In the lobby. In the dining room. On the grounds. Prepared to duck at first sighting. To our ultimate relief, we never saw him and, as far as we were ever able to determine, he never saw us.

We checked out of the Ponte Vedra Club after four days, a move cleverly timed to coincide with the end of the off-season rates.

The departure also came at the same time I exhausted the last of the mix-and-match combinations of the snappy ensemble I picked up on sale at Harry Suffrin's. One more dinner there and it would have been evident to the Ponte Vedra regulars that my wardrobe was largely illusory.

At Daytona Beach, we rented an inexpensive motel room and basked in the pleasant recollections of our four days of elegance at Ponte Vedra.

We ran out of money on the way back to Detroit and lived on oranges until a $25 emergency loan from home caught up with us in the Western Union office in Corbin, Ky.

Now, for the first time in 30 years, we are going back to Ponte Vedra Club to see what's left of the memories.

When I wrote for reservations, Mrs. Ouida Hotch, from the Ponte Vedra Club, sent me a copy of a 30-year-old "Guest History Card." Mrs. Hotch is the mother of Ripley Hotch, the editor responsible for the content of this magazine, a coincidence that confirms my mother's oft-repeated cliche about the size of the world.

The guest history card showed that in 1953 the new Mr. and Mrs. Shine stayed in Room 33 from 1/28 to 1/31 at the rate of $26 a day, American plan.

In the space on the card set aside for remarks, someone had typed: "Very nice." An indication that a proper upbringing, regardless of your station, will see you through in any company.

There's one thing about the trip, however, that saddens me. Benson Ford won't be there.

I would have liked to buy him lunch. ■

Why I won't be going camping this summer

March 10, 1985

It is time again, as March moves us toward better things here in the north temperate zone, to make plans for summer vacation.

Let it be noted here for all to see that I will not be going camping this year.

I believe all that stuff about people who don't learn from history being forced to repeat it, and if there's one thing I want to avoid repeating, it is the Shine family summer camping excursion of 1965.

It is reasonable to expect that 20 years is enough time to soften the memories of that cataclysmic adventure. Whenever the subject is raised, the Shine kids talk about it fondly and laugh at all that happened. To them it was great fun. The very thought of it still makes my stomach hurt.

Like most disasters, it seemed like a good idea at the time.

A friend had offered to loan us a camper mounted on the back of a pickup. We decided that a week or so in the Smoky Mountains would be just the ticket. The kids would like it. We would like it. And the price was right.

So one day, armed with a pound of maps and a list of every campsite between here and Gatlinburg, Tenn., we packed up and headed south — six children, from 18 months to 11 years, and two naive parents.

Since I am a person who sees more in omens than most people, I should have reconsidered the excursion on the first day. That's when we drove away from a Stuckey's somewhere in Ohio, leaving Tom, then 6, in the bathroom.

Only the shouts of his siblings kept us from adding child abandonment to the long list of things that were to go wrong.

We spent a quiet first night in the General Butler State Park near Carrollton, Ky. The next day at the swimming area, Jim, then 9, suddenly appeared on the 20-foot diving board, walked to the end and, while I watched in horror, jumped off. Jim could not swim. He was under water for what seemed like minutes until his head bobbed up and he paddled to shore. He had just taught himself the basics of swimming.

The next stop was at the Cumberland Falls State Park near Corbin, Ky.

For those unfamiliar with the ways of camping, there is a penalty for

109

waiting until dusk to find a place to park your camper. It's called "the overflow area." That can be translated as a place where no campers in their right mind would ever stay unless they had no other options.

The overflow area at the Cumberland Falls park was on the side of a steep incline overlooking a very picturesque gorge.

One of the small problems of that particular site was the tendency of children, especially the baby, to roll out of their beds in a camper parked on a steep hill.

A larger problem was that I had neglected to set the emergency brake and Peggy, 4, playing in the cab of the truck, pulled the gearshift lever out of park, into neutral, and the camper started rolling backward down the hill.

In the back of the camper, my wife was trying to figure a way to strap the baby, Danny, to keep him from rolling out of his bunk. When the camper started to move she assumed I was moving it to a better spot. Actually, it was moving itself toward the cliff when Jim — yesterday's daredevil turned today's hero — pushed the shifter back into park.

Calamity pursued us all the way to the Smoky Mountains. There, Jim, running along a narrow path, lost his footing and fell down the side of a very steep hill.

While other tourists screamed, he rolled and bounced among the trees and boulders for about 100 feet. For reasons I have never understood, he suffered only some very bad bruises.

Since the camper slept only four, the plan was for four of us to sleep in a tent. That plan was scrapped the first night — by me — when a large bear strolled through our campsite.

Another unforeseen unpleasantness had to do with the top-heavy nature of the camper body. Sitting as it was on top of the truck, it had a tendency to rock. Things that have a tendency to rock very often give kids the tendency to throw up, which is what happened. It deteriorated to the point where each kid had to be issued an empty Hawaiian Punch can for emergency use.

On the way home, my wife had a severe attack of asthma and had to be treated at Good Samaritan Hospital in Dayton. The remainder of the trip from Dayton to Detroit was reasonably uneventful.

So if you see me in the woods this summer, take what comfort there is in knowing that I'm probably walking back to my motel room. ■

A father strikes out
with a missing photo

April 28, 1985

Jimmy Shine's memory of that precious day in his young life remains bright.

"I remember the clubhouse and the players getting dressed for the game," he says. "There was a guy with a box of baseballs and he was rubbing them and he gave me one. I remember taking the ball around the room, asking the players to sign it."

Rocky Colavito signed it. So did Al Kaline, Jake Wood, Bubba Morton, Chico Fernandez and Tiger manager Bob Scheffing.

"Don Mossi was on the rubbing table and when I shook hands with him, he asked me not to shake his pitching hand because he was afraid I would hurt it. So I shook his other hand. I thought that was great.

"But mostly I remember Al Kaline. He was the hero. He put me on his lap and showed me how to hold the bat. It seemed like the biggest bat I had ever seen. Then we had our picture taken."

It was 1962, somewhat less than a remarkable year for the Tigers, but to Jimmy Shine at age 6, Tiger baseball was more important that year than the order of finish in the American League.

He was, even at 6, already an irretrievably committed Tiger fan, a condition that has not diminished with the passage of time.

Joe Falls, who was the Free Press baseball writer then, arranged for Jimmy, my oldest son, to visit the Tigers in the clubhouse before the game.

He missed a half-day of school, but it was to be a great adventure, something that would not be matched by anything happening that afternoon in the first grade.

Later in the stands, as the Tigers went through the late-season motions with the Angels before a small crowd, Jimmy read and re-read the signatures on his baseball through the clear plastic sandwich bag in which he had wrapped it.

Then he talked about Al Kaline and sitting on his lap and how good it was that he was going to have a picture of himself with Kaline. "I sure hope it turns out," he said of the picture.

I assured him that the Free Press photographer, Dick Tripp, was a professional and all his pictures turned out.

About two weeks later I began to hound Tripp in earnest for a print of the picture. I told him I was unwilling to go home each night knowing that Jimmy's first question would be: "Did you bring the picture?"

There was, it seems, some understandable skepticism among Jim's first-grade colleagues, who would believe that he had been sitting on Al Kaline's knee only after they saw the picture. Jimmy insisted that photographic evidence of that historic moment would be provided soon.

After about a month, Dick Tripp worked up the nerve to tell me. He had lost the picture and the negative.

Bernice Haun, who worked in the photo department and had a mother's understanding of the situation, had spent a week searching through every negative in the department. It was not to be found.

I asked Tripp if he would mind stopping by my house on his way home from work and telling my son what happened. Tripp, who had six children of his own and understood fully all that was involved in such a task, declined.

That night, in one of the shortest, most difficult conversations of my life, I told Jimmy that there was no picture. That it had been lost and there was no hope of finding it. That I was truly sorry.

He didn't cry. He just turned and went upstairs to his room and closed the door. Although we have talked many times through the years about that day, he never again mentioned the lost photo. Whatever unpleasantness he had to endure from his doubting classmates, he kept to himself.

Jimmy is 29 now and lives in Bradenton, Fla., with his wife, Deanna, and their year-old son Colin. The people at the Bradenton Herald, where he is the retail advertising manager, call him Jim.

It's not possible, really, to go back 23 years and capture a treasured moment that was missed forever one day in a crowded locker room. Special memories aren't easily recaptured and trying to go back often diminishes the importance of it all.

But last month, Jim Shine and Al Kaline got together again at the Tiger spring training camp in Lakeland.

They talked about the 1984 season and about the Tigers' chances in 1985.

Then they stood together by the right field fence and had their picture taken.

It wasn't quite the same as that magic afternoon in 1962, but it was good and it was something worth doing.

And this time the picture turned out. ∎

The thrill of the parent, the roar of the proud

March 23, 1986

The pictures are still on the wall. The trophies are nearby on shelves, picking up dust.

I suppose someday they'll come by and collect all these memories to hang on their own walls.

Or to put someplace where they can get at them easily when they want to tell their children what they did when they were children.

I go up to that empty third-floor bedroom, more often than I should, maybe, and look at the team pictures. Bright young faces shining out from under oversize caps, visors shading everything but the smiles.

I read the inscriptions on the trophies and the medals, look at the dates, and wonder why it seems like such a long time ago.

And why somebody didn't tell me that it wouldn't go on forever.

There were always games. Baseball, basketball, softball, volleyball, hockey.

They interfered with meals, family plans, holidays, vacations and work.

There were times when it seemed that life was simply a succession of bleacher seats and one long, sustained cheer. That my circle of friends consisted only of other parents caught up in the same athletic merry-go-round as I. If this is Tuesday, then this must be basketball.

There may be some deep-seated reason why I took so much delight in the athletic activities of my children — boys and girls.

But I have never done any serious probing for deep-seated reasons, mostly for fear of finding them.

I just liked being there. I liked the way it felt. I liked the way I felt.

It would surprise me if all this had anything to do with my own athletic activities.

All that ended when the Free Press softball team got carried away by a youth movement and the time-tested battery of Neal Shine and Joe Falls got put out to pasture, even though we had more than 60 years of experience between us.

There are a few varsity letters from St. Rose stuck away in a drawer somewhere, and the single trophy I own attests to my active membership on a softball team that won the U.S. Army Tactical Command championship in 1954 in Salzburg, Austria.

113

When the kids were little, one of them knocked it over and broke it and it sat for years on my dresser, a small square of dark marble with a gold-colored figurine leaping to catch the ball. An obviously futile gesture since he had no glove and only half an arm.

When they got older, they got a new, gold ball player, screwed it into the old marble base and gave it to me one Christmas.

I can't remember anymore the last game I went to. Probably a volleyball game at the neighborhood park when Peg and Dan played in a club league.

I try, with some success, not to spend a lot of time thinking about all those games. But when I'm driving home all I have to see to make it all come flooding back is a father hurrying across the street on a spring night to get to the baseball diamond.

A few weeks ago, one of my friends here at the Free Press called me to tell me that his six-year-old son had scored his team's first goal in a hockey playoff game and how wonderful it had all been. All I could think of, with only mild envy, was my friend being able to look forward to a dozen more years of this kind of excitement.

I decided after that phone call that I was going to drive to East Lansing the next day, where my youngest son, Dan, was going to be playing in the semifinals of an intramural basketball league at Michigan State University.

It had been, after all, at least four years since I had seen him play, and even in the snow it's not a bad drive. And since this is his last year there
. . .

The game hadn't started when I arrived and Dan was warming up on the Jenison Field House floor with his teammates on the Theta Chi team, three of whom had played with him on their high school team.

On the sideline, Sean Welsh told me that their opponents, Beta Theta Pi, were formidable.

"They have such a big house," he said, "they use the dining room for a basketball court. After dinner they just move the table out of the way and shoot baskets."

It was a good game. Dan scored seven of his team's 38 points, but they lost by 14 to the guys with the big dining room.

After the game, I hugged Dan. Told him he'd done well and said I was proud of him.

On the way home I felt so good I decided to find out when my friend's six-year-old was going to be playing again. Thought I might go to the game.

It's the least I can do for a friend.   ■

My babies are all grown up, but the memories remain

June 16, 1985

The idea was to have two Father's Day stories in the Free Press that Sunday morning. One by a father with older children, the other by someone to whom fatherhood was still a learning experience.

James S. Pooler, a writer and reporter of considerable talent and a man with grown children, became the designated older father. Neal Shine, a much younger writer and reporter whose journalistic talents were still largely undiscovered, got the other half of the assignment.

The Poolers had four children; the Shines had five and would soon add one more to the three-bedroom house in Center Line, which was already a bit crowded.

The stories ran on Page 3 of the paper on June 17, 1962, set two columns wide down the left side of the page.

Pooler, properly, got the top billing. After all, he had won a Pulitzer Prize for the Free Press when I was only two years old and was still one of the most accomplished writers on the paper.

In an open letter to his children — Mary Ann, Sheila, Pat and Susan — he wrote a touching, nostalgic piece about his memories of past Father's Days, wondering what had made the years go by so quickly.

Mine was a predictable little essay about the kind of gifts I was likely to receive that day. A red stone with white flecks, a live turtle named William, an original crayon drawing of a Titan missile ready for launch and a jelly glass half-filled with water containing a fresh selection of local dandelions (Taraxacum Center Linus).

"There's something about the way little girls look at you when they hand you a bunch of flowers," I wrote in that 1962 story, "that makes you forget about every problem and trouble you ever had."

Jimmy Pooler is dead these many years and I sit here wondering, as he must have wondered 23 years ago, how it all slipped past without me noticing it.

Maybe it was the night work.

I worked nights a lot in those years, sleeping when the kids were getting ready for school, leaving for work when they were coming home. The nature of the business, I told myself. Some people are lucky enough to work 9 to 5, some people are lucky enough to work for morning newspapers.

But every now and then I get the uncomfortable feeling that the old Italian man in the Latin Quarter might have been right. I was assigned to cover a Notre Dame Club of Detroit dinner there one night.

The old man was at the same table as I. He had been born in Italy, he told me, adding proudly that his son-in-law was a Notre Dame alumnus and had brought him to the dinner.

He asked me if I was a Notre Dame graduate. No, I told him, explaining that I was there to cover the dinner and write a story about it for the Free Press.

He was troubled when he found out that I had six children at home and was working nights instead of being home with them.

He told me to go to my boss and demand to work days. If my boss refused, he said, he would hire me and teach me the tile and terrazzo trade. It's an honest living, he said, and you don't have to go to college to learn how to do it. That way, he said, you can work during the day and be home with your family at night. Where you belong.

Otherwise, he warned, "Someday you look around and say, 'Where's my babies?' and somebody tells you they're all grown up and gone away."

Judy, who gave me a turtle once, lives with her husband and two children in the west Michigan countryside near Caledonia. Jim, the crayon artist, lives with his wife and their son in Bradenton, Fla. Sue, who gave me a red stone one Father's Day, is negotiating for a condo in St. Clair Shores. Tom, who dug the stone out of a clay pile for Sue, lives in Wichita, Kan. Peg is spending the summer with a girlfriend in another part of the world and Dan has accepted a summer job on a newspaper in Rochester, N.Y.

All grown up and gone away, just like the man said.

The Father's Day gifts have become progressively more practical over the years. Can't remember the last time I got a stone or a turtle or a bouquet of dandelions, although the creativity of my grandchildren has measurably increased my holdings in crayon art.

In 1962, I wrote that "all the glittering gimmicks in all the shops in the world tarnish in the sunshine of just one little 'I love you, Daddy.' "

No reason for me to change my mind about that sentiment, even after 23 years. ∎

We think of them as children, but this isn't child's play

June 17, 1984

There was never much mystery about the kind of work my father did.

He was a streetcar conductor and did virtually the same things every workday for 40 years. Made change, punched transfers and called out the stops.

But no summer ever passed that my brothers and I did not make at least one round trip on my father's streetcar.

It is important to see your father in a role other than that of parent. Patrick Shine at home was one person. Patrick Shine in charge of his own streetcar was somebody else. The commandant of the Clairmount run in full uniform. Rocking along the rails of the city, meeting schedules, making connections, singing out the streets in a rich tenor voice, the John McCormack of urban transit. Grand opera on the Grand Belt.

When my own children were growing up, all of them spent some time at the Free Press. If the memories worked for me, I reasoned, why shouldn't they work for them?

It has been some time since any of my children spent time at the Free Press. Their lives are busy with other things now, including careers of their own.

Which prompted me to wonder recently if kids ever repaid the favor and took their parents to work with them.

After all, why shouldn't we be as interested in the work our children do as we expect them to be in ours?

So at supper a few weeks ago, I asked Susan Shine if one day she would take me to work with her.

Susan is 27 and a registered nurse. She works in the coronary care unit at Bon Secours Hospital in Grosse Pointe. A couple of Wednesdays ago, she took her father to work with her.

Work starts early in hospitals. It's not quite 7 a.m. and six nurses in green scrub uniforms are sitting at a small table in a windowless room on the second floor.

Susan is assigned this day to the intensive care unit, and the nurses coming on duty are being briefed by Josie Jacques, who has worked the midnight shift.

There are five patients in the unit this morning. One has died during the night. The others are stable.

The discussion is an informal mixture of the personal and the clinical. Amid talk of medication, ventilators and vital signs is a personal concern for each patient. Are they comfortable or restless? Bothered by the ventilator, or irritated by the naso-gastric tube? How are their families doing?

After the briefing, each nurse is assigned a patient and work begins in the unit.

I went to the hospital that morning with Susie, my little girl. One of six children, one of three daughters. As different from her siblings as they are from her.

Susie of the large brown eyes. Who was almost born in the car on the way to the hospital that cold February night in 1957.

Susie, whose wonderful smile could melt the polar ice cap and whose frown would wither the soul of a saint.

Susie in tears on the phone from Madonna College. She was quitting. It was too hard. She couldn't do it.

On the other end of the line her mother, responding with the classic "you're-not-quitting-because-nothing-in-life-that's-worthwhile-is-ever-easy" speech, part of every mother's repertoire.

But inside Bon Secours this bright spring morning I am watching another Susan Shine.

Susan the professional, caring for a critically ill patient with love and warmth and precision. Explaining to me in impressive technical detail how every life function of the patients is measured and monitored.

Telling me later at breakfast how important she thinks her work is. That it was worth all the study — and the tears. Telling me how awesome it can be to have responsibility for the lives of other people and how rewarding it is to be able to help them.

It seems to be part of the nature of things that parents are destined to have a narrow view of their own children.

They are, after all, our children. Depending on us for everything until the day we let them drift out of our lives, confident enough, finally, in their ability to exist on their own.

I learned in one day at Bon Secours that the process doesn't stop there. That it's probably where an important part of it really begins.

In mid-morning on that Wednesday, Dr. Ronald Laskowski walked through intensive care with his daughter Lauren, who will be four in a few weeks. She had come to work with her father.

I couldn't help wondering if it will ever occur to Lauren someday to let her father come to work with her. I hope it does.

It could be a very important day in his life. ■

The winter season passes
as new life springs forth

May 13, 1984

It is Palm Sunday and signs of spring are on the flat, sandy landscape of central Florida.

In the orange groves along Highway 452 in Lake County flashes of green are starting to show against the black trunks of the trees hit hard by last winter's freeze.

Their limbs show white where the dead growth has been cut back. Dried and broken branches lie in piles between the long, straight rows, waiting to be burned.

Flowers have begun to brighten the front gardens of the houses, and even on this gray day it is clear that something important is happening.

It is God's season for rebirth. The season to put winter's harshness behind and to celebrate the hope of new life that spring always brings.

Not far away, in the town of Eustis, in room 498-F of the Waterman Medical Center, the last hours of Edward Knowles' life are being monitored on hospital machines.

He is wired, tubed and restrained. Clear fluid from three soft plastic bags drips imperceptibly into his body.

His heartbeat sends green lines marching across one screen in irregular patterns. On another, red digits silently measure other vital functions.

In the room, the only sound is the soft hiss of oxygen. Life's white sound.

The red hand of a large wall clock sweeps the closing hours of Ted Knowles' life ahead of it, 60 seconds at a time.

He moves in his bed and moans softly in his sleep, either close to his pain or blessedly at peace without it.

Edward Knowles is 73 and his heart has failed.

Outside the hospital window, a Sunday afternoon wind has riled the gray waters of Lake Eustis. Beyond those uninviting waters lie all the memories that accumulate in a lifetime.

Ted, which is what his family called him, spent most of his life in Detroit. He worked 32 years for the city, starting in 1938 cutting grass on the golf courses and retiring in 1970 as chief dispatcher in the department of Motor Transport.

For 31 years, he was my father-in-law. Supportive when it was important to be. Available when he was needed. Out of sight when that was what was called for.

He was divorced when his two children were young and spent more time away from them than he would have liked.

But if his performance as a father was inconsistent, he was the consummate grandfather. His grandchildren became the focus of his life.

He and his wife, Ethel, took them along to Florida on their winter vacations and then built a cottage in Canada so the grandkids could be around in the summers, as well.

When the grandchildren began to outnumber available sleeping spaces at the cottage, he built an addition.

He taught them to fish. Weathered a dozen bone-chilling Thanksgiving Day parades. Overbought on birthdays. Showed up too early every Christmas morning.

Suffered with them through every childhood illness.

Ted Knowles moved to a kind of benign retirement in Florida 14 years ago. Near this quiet place called Eustis. In a small settlement of manufactured houses, with other people from the North living out their lives where the weather, at least, was a little softer.

His grandchildren, grown now, some of them married, were living in other places. The contact was occasional, at best. Letters, some cards, and even a visit now and then. But nothing permanent. Nothing really substantial.

It's one of the things you give up when you retire and move away, he used to say. He didn't like it, but he understood it.

When one of his grandsons, Jim, got a job in Bradenton, Fla., two years ago, and moved there with his wife, Ted was delighted.

When Jim's wife, Deanna, gave birth to their first son before Christmas, once again it seemed that life was going to be what it had always been for Ted Knowles.

But Ted's death on Palm Sunday changed all that.

And on that same day, 14 miles away from the hospital room — past the new growth in the orange groves — in the small front room of Ted and Ethel's home, Colin Patrick Shine, four months into his life, snuffled in his sleep, dreaming whatever it is that babies dream.

Some say he is going to look like his great-grandfather. That he favors Ted. Still a little early to tell. But you never know.

After all, it's spring, and he's got his whole life ahead of him. ■

A place with rainbows
in each and every room

Sept. 5, 1982

Elizabeth Knowles was buried on a warm Tuesday in August in a small country cemetery in St. Clair County, between Almont and Allenton, a few fields away from the farm where she grew up.

She was 77 years old and was buried in the dress she bought for, but never wore to, the wedding of a grandchild. She died in the Hospice of Southeastern Michigan two days before the wedding, among people who had loved her all their lives and people who had loved her for the three weeks they had known her.

During her life, Betty Knowles had more than a suspicion that the world had failed to give her a fair allotment of happiness, something I learned long before I married her daughter.

Betty was divorced when her two children were very young and never remarried. She was Catholic and believed that by not remarrying outside her church, she was keeping her part of a contract she had with God and that, ultimately, He would keep His part.

She worked most of her life in a factory for the Federal-Mogul Corp., but they closed the plant in the mid-1950s and told her they didn't need her anymore. When she reached retirement age, they sent her a pension check each month for $6.09.

Her health had been in decline for years and she seldom left her Center Line apartment for anything other than trips to the doctor and the hospital.

Doctors diagnosed her final illness as cancer. They told her family she had from four to six weeks to live. They suggested she be put in a hospice, which is a place where the balance of a patient's life is measured in weeks or months.

It is also a place where the emphasis is on the dignity of living and not on the certainty of death.

When Betty Knowles arrived at the Hospice of Southeastern Michigan in Southfield, the staff was assembled to greet her. On the front desk was a sign — and a rainbow — bidding her welcome.

Rainbows, in fact, are a pervasive theme at the hospice. On the walls, in the rooms, on the desks, on the uniforms of the staff.

Under the stitching on the right side of his lab coat that spells out "C. O'Shaughnessy, Medical Director," is a rainbow patch with the invitation: "Have a Rainbow Day."

"Why rainbows?" asks Dr. Charles O'Shaughnessy in a brogue as soft as any rainbow that ever settled over a Kildare meadow. "Because after the turmoil of the storm comes this magnificent gift, this free gift of indescribable beauty. Nothing could be more appropriate to what we are concerned with here."

And what they are concerned with there is celebrating those remaining precious moments of life.

"We humanize a natural process," Dr. O'Shaughnessy said. "We don't put it in a straitjacket. We're not staving off the process of death here, we're working with the quality of life. The quality of the days that are left."

Dr. O'Shaughnessy, who was born, reared and educated in Ireland, joined the hospice in December 1980, a month after it opened. Sponsored originally by Sinai, Mt. Carmel, Providence and Northwest Grace hospitals, it is supported now by a consortium of 23 area hospitals.

He likes to compare the work at the hospice with the brilliant victories of Marshal Ney, the French Army officer Napoleon called "the bravest of the brave."

"When Napoleon retreated from Moscow (in 1812) the war was lost, but Marshal Ney fought a rear-guard campaign that was brilliant. A lot of magnificent victories in a losing effort. In that same way, the victories we win here more than substitute emotionally for the inevitable loss.

"When we stop pain, nausea, vomiting, shortness of breath, confusion, agitation or bring it under control, and bring people to the point where they can converse with family and friends, that's a major victory," he said.

After two weeks in the hospice, Betty Knowles felt good enough to ask to go home. She went back to her apartment, and the hospice arranged for a nurse to visit and monitor her condition.

She became seriously ill after 10 days and returned to the hospice. It was a homecoming. The staff gathered to welcome her back and tell her they missed her. For them and for Betty, who has had more rain than rainbows in her life, it was a lovely homecoming.

Betty died the following day. The staff put a card honoring her memory on her bed. Next to it they placed a rose.

They left them there for 24 hours. Then they prepared the room — and a rainbow — for another patient. ■

A four-legged skeleton comes out of the closet

Oct. 6, 1985

There was a time, in our uncomplicated young lives, when you kept your dog until the intervention of one of several inevitable events.

These included, of course, the dog's death, natural or otherwise. In our neighborhood, otherwise was the leading cause of canine mortality, usually in the form of cars and trucks.

My only dog, Mitzi, went the way of all truck chasers — under the wheels of a large oil truck driven by a neighbor.

Then there was the problem of injudicious biting — situations in which dogs bit persons other than kids, especially official persons like mail carriers or meter readers.

There always seemed to be a reasonably high tolerance for dogs biting kids, probably because it usually happened someplace where kids weren't supposed to be, like trying to retrieve a baseball from some grouch's yard.

But people whose careers were jeopardized by dog bites usually called the police, who came and took the dog.

Dogs also disappeared when dogcatchers made periodic sweeps through the neighborhood, always while we were at school, capturing as many unlicensed dogs as they could fit in the truck.

Landlords were a factor in dog ownership, and I can remember no dispute in which the question of "Get rid of the mutt or move out" was ever settled in favor of the dog.

But nowhere in the annals of my memory is there an instance of a kid giving up a dog on orders of an allergist.

At dinner one night several years ago, my wife announced to me and the assembled Shine children that son Tom's allergist had told her to get rid of the dog because it was aggravating Tom's allergic condition.

The ensuing silence was broken by Jim, Tom's older brother, who suggested we keep the dog and get rid of Tom. This was followed quickly by a show of hands, which the dog won, 4-1.

The only vote in favor of Tom came from Dan, the youngest, who took it all very seriously. The court of parental appeals overturned the vote and we kept Tom — and the dog.

The dog has long since died and Tom lives, pet-free, in Kansas. Which leaves my wife as the only person at home these days with allergies aggravated by furry pets.

The fact that we have a dog at home is a secret she has managed to keep from her allergist for a number of years, operating on the principle that if he knew, it would only upset him. Besides, she was not interested in the question coming to a vote some night at supper.

During this past summer, Judy DiForte, a free-lance writer, interviewed me for a story she was doing about front porches, a subject especially dear to me. It was for a publication called Vim, a newsletter for the elderly published by Harper-Grace Hospitals.

Photographs were taken of me on my front porch, sitting there with my daughter Peggy and our dog, Bailey. It was all very homey.

The folks at Harper-Grace liked it so much they took one of the pictures from the article and reprinted it in the fall issue of their Pacemaker magazine.

I thought it was all very nice. My wife looked at it and said, "Oh, my God, what if Dr. Lesesne sees this?"

Dr. John Lesesne is her allergist, the man who has been treating her for years in the unfounded belief that she is from a dogless family.

"He won't see it," I assured her. "Doctors read medical journals, not hospital house organs. His nurse will put it on a table in the waiting room and the next time you go there you can put it in your purse and bring it home."

The next time she went there, in mid-September, Dr. Lesesne was his usual cordial self.

"That was a very nice picture in the Harper-Grace magazine of your husband, your daughter — and your dog," he said.

"You knew I had a dog," she said weakly.

Turning to her file, Dr. Lesesne found a sheet that had been completed 13 or 14 years earlier. He quoted from it: "Will get rid of pets."

What she did not tell him last month was that Bailey is our third dog since she made that unkept promise.

Dr. Lesesne has modified her medicine to accommodate this new information about his patient, which prompts me to take the whole thing one step further.

In the interests of promoting a more open relationship between journalism and medicine, I think it represents a demonstration of good faith to give him one additional bit of information.

We've got a cat, too.   ∎

5. Inside the Morning Friendly

First day on the job,
and the job wasn't there

Jan. 5, 1986

The day I realized that I had worked at the Free Press for 10 years, I found it difficult to believe the time had passed so quickly.

The second 10 years slipped by even faster.

Since then I have tried not to think about it.

But when I closed my 1985 American Heritage Century Desk Calendar last Tuesday, I couldn't escape the truth that I was closing in on 35 years at this newspaper.

Tenure can be a wonderful thing. It improves the multiple on the pension plan, sounds impressive when you're being introduced at gatherings and somehow always seems to convey the image that length of service and professional wisdom are inseparable qualities.

Tell somebody you've worked for the same company 35 years and, depending on their age, they will either praise your loyalty and perseverance or ask you if they had movable type when you started working.

I have become accustomed, more or less, to being told by new reporters that when they were born I had already been working at the Free Press for 10 years.

Whenever that happens I just remind myself that people who had been at the Free Press 35 years ago, when I started work here, were hired in 1915. It helps me maintain some perspective.

The only problem I have with all this is believing what the calendar tells me. That in 1950 I walked into the Free Press newsroom, talked the night city editor into hiring me as a copyboy, and I have been here ever since.

And, for reasons I will explain later, I am quietly pleased that the tile in the men's lavatory in the east end of the newsroom is starting to deteriorate.

Though a lot of what has happened to me since is compressed into a kind of fast-forward blur, that Wednesday in 1950 is as fresh to me as anything that happened yesterday.

The night editor, Charlie Haun, said I could work one day a week and told me to report for work at 9 a.m. Saturday.

When I showed up Saturday, another editor, Bob Sturgis, told me they didn't need any new copyboys, and even if they did, Charlie Haun wasn't authorized to hire them.

What Mr. Sturgis didn't understand that morning was that for the past three days I had gotten myself quite used to the idea of being a Free Press employe and I was not going to be turned back by weak statements about hiring authority or current openings for copyboys.

I began to argue with him. When it became clear that I was not going to go quietly, he suggested I try the News. I suggested he call Charlie Haun at home and clear up the question of my employment at the Free Press.

Finally, I held up my lunch bag and asked him if he had any suggestions about what I could tell my mother, who had packed it lovingly that morning in the sincere belief that the Free Press, an honorable institution, had agreed to employ her son.

I think it was at that point that I pulled ahead.

He told me to sit on the bench under the clock, and when the chief copyboy came in, he'd let him worry about it.

The chief copyboy, Archie Hilton, who had more authority than the Free Press ever intended, validated my hiring.

Now about that tile. One day nearly 20 years ago, when I was city editor, I went looking for a reporter who was late leaving for an assignment. I found him in the men's room watching a workman lay ceramic tile.

We're crazy to be doing what we're doing, the reporter told me. Our work has no boundary, no scope, no dimensions, no permanence. We put every bit of ourselves into our writing, he said, and it's forgotten in days.

Fifty years from now, he said, when nobody remembers who we were, this tile-setter's work will be as good as the day he did it. We should get out of journalism, he said, and into the tile business.

It has, in fact, been a very good 35 years and I do not need to see broken tile in the men's room to reinforce that feeling.

A large number of very good people have passed through my life, and many of them are still part of it.

Charlie Haun, who made it all possible, is retired and does a little organic farming in the Thumb, where he avoids using insecticides, choosing instead to knock bugs off his plants with a stick while cursing at them.

Archie Hilton sells real estate in Petoskey, but I'm afraid I've lost track of Bob Sturgis. Which is a pity.

I have always wanted to tell him I packed my own lunch that day. ∎

A little outside profit
In crumpled cigaret packs

Aug. 1, 1982

Walter Pierre, who had been an editor at the Free Press, died a few weeks ago and it was reason enough to call Bill Sudomier to talk about Walt's passing.

Sudomier had a long and colorful background at the Free Press as a reporter and city editor before joining the Detroit News, where he is an assistant news editor.

We agreed that we would probably never work for an editor who was any better at what he did than Walt Pierre.

Then we rolled around for a while in the kind of nostalgia that always wears well. Recollections that are shaped and softened by the passage of time to the point where it becomes terribly easy to convince yourself that those really were good times and it will never be as good again.

We talked about how quickly Walt could edit a wire service story or write a headline or lay out a page. Then Sudomier added: "And he never hassled us over the 'We Never Sleep News Agency.'"

And that, friends, is another whole story.

By way of background, I first met Bill Sudomier in an American Literature class at the University of Detroit. I found it remarkable that he was able to make good grades even though he spent most of his time in class reading the Racing Form and making small marks in the margins.

He was, it turned out, a copyboy at the Free Press and also — under the name "Old Rosebud" — a handicapper of thoroughbred horse racing, whose picks, worked out carefully every morning in American Lit, appeared in the Free Press sports section.

It was Sudomier who helped me successfully direct my previously unsuccessful efforts to find work as a copyboy at the Free Press.

I joined that group in 1950 and soon learned that there were ways to enhance my copyboy salary which was, by any measure you care to apply, less than modest.

The most impressive of these income-enhancers was participation in a questionable endeavor, operating without the permission or knowledge of Free Press management, known to the copyboys as the "We Never Sleep News Agency." What was least impressive about the WNSNA was that its activities probably violated several state, local and federal statutes, let alone what passed then for Free Press policy governing the conduct of its employes.

What the "agency" did, actually, was supply horse racing information from Free Press wire services to persons whose access to such information was limited by the nature of their employment, namely bookies and people who ran a game of chance in Detroit called numbers.

By virtue of his position as head of the Copyboys' Protective Association, Sudomier was also in charge of our covert news agency. He dealt with the "clients" and gave the rest of us our assignments. We got the race information off the wire, called a number and recited the information to a voice that repeated the information and then hung up without saying thanks or goodby.

We were compensated weekly by a shadowy figure who drove a Chrysler slowly through the alley behind the Free Press loading dock. While we watched from a doorway, the driver rolled down his window and tossed out a crumpled cigaret package which contained the fee for our services.

I'm not quite sure of the reason for the melodramatics involved here except that it might have been an indication that the bookies were having as much fun doing this as we were.

My recollection now is that there wasn't a whole lot of money involved — perhaps $40 a week split four or five ways — which didn't bother us much at the time. We simply assumed that bookmaking was a business where the profit potential was obviously marginal. And none of us was inclined to stop the guy in the Chrysler to ask for an increase.

Somewhere during that time, the need for our services was interrupted permanently by some official agency which, if it did not turn our mysterious benefactors to more productive lives, at least disconnected their phones. Whatever happened, we never heard from them again.

It will serve no higher purpose here to mention the names of others involved in this little venture, even though the statute of limitations protects us all. They have gone on to make their way in business, industry, government and the professions and don't need any public reminders of their shadowy past.

I was even going to leave Sudomier out of it but, as much as I like him, I'm really not inclined these days to do favors for people who work for the Detroit News. ■

That bear of a city editor
kept a cub reporter humble

July 24, 1983

There are people who pass through our lives, however briefly, who make such a searing impression on our consciousness that every memory of our dealings with them remains vivid despite the passage of time.

Ask newspaper people, for example, if they remember their first city editor. You will hear, in meticulous detail, several chapters of material, including anecdotes and horror stories, about that individual.

By definition, a city editor is responsible for a newspaper's local coverage and for the reporters who cover local events. Trying to define exactly what a city editor is is a bit more difficult.

In 1934, Stanley Walker, then city editor of the New York Herald Tribune, gave this partial definition of the job:

"He invents strange devices for the torture of reporters, this mythical agate-eyed Torqeumada with the paste pots and scissors. Even his laugh, usually directed at something sacred, is part sneer. His terrible curses cause flowers to wither, as the grass died under the hoofbeats of the horse of Attila the Hun. A chilly, monstrous figure, sleepless, nerveless and facing with ribald mockery the certain hell which awaits him."

In the 1920s, the live prototype of Stanley Walker's city editor was Charles Chapin of the New York Evening World, who had fired 108 reporters in his 20 years in that job.

And when Chapin murdered his wife in their hotel room, he was violently critical of the way the newspapers handled stories about his crime. From his cell he demanded to know: "What's the newspaper business coming to?"

Of course, no discussion of this topic would be complete without at least some mention of Frederick L. Olmsted, who was named city editor of the Free Press in 1955. It was the same year the newspaper, in its questionable wisdom, agreed to give me a six-month tryout as a reporter, since it appeared my career as a copyboy was going nowhere at a discouraging rate.

Olmsted came to the Free Press in 1948 as a reporter and, before he was named city editor, was one of the best rewrite men in the business.

It would not be fair to call Fred Olmsted a tyrant, although the copyboys agreed it would certainly be nice if he had his own Caribbean country to run. A better word might be intense.

His intensity put our newsroom phone system on "loss leader" status with Michigan Bell, since Olmsted often terminated unpleasant phone conversations by demolishing the telephone.

And it might not be reasonable, but it would be honest, to say I was terrified of Fred Olmsted to the point of daily exhaustion.

He had one journalistic standard: high. He demanded it consistently and accepted no excuses for error or inaccuracy, though I was prepared at all times to plead youth, inexperience and a disadvantaged childhood to escape his wrath.

To him, there was no such thing as a small mistake. And when you made one, you dealt with the full force of his displeasure, standing at his desk while he explained, in a voice loud enough to be heard throughout downtown, that you were a hopeless journalistic case and should seek some line of work that required less thinking.

It was difficult for me, in those early months, to write any story through in one try, so I used more than my share of the copybooks with built-in carbon sheets that the Free Press provided.

One day Fred Olmsted checked my wastebasket and publicly estimated that I was costing the Free Press 50 percent of my salary in wasted paper.

From that point on, every time I made a false start on a story I quietly removed the copybooks from the typewriter, folded them and put them in my inside coat pockets.

I would leave the Free Press each night in a panic that Olmsted might notice I had stuffed several pounds of his precious copybooks inside my coat, in my belt and under my shirt and was planning to shove them down a catch basin in the alley behind the American Legion hall at Cass and Lafayette.

It also troubled me that he might think I had found a suitable repository for my work and would suggest the arrangement be continued until it created an unacceptable burden on Detroit's sewer system.

Olmsted retired in 1970. He's 78 now and still lives in the Detroit area.

I have one concern about writing this.

That Fred Olmsted won't like it and will show up in the city room to tell me — and everyone else — exactly why. ∎

Memories of an unsolved kidnapping still linger

Feb. 14, 1982

The Browe family moved on our block sometime in the spring of 1938, and from the start it was evident to the other kids in the neighborhood that there was something special about them. They lived two doors from us on Beniteau and had come from the west side under circumstances that were mysterious only because nobody would talk about them.

Whenever neighbors gathered in somebody's front yard, the conversations would trail off into silence if Mrs. Browe passed by. The silence would linger as they watched her walk up the street. And then the gathering would suddenly be over, and the people would return quietly to their yard work or go back inside their houses.

I can remember my mother watching Mrs. Browe from behind our curtains and saying softly, "God help her."

The Browe children, at least Chuckie and Eddie, the ones my brother and I played with, seemed no different than any of the many other kids we knew.

But the difference was that at 4:30 p.m. on a warm September day in 1936, Chuckie Browe, then 9, and his brother Eddie, 7, took their baby brother in his carriage to Clark Park, on the west side about a mile from where the family lived on Seventeenth Street.

In the park, a woman gave them five cents to buy some ice cream. A man with her gave them three cents for candy. The woman said she would watch the baby while Chuckie and Eddie went to a nearby confectionary store.

When the two boys returned minutes later, the carriage stood empty by a park bench. Their brother, Harry, 19 months, who was called "Buddy" by his family, was gone.

If, two years after the event, Chuckie and Eddie Browe had been damaged by this tragedy in their young lives, it was not apparent as we played stick tag in the alleys or ranged happily through the empty fields along the river.

The shelf-life of childhood trauma is blessedly short, and though talk of the kidnapping continued to darken the faces of our parents, it did not spill over to the street to dampen the games children played. And only momentarily in those months did I ever reflect seriously on whether I could ever play again if someone stole my brother while he was in my care.

Harry Browe was never found. No ransom demand was ever made, which surprised no one. A family with six children and little money was hardly the kind that attracted kidnappers whose motive was profit. Not like the Lindberghs, people said.

Somebody who wanted a baby of their own, the police theorized. Probably a "crazed woman," a command officer told reporters.

After two years, there were only occasional stories about the kidnapping. The deadline to collect the $650 in reward money had passed, and the Browes decided to move across town to the east side, away from the memories of Clark Park. They would later move back to their old west side neighborhood, into a flat on W. Vernor, just in case someone would come looking for them to give them back their baby.

Tragedy continued to pursue the Browes. In 1950, Mrs. Browe was struck and killed by a car that crippled her husband as they walked near their Dearborn Township home. Two years later, Chuckie died when the oil truck he was driving rammed another truck near Monroe.

And it was in 1962, a few weeks after one of the periodic stories about the case, that I answered the phone on the Free Press City Desk, where I was working nights as a reporter, and talked to a man who said he thought he was Harry Browe.

He was nervous and spoke slowly and quietly. He said the woman he always believed was his mother told him before she died some years before, "You are some other mother's baby. I took you, and I have never been sorry, except for breaking that woman's heart."

The story about the kidnapping worried him. He was the right age. Like Harry Browe, his eyes were blue. Like Harry Browe, he had a mastoid operation scar behind each ear. He had no physical resemblance to the woman he thought was his mother. And he wasn't sure he wanted to find out the truth.

We talked twice more by phone. He said, finally, that he didn't think he wanted to complicate his life by pursuing the question. He never gave me his name or told me what he did for a living, except that parts of the conversation led me to think he was a cook in a hotel kitchen.

I spent some time in hotel kitchens over the next six months. Lots of blue eyes. No mastoid scars. No Harry Browe.

In the Free Press library is a three-page summary of the kidnapping, prepared for publication by a forgotten rewrite man who signed it simply, "cummings . . . rewrite." It is dated Dec. 16, 1936, and marked "(. . . for use when and if Harry Browe is found)." It remains filed under "Browe, Harry. Kidnapped baby." ∎

He probably brushed past God to find Jerry Buckley

Aug. 15, 1982

It was at the absolute height of Riley Murray's storytelling years that Ed Lahey warned me about growing old in the newspaper business.

"You'll find as the years go by," he said, "that nothing in this business will seem as good as it was when you were younger. That everything — the stories, the reporters, the editors — was invariably better in the old days. And when some young reporter gets excited about a murder story, you're going to give him a sympathetic little smile and say: "You call that a murder? Hell, in the old days that's two paragraphs back by the truss ads. The car barn murders, now that was a murder.'"

And then, Lahey said, you will proceed to bore those around you with endless stories about how good it was when the business had some substance to it and when reporters knew a first-rate murder story from a routine killing.

The late Mr. Lahey was then chief of the Washington Bureau for Knight Newspapers. He was one of the best to come out of that era of Chicago journalism — the 1920s and 1930s — which guaranteed all those involved in the newspaper business in those years the right to be referred to in their obituaries as either colorful or legendary.

Riley Murray was a Free Press reporter who could probably be ranked, even by the most rigid standard, as a local legend. Maybe even a regional legend.

So a couple of things struck me about Ed Lahey's portentous warning, which was delivered in the Free Press newsroom one night in the late 1950s. One was that nothing he said applied directly to me, since at that time I had no firm plans to grow any older. Secondly, he was describing Riley Murray with frightening accuracy and I had already been convinced by Riley that the newspaper business was not as glamorous and exciting as it used to be and neither were the stories.

If you talked about mass tragedy, Riley would tell you about the Eastland disaster in which 812 people drowned when an excursion steamer capsized in the Chicago River in 1915. His father was a Chicago fireman and was one of the first on the scene, and Riley remembered every heart-rending detail.

Talk about contemporary gangs and Riley would scoff and compare them loosely to his parish altar society and then recite membership, pedigree and exploits of the Purple Gang, the Little Navy Gang and the Myrtle Street Gang.

Mass murders? There'd never be another like the Collingwood Massacre or the Benny Evangelista cult killings.

He rejoiced in the stories he had covered and mourned endlessly for the ones he had missed. Like the Jerry Buckley story.

Buckley was a radio commentator and a friend of Riley Murray. On the air he was a noisy critic of public corruption and told Riley over a beer one night in 1930 that he thought someone might try to kill him to keep him from broadcasting what he knew.

Riley advised Buckley to put everything he knew on paper, put it in a safe-deposit box and send him the key. "I told him that if anything happened to him," Riley used to tell us, "then I'd make sure that the information was made public." Buckley agreed to the plan and told Riley he'd send him the key.

A few days later, shortly after one of his broadcasts, Buckley was shot to death in the lobby of the LaSalle Hotel at Woodward and Adelaide. Riley never got a key, although he was convinced that Buckley was serious about the plan.

Thirty years after the shooting he would still wonder what went wrong. "Maybe he just didn't have the time," he would say. "Or maybe he did it and didn't get a chance to send me the key." Then Riley would stop talking, take a drag on his cigaret and stare out the window at the darkness of the city, thinking about the story, his story, languishing all these years in some dusty safe-deposit box.

Riley Murray retired from the Free Press in 1972 after working here for 44 years. Leaving nothing to chance, he had prepared his own obituary in 1961, pointing out that he was born in Chicago in 1904 and started newspapering there in 1922. His list of career highlights were, not surprisingly, heavily weighted toward events in the 1930s.

Riley Murray died in January 1981. His funeral mass at St. Theodore Church in Westland was attended by fewer than 20 people, a turnout hardly befitting a legend, even one that had outlived most of his contemporaries.

I remember thinking that day in church that Riley, who was an expert at counting crowds on assignments he covered, would not have had much trouble with this crowd.

I also remember thinking that now maybe Riley Murray would find out from Jerry Buckley what went wrong with the plan they worked out so carefully that July night in 1930. ■

They stood and applauded
when Ken McCormick returned

April 11, 1982

The one indisputable fact at the Free Press in the early 1950s was that the people who knew the most about what was going on at the paper were the copyboys.

When I joined that questionable group in 1950, the unofficial orientation included a detailed rundown of the reporting staff. Which ones were the drunks, which ones treated the copyboys like serfs, which ones were good at what they did and which ones were in over their heads.

When they told me that the best reporter on the staff — and probably the best in the city — was Ken McCormick, I had no reason not to believe them. Over the years I learned how right they were.

My own affection for Ken McCormick was entirely personal.

After five years as a copyboy, I was given a tryout on the reporting staff. As I sat there that Monday morning waiting for my first assignment, McCormick came up to me, handed me a dollar and said: "How about getting me a coffee, and get one for yourself."

Nobody had told McCormick that Friday's copyboy was Monday's reporter. I held the dollar, wondering whether to explain my new status or just go and get the coffee. I decided that the moment called for a break with the past.

When I told him I was starting my reporter tryout, he grabbed the dollar and asked me, "How do you want your coffee?" Then he went down to the coffee shop and brought back two coffees. I have never forgotten that gesture.

McCormick came to the Free Press in the fall of 1931. He had started in the business two years before as office boy to the advertising manager of the Cleveland Press.

"There was a coffee shop on the ground floor of the (Press) building," McCormick recalls, "and it was clear to me that the people in there who seemed to be having the most fun at their jobs were the reporters."

So McCormick went back to his boss and said he'd like to be a reporter. All things being possible in 1929, he was assigned to the police beat reporter to learn the business.

"After a little while on the police beat, they decided I'd progress faster on a smaller paper and sent me to the Indianapolis Times," McCormick says. "I hated Indianapolis, so I started writing every paper in the country telling them they'd be chumps if they didn't hire me."

He heard from a Free Press editor who told him he might have a job open in 10 days or so.

"I took the next bus to Detroit and started sitting around the newsroom waiting for the job to open," McCormick says. "After a couple of days, they decided I was determined to work there and they hired me."

McCormick started on the police beat for $21 a week and alternated his coverage of police news with his responsibilities as part of the round-the-clock poker game in the pressroom.

"It was a game that never ended," McCormick remembers. "When a new shift of reporters showed up for work, they replaced the guys in the game, and it just kept going. I know that at one point the game lasted for at least three years without stopping."

It was the poker game that occasioned McCormick's first fight in Detroit. A Detroit Times reporter spent so much of his time needling the new Free Press man that McCormick followed him to the men's room one day and knocked him cold.

McCormick's last recorded instance of physical conflict was his memorable — though hardly illustrious — flattening of Milky, the Twin Pines clown, in the Detroit Press Club in 1960, where McCormick, the club's president, decided the clown was making a nuisance of himself.

In 1945, McCormick won the Pulitzer Gold Medal for the Free Press for his exposure of corruption in state government. As a result of his investigation, 101 people were indicted, including legislators, lobbyists and state officials. Sixty were convicted, and 25 of them went to prison.

McCormick left the Free Press in 1962 to work for Michigan Energy Resources Co. where, at 76, he still works as a consultant.

He has been back to the Free Press city room only once since that time. He was walking into the managing editor's office when it happened. The people in the newsroom stood and began to clap. Soon the entire room was on its feet, applauding Ken McCormick. A unique reaction from a group of people not usually given to such spontaneous displays of approval — especially to other reporters.

And there was a moment that day when we thought we were going to see Ken McCormick, tough-talking reporter, cry. ∎

Martin Street's old hag
knew how to dish out fear

April 18, 1982

Some of you may already have drawn the inference that I have a cautious respect for phenomena I do not fully understand. Like ghosts.

No one has ever proved to my complete satisfaction that there are no such things as ghosts, so excuse me if — in the absence of incontrovertible scientific evidence to the contrary — I refuse to write off the spirit world as storybook stuff.

But let the record show that I have never let personal quirks interfere with my professional performance. Absolute proof of this came one October night in 1962 when an editor sent me with a photographer to check a report that a family on the west side had fled their home in terror, chased out by the ghostly presence of an old hag.

The house was on Martin Street, near McGraw. When I got there the lights were on, but the house was empty. Through the windows I could see food on the table, dishes in the sink.

A neighbor told me the couple who lived there had told her that strange and horrible things were happening in the house and that they were going to move in with a relative in Dearborn until they could make arrangements to move their belongings.

We found the family in Dearborn. Reluctantly, they told us of a series of strange happenings in the house that culminated with the appearance of a ghostly old woman with stringy gray hair and a smile like death. The couple, and a relative visiting from out of town, all had seen her.

My photographer, Jerry Heiman, asked if one of them would go back with us to the house and let us look around. They refused. I was relieved.

But Heiman pressed, as only photographers can, and the visiting relative agreed to return to the house with us, but said he would not set foot inside the bedroom where the hag had appeared.

Back at the house on Martin Street I stood in the empty front room, determined to go no further. The photographer insisted on seeing the bedroom. I found myself hoping the old hag would get him.

Our guide told us where it was, but refused to show us. He also suggested that only one of us go since the hag never appeared when there was more than one person. Heiman said that since I was the reporter, I should be the one to go. I decided that if the hag didn't get him I would.

I also knew that if I refused to go into the dreaded room, the story of my cowardice would be all over the newsroom by breakfast.

Before I walked to that back room, I told Heiman to focus his camera on the French doors that separated the kitchen from a hallway that led to the bedroom. If I heard, or saw — or even sensed — anything in that room, I told him, he would get a prize winning shot of me crashing through those closed doors.

I spent about 90 skin-crawling, shirt-dampening uneventful seconds in the room, my thoughts about getting out of there crowding out every other emotion.

The story caused a minor sensation. Hundreds of people showed up at the house. Police from the McGraw Station had to barricade the street, and the day shift had to be held over to help handle the crowd.

The city editor was prepared to go the distance on the story. I found I was less prepared when he called me in and told me: "I want you to spend the night in that house."

I tried to remain calm. "It's my day off," I said.

"I'll pay you overtime," he said.

I realized that I would eventually lose this fencing match, so I told him there was not enough money in town to get me to stay all night in that house.

"You mean you believe in ghosts?" he asked me, stunned.

"I believe in that one," I said.

Gentle Jimmy Pooler was the reporter finally assigned to spend the night there, but as he approached the house a bunch of kids, pursued by the police, knocked him down, breaking his arm.

The city editor thought it was an unfortunate accident. I saw it as a sign.

In 1973 a Free Press reporter returned to the house to do a follow-up story.

He was told by the woman who lived there then that the only unusual thing that happened was that one day a crashing sound — like a cascade of broken dishes — came from the kitchen. When they rushed to the kitchen, they found the dishes unbroken and stacked neatly in the cupboards.

A few weeks ago I knocked on the door of the house on Martin Street. The first time I had been there since that night in 1962. I spoke with the daughter of the woman the Free Press had interviewed in 1973. She told me her mother had died three years ago.

"Has anything unusual been happening?" I asked.

She thought for a moment, then said: "No. Nothing. Except every now and then we still hear the sound like dishes breaking." ■

Lou Cook has taken leave
of the place where he belonged

April 15, 1984

If there's a hierarchy in the newspaper business (and I'm still not sure there is), copyboy is an unlisted position.

So in 1955, I took advantage of an offer to move from the relative security of five years on the copyboy bench to a six-month tryout as a reporter.

I viewed the move less as an opportunity for advancement than I did as the chance to self-destruct in a position where failure was a high-risk possibility, if not a sure thing.

But failure was not to be — at least not then — largely because I prayed regularly and got a lot of help from Lou Cook.

Lou had been a writer at the Free Press since 1951 and now he became my personal writing coach, my counselor, adviser and guide.

He convinced me that terror and self-doubt were normal emotions in the life of a reporter.

He was there when I needed him and even when I didn't. Rewriting my leads. Explaining why only half my story appeared in the paper. Reassuring me that not all editors were fools and milksops, insensitive to the wonders of language, but that a lot of the time it would appear to be the case.

Now Lou Cook has retired and the whole thing makes me a bit nervous.

It should not be necessary, at this stage of my career, to feel comfortable at work only if Lou Cook is within walking distance. I can do a lot of things on my own nowadays.

I deal with self-doubt on its own terms and terror is only an occasional interrupter of my day. And editors don't fuss with my writing the way they once did.

Nevertheless, it was a good feeling knowing that Lou was around. Just in case.

But a few Fridays ago he piled his career into a few cardboard boxes and took them home. Just like that.

Before he came to the Free Press, Lou Cook had worked since 1937 as a reporter on the Des Moines Register.

Before that he had taught Shakespeare at the University of Iowa, his alma mater. He quit to become a section hand on the Chicago, North

Western, working out of Honey Creek, Iowa. Where, he said, the pay was higher and the companionship more interesting.

Later he worked as a ditch-digger on the Indian Creek Flood Control Project and wrote stories for the Council Bluffs Nonpareil at five cents an inch.

My earliest memory of Lou Cook is watching him stride (he strides as well as any person I know) through the newsroom wearing a heavy brown leather greatcoat and carrying a violin case under his arm.

The coat came from a German officer, a functional trophy of Lou's service with the Army in Europe in World War II. The violin was his own.

My most personal memory of Lou Cook is a conversation we had in the rain late one fall night in 1960 on the corner of Cass and Lafayette.

Newspapers, you must understand, are places where personal turmoil is a quality present in abundant amounts. It finds expression among newspaper people in, among other places, old saloons and inexpensive diners.

I had just left the basement bar of the old American Legion Hall where I had spent the evening with my night-shift colleagues discussing the Free Press, its editors and its owners in terms that can be safely described as uncomplimentary.

Lou Cook had come in around midnight looking splendid — if out of place — in black-tie. He was writing about music and drama for the Free Press those days and was the only guy on the staff with his own tuxedo.

He followed me when I left and stopped me on the street to talk about the level of my participation in the night's conversation. He said the kind of talk he had heard that night was not worthy of me.

My friends of the evening, he said, would always be malcontents. Marginally talented journalists who would end their days butchering stories on the copy desk of some paper nobody ever heard of, still complaining about the people they worked for.

"But you and I will still be here," he said, "because this is our paper. This is where we belong."

I did not feel good about myself that night.

Now Lou is gone and I'm left.

He says he's going to work in his garden, sail in his boat, play his violin in the Grosse Pointe Symphony and drink some gin.

I am prepared to interrupt him in the middle of any one of those endeavors, should the need arise.

You never know when you might need a friend to help you face some terror or overcome some self-doubt. ∎

We got the story at any cost, and the price couldn't be beat

Jan. 27, 1985

One of the more mundane management responsibilities which falls to me each week is approving the expense sheets of the reporting and editing staff of the Free Press. Lunches, dinners, mileage, travel, miscellaneous items such as "batteries for tape recorder" or "pizza for source."

What impresses me most is the great leap forward we have made in getting reporters to the scene of breaking stories. Commercial airlines when news circumstances permit, chartered planes or helicopters when time is a major factor.

In other years, I promised myself that if I lived past 50 in this business I would not adopt the posture of the old editor who spends his time telling his younger colleagues about how tough it was in the old days. Just like I promised never to tell my kids how far I had to walk to school in the snow.

But yesterday's promise is today's temptation, and the way I see it, why forgo something as eminently enjoyable as conversations which you can open with "You think you've got it tough today. ... "

Time was when a trip to Grand Rapids by a Free Press reporter was a major excursion requiring more approvals than it takes to activate a missile silo.

After the approvals, the next management decision centered on the question of what's the cheapest way to do this.

A personal example. In July 1960, a woman from the Detroit area was found murdered on Mackinac Island. At the Free Press, a decision was made — at a level where travel decisions were not allowed to be made — to send reporter Shine to Mackinac.

The people with power to make the decisions said it was all right to send the reporter, as long as it didn't cost anything.

In those days, the Free Press circulation department flew its early editions by cargo plane to Tri-City Airport near Bay City where the papers were picked up by trucks and carried to all parts of the state.

Somebody from circulation got me a ride on the old DC-3 and told me when I got to Tri-City to find the truck heading for the St. Ignace and hitch a ride.

It's never bothered me to fly in aircraft that look like they were meant to be flown. But planes whose vintage suggests that safety would be best served if they were on display at Greenfield Village are something else.

And it did not help when the pilot of this relic complained to his supervisor that the plane was overloaded and that this was the last time he would ever fly with that many bundles of papers on board.

The only seat for me on the plane was a tool box behind the co-pilot, and it was on that spot I sat, as we lumbered down the runway, listening to the pilot pleading with the plane to take off.

"Come on, baby. Up! Up!" he said. It was not a reassuring conversation.

In Bay City I hooked up with a truck driver named Leo, who told me he would be glad to have me ride with him to Mackinaw City. One problem, he said. There was only one seat in his truck. He took out the passenger seat so he could carry more papers.

It hurts your time to the Straits when you have to stop every few miles and drop off copies of the Free Press. And although Leo insisted that I try to sleep, I was fascinated watching him reading his manifest, counting papers and trying to keep from running off the highway.

I told Leo that if he would concentrate on driving, I would count the papers and wrap them. He declined the offer, saying I should get some sleep, even though by this time he was distributing the papers from the bundle that was my seat.

By the time we hit Topinabee, the overloaded DC-3 was beginning to look like an appealing travel option.

We got to Mackinaw City as the sun was coming up and the ferries had not begun to operate for the day.

Two young men putting boxes on a boat told me they'd take me to Mackinac Island if I'd help them finish loading the boat. Even though I had money enough for the ferry, I knew my editors would be pleased that I worked my way across.

I spent three or four days on the island, covered the story, stayed free at the summer home of an editor's friend and caught a ride back to Detroit in a State Police car.

The following Monday some editor approved my expense sheet, the only irregularity being a pound of fudge disguised as lunch.

The total outlay of Free Press funds for that assignment was, as I recall, somewhat less than the total I approved the other day for "pizza for source." ■

6. War stories

Bubble Gum WAR CARD NO. 426

P-51 MUSTANG

One family's steep payment
to two wars of our nation

Nov. 10, 1985

> Here we dead lie because we did not choose
> To live and shame the land from which we
> sprung.
> Life, to be sure, is nothing much to lose,
> But young men think it is, and we were
> young.
> — A.E. Housman

Even before they saw the man from Western Union come up the walk, most of the neighbors knew that one of the Ingalls boys had been killed in the war.

The word had come down from L'Anse, in Michigan's Upper Peninsula, where the Ingalls used to live. Someone there had heard from a relative in the service that one of the Ingalls brothers — Dick, Bill or Vince — had died.

None of the neighbors was able to tell the Ingallses, so they waited. They knew that one day the telegram would come.

It came one hot day in the middle of July 1945. Cleo Ingalls was home alone. She was 15.

"When I answered the door," she says, "a Western Union man stood there with a telegram in his hand. When he heard that I was alone he told me they were not allowed to leave a telegram except with the parents, but he said it was a long way out here. He told me if I would open it while he was there, he would leave it."

Cleo Ingalls opened the telegram. It was Vince.

Cpl. Vincent Lansford Ingalls, 22, U.S. Marine Corps, son of Mr. and Mrs. Leo V. Ingalls, 14231 Crescent, Detroit, had been killed in action on Okinawa one day before the Japanese surrendered the island.

"A neighbor came over when he saw the Western Union man come up the walk," she continued, "and he called my father at work — he worked in a factory in Ferndale — and told him."

Leo Ingalls came home and waited for his wife to return from a visit to her father. She could not be reached by phone.

"She didn't get home until 10 o'clock that night," Cleo Ingalls recalls. "I can still remember lying in bed with my younger sister, listening to her footsteps as she came down the street."

The death of Vincent Ingalls was reported in the Free Press on Aug. 15, 1945, the day after V-J Day.

I mentioned that report in a column last summer in which I talked about how the war had changed us in those four years from Pearl Harbor to V-J Day. And how that casualty report, buried in a corner of the Free Press on the day we celebrated peace, was a reminder that the cost of victory was a personal one.

After the column appeared, I heard from Cleo Ingalls, now Cleo Neynaber, about her brother.

"His legal name was Lansford Vincent Ingalls," she wrote, "but he always went by Vince. They day after the war was declared he went down to join the Marines.

"They told him that he would have to use the name Lansford, since it was his legal name. He told them he was not going to go through the Marines with that name.

"My mother was doing the wash when he came home and asked her if she would go down with him to the city hall to change his name."

They took the bus downtown and had his name changed. Mrs. Ingalls went home. Vincent Ingalls went back and joined the Marines.

"He was sworn in at a special ceremony at Briggs Stadium on July 4, and taken to the train station after the game," Cleo remembers. "We never saw him again."

Vince Ingalls was buried on Okinawa and his brother, Dick, who saw him from time to time in the Pacific, saw the grave.

"He told my mother that if she ever saw what a beautiful cemetery he was buried in, she'd leave him there," Cleo said.

But in 1948 the government notified the Ingallses that the bodies were going to be removed to a cemetery in Hawaii, so the family decided to bring him home.

"My family often talked of him," his sister says, "and what he would be doing if he were still with us. Would he be married? How many children? Where would he be living? Recently it has been, where would he be retiring from?

"Now we have added our son to all of those same questions. Vincent and our son, Rusty, are both buried in the family plot. One from World War II and one from Vietnam."

Russell (Rusty) Neynaber, a Navy airman, son of Cleo and Clifford Neynaber of Pontiac, the oldest of their four children, was killed Nov. 29, 1972, in an airplane crash. He is buried in a quiet corner of Acacia Park Cemetery with his uncle, Vincent Lansford Ingalls. They are both 22. ∎

Good soldiers for the Empire rest in peace far from 'Wipers'

Nov. 11, 1984

They buried Harry Knowles in a back section of the cemetery, near the wall that separates the graves from the soccer pitch where the kids from St. Sever play after school.

In the files of Britain's Commonwealth War Graves Commission this place is officially the St. Sever Cemetery Extension.

In St. Sever, a small town near Rouen, France, it is known simply as *le cimetiere militaire Anglais.*

There are 12,000 war dead of the British Empire buried here, rank upon rank of headstones among well-tended flowering shrubs and clipped grass. Part of a generation of young men who came to France from 1914 to 1918 and died there.

The stones list their last names, a first initial, the date they died and the places they came from. Durham, Lancashire, Sussex, London, Canterbury, York, Staffordshire, Northumberland, Shropshire, Gloucestershire, Middlesex. There are Canadians among their number. And New Zealanders, Australians, West Indians, South Africans and Indians.

And they died — depending on whether you listen to the patriots or the poets — either for king and country or for a botched civilization.

These were the best the Empire had to offer. The Argyll and Sutherland Highlanders, the Grenadier Guards, the Royal Irish Regiment, the Leinster Regiment, the Durham Light Infantry, the Royal Newfoundland Regiment, the London Irish Rifles.

Harry Knowles was from Peterborough, Ontario. He was a driver in the 33d Battery, 5th Brigade, Canadian Field Artillery. He died on Nov. 1, 1917, of injuries suffered in a gas attack during the Third Battle of Ypres, sometimes called the battle of Passchendaele. He was 46.

The government sent a small metal cross with his name engraved on it to his wife, Elizabeth, back in Peterborough. A daughter, Elsie Batterson of Windsor, one of the eight children he left behind, still has the cross.

Mrs. Batterson, who was three months old when her father died, said he joined the Army because he needed some way to support his family.

"It was a question of money," Mrs. Batterson says. "It was a very hard time for our family then. In Peterborough, my father drove a hackney (a horse-drawn taxi) and had done the same in England before he moved the family to Canada."

But it was not steady work the way soldiering was, and Harry Knowles took his skill with horses to the field artillery, where cannons were still pulled by horses.

And in the mud of Flanders, his brigade joined the battle for the medieval Belgian town of Ypres. It was the place the British troops called "Wipers" with the same wry humor they called the noisy German artillery shells "whizbangs."

The fighting for that piece of Europe began on June 7, 1917, and when it ended on Nov. 12, 1917, it would be remembered only for its dreadful cost in human life. The Third Battle of Ypres, with its 244,897 British casualties, would take its questionable place in history with Verdun and the Somme and the other bloody places of that war.

We had gone looking for Harry Knowles' grave this summer because he was my wife's grandfather.

The family knew little of what happened to him except that he went to war and never returned.

Another grandchild, Diane Chave, had learned from the War Graves Commission where he was buried.

The cemetery is an extension of the St. Sever town cemetery. It is cared for by six English gardeners who, not surprisingly, keep this corner of France looking very much like an English garden.

There are no other visitors in the cemetery, and in the quiet of this August afternoon we stand by the grave of this man none of us ever knew, each with our own thoughts.

I find myself thinking of the gas. Greenish-yellow clouds moving lazily on a light breeze toward Harry Knowles and his comrades, turning to a deadly, choking bluish-white mist in the dampness of Flanders.

From the other side of the cemetery's brick wall, beyond the soccer pitch, the chimes of an ice cream van can be heard.

But I keep thinking of other music. Of the weary, muddy ranks of British and Canadian soldiers caught in that terrible war and of the song they sang at this deadly place they called "Wipers."

"Far, far from Wipers, I long to be.
Where German snipers can't get at me.
Damp is my dugout, cold are my feet
Waiting for whizbangs to send me to sleep." ■

A name on a gravestone
and a missing testimonial

April 20, 1986

Even when it had the light all the way, the streetcar always slowed down for the right turn off Kercheval onto Mt. Elliott.

While the trolley started to pick up speed as it passed the cemetery, I'd watch for the gravestone.

It stood just inside the iron fence, facing the street.

Serg't William A. Ruedisale

Killed in France

Aug. 5, 1918

Co C 125 Inf

32 Div

Riding the Fort-Kercheval streetcar with my father, the conductor, from its east side terminus at Lycaste and Jefferson to the end of the line beyond the unexplored territories west of Woodward, was a regular summertime excursion.

And as the streetcar continued on its journey to Wyandotte, where people had big fields for backyards and kept goats tied up in them, I would think about the dead soldier.

Who was he? Did he have brothers or sisters? A sweetheart? How did he die? Where did his father work? Who cried for him? Who loved him?

I had a particular fascination with the Great War. My father fought in France, and Richard Conover's father still limped from his wounds, but he had brought home his helmet, and Richard, when he was in the mood, would let us take turns wearing it.

Even when I grew older, I continued to be intrigued by a man who was still only a name carved on a headstone.

Once I went in the cemetery and saw the graves of his mother and father in the same plot. They had died in 1928.

Then one day I decided to see if I could find out more about Sgt. Ruedisale.

Irene Aust, who runs the cemetery office, pulled out the heavy ledgers. Sgt. Ruedisale's body was returned from France in 1921 and he was buried on July 30 that year. The funeral was from St. Catherine's. On Oct. 20, 1949, a Sylvester Ruedisale of Detroit paid $100 for perpetual care of the grave.

I found Sylvester Ruedisale in the phone book. He is 82 and lives in St.

Clair Shores. He is Sgt. Ruedisale's youngest brother.

He told me that his brother, the oldest of seven children — four girls and three boys — was 27 when he died. "They're all dead now, except me," he said.

Reports differ on where William Ruedisale was killed. It was either at Chateau Thierry or in Alsace-Lorraine. He won the Distinguished Service Cross and the French Croix de Guerre for gallantry.

"My father had been a woodcarver," Sylvester said, "and he made the wooden street signs for the city on a carving machine in a small shop behind our house.

"When the war started, Bill was running his own music store on Gratiot and Van Dyke, and he closed it down and enlisted. We had to sell all the pianos and an organ and boxes of sheet music and the records and piano rolls.

"I guess you could say he was my hero, even though he was 14 years older. He was quite a ball player and took me with him to the games. In 1910, he pitched a no-hitter at Mack Park."

Sylvester's photo album is fat with memories of his brother. Bill and his friends mugging for the camera at the family cottage in New Baltimore. Bill getting ready to dive in the water from the top of a pile driver in Fair Haven. Bill in uniform at Camp Grayling, and later in combat gear, pictures identified only as "Somewhere in France."

The last one is dated July 4, 1918, a month, almost to the day, before he was killed.

After his death, the neighbors got the city to change the name of the street beside the Ruedisale house at 4130 Van Dyke to Ruedisale Court.

Bill Ruedisale's father made the sign in his shop, and put a gold star after his son's name. When the old wooden signs were replaced, the family tried without success to get the one with the star.

The house still stands on that corner, but the signs marking it as Ruedisale Court are gone. Torn down by vandals and never replaced.

I'm going to ask the city to put the signs up again to remind all of us that people who die in our wars are, for all that, real people, not just names on cold stone.

I'll add the gold star.   ■

Of bombs, Pearl Harbor
and bubble gum cards

July 10, 1983

The mere involvement in the process of growing up provides kids with a unique roster of special anxieties.

These include, but are certainly not limited to, concerns about school, the social graces, puberty, complexion, popularity and personal relationships with parents, siblings and peers.

Now, because of the workmanlike job we have done in perfecting weapons ultimately capable of accomplishing the destruction of large sections of the world and its inhabitants, we seem to have added significantly to that burden.

Surveys show that a high percentage of kids, from the grade school level through high school graduation, have added the fear of nuclear war to the list of things that trouble them.

The real possibility of lots of us disappearing someday in a misty vapor has not escaped them. And their concern about it has altered their ideas of what their future might be.

All of this invites the inevitable comparison to the reaction of children 42 years ago, when war became the most exciting thing in their young lives.

With the exception of momentary panic inspired by a some war cards providing exceptionally graphic, full-color representations of the tragic results of bombings in Shanghai, I do not recall being particularly concerned that the war would be a bad thing for me or for any of my friends.

In fact, it became a frantic and exciting activity around which our lives would be centered for the next 3½ years.

The day after Pearl Harbor it was impossible to contain our excitement when fighter planes from Selfridge Field flew in noisy formation over our houses.

The word spread quickly through the neighborhood that Waterworks Park had been fortified. We ran the 14 blocks to the park to find soldiers with rifles and helmets guarding the gates and others setting up a machine gun at the arch of the Hurlbut Memorial, the park's main entrance.

Our lives quickly became one-dimensional, the conduct of the war our dominant concern and victory merely a matter of time.

Baseball cards became secondary attractions, and war card collections became prized possessions. The back of each one explained that the purpose of the carnage depicted on the reverse side was to educate the young to the horrors of war. We also understood, and accepted, their primary function — the sale of bubble gum.

The cards became instruments of trade and barter and, in some cases, legal tender. Collections were enhanced or diminished by a process known as "flipping," wherein cards were spun end-over-end to the sidewalk to determine odds or evens, win or lose.

We became volunteer air spotters and spent hours studying silhouettes of enemy aircraft and countless more hours looking skyward for a glimpse of any Zeros, Stukas or Messerschmitts foolish enough to fly into our area of responsibility.

We argued about whose father was contributing more to the "war effort" and whether it was more important to work in a factory building tanks than it was to build trucks for the Army.

We learned that singing during an air raid protected your ears from concussion, that it was better to throw sand on an incendiary bomb instead of squirting it with water, and how to tell the difference between the Chinese and the Japanese.

Those of us unlucky enough not to have any older brothers listened in jealous silence while those who did recounted their adventures in full and glorious detail or read their V-mail letters in front of the class.

I do, however, recall thinking one morning, at a memorial mass for the war dead of the parish, that maybe I was lucky after all in not having an older brother. Two boys in my class, Joe Callahan and Joe Warakomski, had brothers who never returned from the war.

If our psyches were damaged by any of this, we were not sophisticated enough to notice.

Bolstered by our own inflexible optimism, it never once occurred to us that we would not win. And, despite our precautions and preparations, we never seriously believed that the war would ever touch us personally. So there was really nothing to worry about.

It would be more emotionally convenient for today's children if things were in the same neat package as they were in the 1940s. The same sense of national purpose, the same strong confidence in the outcome.

But nothing stays the same, and the fear of nuclear obliteration is a real one for these young people.

It's a fear I share for my own children and for my grandchildren.■

We fought the big one
in the trenches of St. Jean

March 28, 1982

They tore down the East End Theatre a while back.

It was a routine passing in a city where more buildings come down than go up.

But somebody once told me that combat veterans have a special and lasting affinity for the places where they fought their wars. Maybe that explains the tinge of sadness I still feel whenever I pass that empty lot at E. Jefferson and Glover.

Because from 1942 to 1945, mostly from somewhere in the first 10 rows, I gathered with the rest of the kids from the neighborhood to fight World War II.

A least three times a week, my allowance and the Legion of Decency willing, I joined the lower east side irregulars as we helped Randolph Scott destroy enemy hordes in "Gung Ho!", slipped "Behind the Rising Sun" with a courageous Tom Neal and faced defeat with dignity on the "rock" with the cast of "Corregidor."

It was painfully serious business. So much so that once, in the final dramatic moments of "Bataan," Lefty Brosnan jumped up and threw a golf ball through the movie screen in a futile attempt to turn back the Japanese attackers and save Robert Taylor.

When we assembled two years later to watch "Back to Bataan," we considered it nothing less than a personal triumph for Lefty.

The manager of the East End never quite found it in his heart to forgive Lefty, failing to recognize that fine line between patriotic fervor and vandalism.

There were personal sacrifices as well. I decided not to continue my fantasy love affair with Judy Garland until we had made the world safe for democracy.

Some months earlier, Judy had replaced Deanna Durbin in my affections when I decided, after some painful reflection, that living on Lycaste probably would not appeal to Deanna. Judy seemed more right for the neighborhood.

The war dragged on, but there was no weakening in our resolve to see it through with the bravest Hollywood had to offer.

"Bomber's Moon," "Corvette K-225," "The Sands of Iwo Jima," "They Came to Blow Up America." "Guadalcanal Diary," "Thirty

Seconds Over Tokyo," "Sahara," "Fighting Seabees," "The Purple Heart," "Burma Convoy," "Crash Dive," "Calling All Marines," "Lifeboat," "Destination Tokyo."

We all agreed that although "Mrs. Miniver" was a nice lady, her movie — measured against standard combat fare — was a bit sappy.

We learned to hate Benson Fong and Richard Loo. Though they were Chinese, they played Japanese roles, forfeiting any claim to special ethnic consideration. Equally hated were Helmut Dantine, Erich von Stroheim and all the Kruegers (Kurt, Karl and Otto).

In our spare time, we followed people with accents we thought might be German and set up a loose surveillance on the Canton Chinese Laundry on Jefferson and Beniteau. We knew the Chinese were on our side, but if Benson Fong and Richard Loo had turned, anything was possible.

It wasn't, however, all death and destruction. Recognizing that even the East End wasn't immune to the dangers of celluloid combat fatigue, Hollywood took some pains to demonstrate that war isn't necessarily hell.

We were treated to Ann Miller's tap dancing in "Reveille with Beverly" and the singing of Bing Crosby and Betty Hutton in "Here Come the Waves."

Then, with only a passing thought about why Sonny Tufts was not in the service, it was back to the war.

We forgave Edward G. Robinson his criminal past and joined him on the bridge in "Destroyer." We envied the "Boy from Stalingrad" and prepared against the day we would be called on to defend Detroit. We always assumed the push would come from the west and vowed that we would hold the line — at any cost — at St. Jean. If they came east along Eight Mile, that was somebody else's problem. We were strictly a neighborhood defense force with no military responsibility outside the parish boundaries.

Then 1945 came, and the tide of the war turned just about the time John Wayne got involved.

The job was done. The east side irregulars grew up and went their own ways. Two of them would die in Korea, a war that was uncomfortably real to all of us but got little attention from Hollywood.

And my relationship with Judy Garland never got past the first 10 rows, perhaps for the better. I was probably kidding myself about her being right for the neighborhood. ■

Recalling the war, the spy and the kid from Germany

May 5, 1985

There are still some people who call it World War II, to distinguish it from the Great War and from the hostilities that have intervened in their lives since 1945.

But to so many of us, it will always be simply "The War." No Roman numerals, no dates or delineations. The War. The standard by which we will forever measure global conflict.

I was 11 years old when Pearl Harbor was bombed, not quite 16 when the Germans surrendered. Nothing before or since has had the kind of impact on me as that war.

It's difficult now to believe that nearly 40 years have elapsed since the end of the war. Difficult because the memories of those years are as clear as FDR's voice coming from the old Majestic radio in our upstairs flat, declaring that a state of war existed between the United States and the Empire of Japan.

My involvement in the hostilities, by virtue of age, was peripheral. But it was good enough for me.

On Dec. 8, 1941, the neighborhood kids gathered to decide which patriotic course to pursue. Since we preferred something quick and close, we decided to head for Waterworks Park and secure the city's water supply lest it be contaminated by Axis spies, who were probably already in place, working their espionage in Detroit.

Unfortunately, the Army had already acted and had the gates guarded. We stood around for a while and watched the soldiers, concerned that our participation in this great adventure would be diminished considerably if local involvement in the war was going to be handled by uniformed interlopers from outside the neighborhood.

As the months passed, we turned our attention to what seemed to be the country's prevailing security menace, the dreaded Fifth Column.

We were not really sure in those early days how international loyalties were being worked out, so we decided the most prudent course would be to suspect all persons with accents to whom we were not related.

Our first serious investigation involved a man who lived in a rooming house on Hart. Our suspicion was provoked not by his accent — none of us had ever heard him speak — but by his slouch hat and long black overcoat. Spy apparel, if we had ever seen it. There was also a strange-looking aerial on the roof of the rooming house, which we decided faced the general direction of Berlin.

So we followed him every night to the restaurant on the corner and then back to his rooming house. When he went inside, we sat on the curb across the street and watched the aerial, convinced that all the loose talk our agent had picked up at the counter of the Hart Grill was now a coded message, speeding toward the Third Reich. Our surveillance was suspended when he moved out of the neighborhood without notifying us.

We joined the junior sky-watchers corps and memorized the menacing silhouettes of Zeros, Stukas, Messerschmitts and Mitsubishis. In the playground at Lingemann School, the Civil Defense people showed us how to use sand to smother incendiary bombs. We took first-aid courses, pasted 10-cent war stamps in fat books, and sold tin cans, old inner tubes and fat drippings for a few pennies a pound, all in support of the war effort.

The fact that each night we retrieved the rubber we sold during the day, and resold it the next day, was viewed by us not as unpatriotic but as our way of improving the economic condition of the neighborhood.

Kids with older brothers and uncles in the service plastered their sweaters and jackets with chevrons, unit patches and brass badges, inspiring a quiet envy in those of us without close kin in the military.

War's painful reality came later. Gold stars in the windows of the Callahans, the Diehls, the Buckleys, the Warakomskis and others.

And a kind of personal pain one summer day in 1944 on a Lake Erie beach in Canada.

We went there some summers and rented a cottage. On the beach one day we met a kid our age. He was by himself and we invited him to join us in whatever game we were playing. He hesitated and said he thought he should tell us something first.

He was German, he said, and if we didn't want to play with him, it was OK. He would understand. There were other kids who didn't play with him for that reason.

We played together for the rest of that summer and tried to understand what the war had to do with kids refusing to play with a blond boy named Rudy whose parents were from Germany. My father said: "War can make people act that way."

I didn't understand it then. I still don't.　■

Counter-surveillance
at the St. Rose Sweet Shop

Oct. 31, 1982

It's difficult to remember now just when it was that the count and countess bought the neighborhood candy store.

It was not long after the war and shortly after the countess had been released from prison where she had served a four-year term for being a Nazi spy. Her emergence as co-owner of the St. Rose Sweet Shop at Kercheval and Beniteau may not have given the place an air of international intrigue, but it sure did a lot for its stature as an after-school hangout.

Actually, it was some time before we learned that the nice lady with the German accent known to us as "Mrs. Miller" was actually Countess Marianna von Moltke, a genuine aristocrat and a convicted spy.

Her husband, and partner in the store, was Count Heinrich von Moltke, who lost his job as a professor of German at Wayne University when she was arrested in 1943. It had always seemed to me that operating a candy shop near a school in a working-class neighborhood was pre-destined to be a non-profit venture.

Consumer traffic never seemed to be a problem. The little store was always jammed. Consumer spending, however, was entirely another matter.

The purchasing power of kids in that neighborhood was not the answer to an entrepreneuer's dream and even before we understood things like cash flow we understood that very little of it flowed in the St. Rose Sweet Shop.

The identity of the von Moltkes was made public when the countess called the police about a disturbance in the neighborhood, and a Detroit Times reporter saw her real name on the police report.

We decided quickly that it made little difference to us that "Mrs. Miller" was really a countess who had done time for espionage. We also decided that it was probably a good thing that the Spike Jones recording of "The Fuehrer's Face" had been taken off the jukebox some months earlier.

However, that attitude did not prevail in the neighborhood.

The war was over, but there were still gold stars in some of the windows and there were people who wanted the von Moltkes gone.

The pastor of our church joined those who thought the community would be better off without the German couple.

Historically, the separation of church and candy store in our neighborhood had never been fully realized. The sweet shop had been characterized as a workshop where the devil was in regular attendance, having his way with an abundance of wonderfully idle minds.

The pastor became convinced that the devil's work was being supplemented by Nazi propaganda supplied by the von Moltkes.

Nothing ever came of the move to move the von Moltkes. I remember the kids in the high school getting signatures on a petition in support of the couple. It pointed out that they were good people and had never even spoken about Hitler or Germany and since the countess had paid for her mistakes, the past should not be held against them.

It was quite an impressive document, and most of the kids in the school signed it. But the circulators didn't know what to do with it after it was signed, so somebody gave it to the von Moltkes.

There was always a measure of curiosity, even mystery, about the extent of Countess von Moltke's treason. None of us really knew what she went to prison for.

We had our own string of scenarios that included trying to put poison in the pipeline at Waterworks Park and conspiring to blow up the bomber plant at Willow Run.

As best as I can determine from the clips in the Free Press library, Countess von Moltke's crime was hardly a spectacular example of international espionage. It appears she was more than a little sympathetic to the Nazi regime and fell in with a crowd of pro-Nazis, including Grace Buchanan-Dineen, a real German agent who agreed to work for the FBI when her identity was uncovered.

One of the things of which the countess was accused was providing Buchanan-Dineen with addresses in Switzerland so letters could be forwarded to Germany. Countess von Moltke pleaded guilty and was sentenced to four years in prison.

Some time in the early 1950s the von Moltkes sold the candy store and disappeared.

Harry Okrent, the court-appointed attorney who represented her on the espionage charge, is retired now and says the countess and her husband are dead.

The candy store was torn down a few years ago to provide more parking for the church. Nobody knows whatever became of the petition. ■

A POW's diary of survival on faded photographs

Dec. 8, 1985

For Syd Goodman it was, in many ways, an exercise of the spirit.

A way to keep some small hold on the reality he feared might elude him.

So every day from Dec. 17, 1944, until March 28, 1945, in tiny script on the backs of 36 snapshots, Goodman recorded the days of his life in a place called Stalag IX B in Bad Orb, Germany.

Pvt. Sydney L. Goodman, who lived at 3250 Calvert, was captured by the German Army in Luxembourg on Dec. 17, 1944.

He started writing his diary the day the Germans took him prisoner.

Dec. 17, Sunday: "... I was taken to a group of officers who questioned me. ... I was taken to Waulhausen — and from there to another town where I spent the night."

"They took us to a small room," he recalls, "and made us take everything out of our pockets and put it all in our helmet liners."

Among Goodman's personal belongings was a packet of photographs from home. The kind of pictures soldiers carry. Snapshots of family; of his wife, Grace, but mostly of his little girl, Karen, who was not quite two years old. A dark-eyed child, looking up at the camera the way children do, momentarily co-operative but eager to get back to whatever it was they were doing before the interruption.

There is Karen in her playpen. Karen on the front porch of the flat on Calvert, dragging a cloth doll by one arm. Asleep on the front seat of the car. Playing in shallow water at the beach. Sitting patiently on a potty chair.

The Germans gave Goodman back the pictures, and they became the pages of his diary.

Jan. 2, 1945: "The fuel situation is desperate. Not enough heat to warm the stove, let alone the room. Nothing to do, and life is down to one of its lowest ebbs for me. All I think of is home and food. I wonder if Grace knows anything?"

Syd Goodman was 26 when he was drafted in 1943. He graduated from Central High in 1935 and from Wayne University four years later. In 1940, he married Grace Goldberg and started a small body-shop supply business of his own. Karen was born in 1941.

He is 68 now and retired from his business. Karen, of the serious dark eyes, lives in Connecticut. She has two children. Goodman's two other daughters live in California.

Jan. 14, Sunday: "Prot. and Cath. serv. this morning. I listen in because it's religious and I miss our own serv. I have a New Test. and I don't think it's harmful that I pray with it even though it's not my own rel. There isn't a Jewish chaplain or even a Jewish officer here. Thought of home today and I couldn't keep from crying. I miss Grace & Karen & the folks so very much. Dear God, I hope it's not too long."

"I wrote something every day," Goodman says now, "mostly during the afternoon. It was something to look forward to, something to plan on. Something to keep me going.

"So many others just gave up. One day they wouldn't get out of bed and would tell us, 'Just leave me here,' and pretty soon they would just die."

Goodman kept a list of those who died so that there would be something to show that they had been here, that somebody in a world gone mad had thought enough of them to mark their passing by putting their names on the back of an old photograph. When it was over, there were 70 names on the list.

Jan. 18, Thursday: "All Jewish boys to be separated tonight into where the officers formerly lived. Very cold. I wonder what the future holds in store for us?"

"An American officer came in and told us it was the policy of the German government to segregate the Jewish soldiers from the rest," Goodman remembers. "He asked all Jewish soldiers to identify themselves. Only a few did. He said he didn't want to frighten us, but said, 'If some of you guys are Jewish and they find out about it, dire things could happen.'

"A little later," Goodman says, "he came back with a list of names that sounded Jewish, and we were all moved to another barracks and locked in."

At the end of February, most of those in the camp, including the Jewish soldiers, were moved to another location at Berga, Germany. They had been moved from that camp and were being marched deeper into Germany when they were liberated by advancing American troops in April 1945.

Goodman says he can't remember the last time he read the words he wrote on the back of the pictures.

"I guess I didn't write it so I'd have something to read someday," he says.

"I wrote it so I could survive." ∎

Germans were holding the bag when payday rolled around

Feb. 3, 1985

On Dec. 14, 1944, 1st Lt. Robert E. Rutt was given a sack of money at the headquarters of the 422d Infantry Regiment of the 106th Division in St. Vith, Belgium, and told to take it to the front lines and pay the unit's officers.

On Dec. 16, the German Army, displaying an absolute lack of concern for Lt. Rutt's fiscal mission, counter-attacked in what came to be known as the Battle of the Bulge.

A week later, Lt. Rutt, still carrying most of the money, was taken prisoner.

On Sept. 14, 1945, the Office of the Fiscal Director, Headquarters Army Service Forces, Washington 25, D.C., sent Mr. Robert E. Rutt, Detroit civilian, a letter.

A textbook example of the stiff but correct "TO: FROM: and SUBJECT:" military communication, it informed Rutt that a board of officers had been convened "to investigate the loss of funds in the amount of $14,936.04 intrusted (sic) to you in December, 1944. ... "

"If the funds are still in your possession," the letter went on, "it is requested that a certified check or money order in the amount of $14,936.04 be forwarded to this office. ..."

"The frightening thing about it," Rutt says today, "was that besides what was left of my mustering-out pay, I had no money in the world and the Army wanted me to send them nearly $15,000. I think I even had to borrow the stamp to answer the letter."

His wife, Lucille, he says, was pregnant with their second child. "She just kept saying, 'What are we going to do?' "

Rutt, who was in law school at the University of Detroit before he went into the Army, did what any serious student of the law would have done. He answered the Army's letter with one that was a full page longer.

Rutt, now a partner in the law firm of Plunkett, Cooney, Rutt, Watters, Stanczyk & Pedersen, explained to the Army that the vouchers for the money he had disbursed were given to other officers and were eventually lost in the confusion of battle.

What remained of the money had been taken by the Germans, despite his protests that it rightfully belonged to the U.S. Government.

Actually, Rutt says, he doesn't really know how much of the money he had left when he was captured.

"The officers I was paying were on a front of about 10 miles," Rutt says, "and it wasn't easy getting to some of them. When the Germans started their drive into the Ardennes we were hit pretty hard, and by that time getting paid wasn't as important to the officers as it had been earlier."

So when the Germans surrounded his unit, Rutt was still carrying most of the payroll.

"It was in Belgian francs," he says, "and included a bag of coins that weighed about 10 pounds. When it got bad, I asked a private if he'd like some money and gave him the bag of coins. I took the rest of it and stuffed some of it in every pocket I had."

He and another officer tried to break out of the encirclement but were captured by a German armored unit.

"Every time I got searched," he says, "they found some of the money, but it took about a month before they got it all."

Even as a prisoner, Rutt says, he knew that someone, someday, would want to know what happened to the money. So he did what any reasonable person who understood the military bureaucracy would do.

"I asked the Germans for a receipt. I told them it wasn't my money, and if they were going to take it then they were going to have to give me a receipt for it."

After their initial astonishment at the demand from a person so obviously in no position to make demands of any kind, Rutt got two receipts from the Germans for the money.

On one of the receipts Rutt asked a German officer to specify that Rutt's personal money, some 2,060 Belgian francs, was found in his wallet, separate from the Army's funds. The German officer made the notation and listed the amounts separately.

In his letter to Washington, Rutt pointed out that he had not, as yet, been reimbursed for the 2,060 francs, although he had filed a claim in August.

"I also told the Army that the Germans had taken the money before I had a chance to pay myself," Rutt said. "I told them the Army still owed me my pay for November 1944."

The Army sent Rutt a check and has made no further inquiries about the $14,936.04.

Rutt expects to hear no more. "I think the statute's probably run out on that by now." ∎

Snuffy was a certified war hero, but he wasn't always on the mark

Sept. 2, 1984

Snuffy would have liked the obituaries.

The newspapers in Michigan and Florida that marked his passing carried the version of his exploits he would have approved of. His own personal rearrangement of those terrible minutes in a burning bomber over the English Channel on May 1, 1943.

Maynard Harrison Smith, 72, Medal of Honor recipient, "Snuffy" to his friends in the Army Air Force and "Hokey" to those who remember him as a troublesome kid in Caro, Mich., died last May 11 in the Bay Pines VA Hospital near St. Petersburg, Fla.

His heroism following a raid on St. Nazaire, France, saved the lives of his fellow crew members, and Secretary of War Henry L. Stimson flew to England to hang the medal around Snuffy's neck.

Back in Caro, folks downplayed what they called his "Peck's Bad Boy" reputation and welcomed him home with a giant celebration.

There were some speeches from a bunting-draped podium on the porch of the Hotel Montague. Then a parade down S. State Street, with Snuffy riding in an open car with his mother and Gov. Harry F. Kelly.

He left Caro after the festivities, and if he ever went back, no one really remembers. There was not, Snuffy would say in later years, an abundance of love lost between him and his hometown.

And in the years after the war, about the only thing that improved steadily in Maynard Smith's troubled life was his version of what happened that angry day in 1943.

He had, indeed, stayed with the burning B-17 while three of his crew members bailed out. He fought and extinguished the fire himself, jettisoned ammunition cases, tended a wounded crew member and drove off attacking German planes with machine-gun fire, and the pilot was able to fly the plane safely home.

That was enough, a grateful nation decided, to confer our highest award for valor on the little guy from the Thumb.

But little by little, Snuffy upgraded the extent of the heroics. He embroidered the story a bit, embellished a point here and there, improving it until he had worked it into a version he found acceptable.

The 98-pound ammunition cases became 250-pound cases. The 20 German fighters that had attacked the bombers grew to 400.

And Snuffy elevated his ultimate participation in this bit of military history by claiming that after he put the fire out he rushed to the cockpit, pulled the wounded pilot and co-pilot from their seats, gave them first aid, and then — although he had never flown before — piloted the crippled bomber back to England and landed it safely.

But it was, after all, a harmless kind of dissembling. The kind of permissible exaggeration we allow our heroes, and Snuffy Smith was a hero.

We extend this kind of indulgence to the people who fight our wars. Maybe because we're relieved that they are the ones who faced the danger and not us. Perhaps because we are never sure enough of ourselves to predict with any honesty how we would react in a personal confrontation with death.

But also because the world loves a hero, and we have attached certain rights and privileges to that high station. Among them, the right to tell their stories to those who will appreciate the quality of their heroism and accept it as it is offered. Revisions and all.

So we sit over beer in smoky American Legion halls or at veterans reunions or walk with them on the peaceful beaches of Normandy and listen to their memories and think no less of them if the stories improve with each telling.

Snuffy Smith was no different from the hundreds of thousands who came out of that war with their own personal versions of what it was like.

And though they gave him a medal for his efforts, Snuffy never traded on that. Being able to tell the story was always enough.

On May 13, they had a service for Maynard Smith in the main chapel of the David C. Gross Funeral Home in St. Petersburg. There was an honor guard from MacDill Air Force Base and about 100 people showed up.

Two days later, Snuffy was buried in Arlington National Cemetery. In Section 66, Grave No. 7375, with "modified honors" — body bearers, firing party, horse-drawn caisson. Rites commensurate with his status as an American hero.

Back in Caro, the Tuscola County Advertiser carried Snuffy's obit on Page 16, just above the recipe for Easy Penuche Frosting.

But the version was pure Snuffy, down to the last detail. He would have appreciated the irony of it all.   ∎

7. It happened in Detroit

West-siders: They're green
with pointy ears, right?

March 6, 1983

It's not clear to me now, nor has it ever been, why we have allowed ourselves to become separated, one from another, by Woodward Avenue.

We are divided, socially and culturally, by a street. And it is a division we have never seriously resisted.

In some kind of final accounting we may consider ourselves Detroiters, but in our hearts we know what we really are. We are east-siders or we are west-siders, and nothing will ever change that.

The disturbing dimensions of this urban separation are part of virtually every conversation about growing up in Detroit. But nothing illustrates it more clearly to me that an occurrence one frigid morning in the winter of 1954.

I had agreed the year before, with some sincere prodding by the Selective Service, to serve my country in whatever capacity the government might deem the most advantageous use of my talents. The government made me a private in the Army and sent me to Austria to help keep the peace.

On that frigid morning in 1954, I was standing guard, in deep snow, over a battalion of sleeping American soldiers in a beautiful Alpine valley near the Austrian village of Lofer. We were there on military maneuvers, exercises that were scheduled whenever the weather got bad enough.

Across the road, standing guard at what I think now was a signal battalion, was a soldier who looked as cold as I felt.

We met in the middle of the narrow road and began to talk. Priority conversation. How cold it was. How much we hated being there. How much longer to go in the Army. Hometowns.

"Detroit," he said.

"Me, too."

We took off the heavy woolen gloves and shook hands.

"What part of Detroit?" I asked.

"West side," he said.

He did not misunderstand my hesitation in responding.

"You from the east side?"

I nodded.

He looked at me for a few seconds from beneath the hood of his parka and said finally: "Well, stay warm and take it easy. Maybe see you back in Detroit." He walked off into the darkness of that Austrian valley knowing, as I did, that further conversation about Detroit would have been a waste of time.

His Detroit world — schools, playgrounds, neighborhoods, hangouts — was on one side of Woodward, mine on the other. It was a difference we both understood.

One of the reasons for this discussion today derives from the amount of mail I receive containing the phrase: " . . . but how come you never write about the west side?"

To say it's the same reason I never write about Irkutsk would be overstating it, but not by much.

So I called west-sider Saul Wineman, who is known as Paul Winter to those who hear him on Channel 56 or on WQRS, and as Solly to his west-side pals. He is also an assistant professor of humanities in Wayne State's College of Lifelong Learning.

I was seeking to find out what it was that made us different, east-siders and west-siders. He didn't really know, either.

"One of the things I find," he said, "is that I don't think the west-side people have the range of anecdotal recollections that east-siders have. I don't have them, and I don't know any of my peers who have them."

Beyond that statement, which I would not want to defend in any kind of open forum, what we did mostly during our downtown lunch was reinforce what we already knew.

"It was an entirely enclosed existence in those neighborhoods," Wineman said. "There were some east-side lures for us — Belle Isle, Jefferson Beach, Eastwood Park, the river — but outside the neighborhood usually meant the Main Library or downtown. I never had any real sense of the east side except that it was another country."

Our conversation did reveal, however, the shared myth that certain ethnic and social groups had specific "push days," when they gathered downtown to push people for whom they harbored some kind of antagonism.

But we could not resolve any definable difference tied specifically to living on one side of town or the other. Which leads to the reasonable conclusion that there may not be any.

We played the same alley games, danced to the same songs, had the same movie heroes. We just didn't cross Woodward a lot.

After lunch, Saul Wineman and I walked down Woodward and talked some more. "Where is your car parked?" I asked him.

"This way," he said. Pointing west. ∎

The Field and Jefferson gang
— maybe not so tough after all

Dec. 11, 1983

I remember the Field and Jefferson gang. They were in charge of Belle Isle.

It's not that I ever remember running into any one of them personally. But on the east side it was understood that their territorial imperative included not only the island, but Gabriel Richard Park and the bridge.

Nobody questioned it. You just operated on the assumption that your activities in those areas were at the sufferance of the Field and Jefferson gang.

After all, these were the guys who jumped off the Belle Isle bridge just for fun. Who used to run full speed up the gangplank of the U.S.S. Dubuque, the training ship anchored behind the Naval Armory, across the deck, past the guard and over the rail and into the river. Including one kid who carried an inner tube because he couldn't swim.

So when I got a letter inviting me to the annual reunion of the Field and Jefferson gang I was intrigued enough by the history of that organization to accept immediately.

They had gathered on a rainy night in October in an American Legion Hall on Whittier for a party put together by Joyce Fiott, Bobbie Hargis and Ronnie Loepp. None of them seemed nearly as tough as the legend.

Ray Brewington, who retired seven years ago after 25 years as a Detroit policeman and is now an enforcement officer for the Friend of the Court in Macomb County, calls them "the boys with the grandfather faces."

Jerry "Terrible" Donovan was an informal master of ceremonies that night. His friends from the corner remember him as a scrapper who fought several years as an amateur in the bantam, feather and lightweight classes and for his excellent impressions of Richard Widmark.

He spoke that night of the special affection all of them had for Joe Radkin, proprietor of Isle Recreation, the poolroom that was the center of their existence in the 1930s and into the 1950s.

"He was the father figure for us all," Terrible Donovan said, "and we will never forget him."

The reunion, in many ways, was a tribute to Radkin from the men who had been the boys in his life.

171

Nor would they forget "Mrs. Joe," Donovan said.

Miriam Radkin, Joe's wife, took over the poolroom when Joe got drafted in World War II. One of the first things she did was prohibit swearing in the poolroom.

"If you missed a shot," Donovan said, "you had to go outside and swear. It had to be the only poolroom in the city where you couldn't swear."

There was talk that night of the people who made the corner a place of memories. Ted the Milkman, Murphy the Bum, Cloppy Joe, Dick the Paper Boy, Fuzzy and Stumpy.

There was news that one of the last of the "kids" left in the old neighborhood, Honest John Monazym, had sold his bar on Field. That Buff Gesquiere, who had brought the neighborhood glory by winning the state senior men's speed skating title, was ill and couldn't attend.

They talked about the neighborhood chagrin when word got back that Doug Kaake, who was in the Navy, had fired on an American plane.

And Tommy Thomas was identified as the kid who jumped off the Dubuque with the inner tube.

They talked about singing in the choir at the Church of the Messiah on Lafayette and the Boulevard, information that was not current outside the neighborhood in the '30s and '40s. Their reputation as a tough crowd was largely the result of "fringers," says Jack Fiott, director of environmental services at Oakwood General Hospital.

"Guys like Knifey and Joe the Rat and Jitterbug Joe," he said. "They came around from time to time, but were never really part of the group."

Then he recalled the time the police arrested Jitterbug Joe in the middle of a softball game on Belle Isle.

"He was pitching and two detectives walked right out to the mound and handcuffed him and took him away," Fiott said. "When they were putting him in the car he turned and said, 'See you guys in about three to five years.'"

Jack Francis is principal of Utica High School and says it's hard to describe how he and his friends feel about that neighborhood.

"It's not loyalty, exactly," he says, "it goes deeper than that. We really didn't owe the neighborhood loyalty because it gave nothing to us."

Jack Fiott disagreed.

"What it gave us," he said, "was each other." ■

172

Enriching experiences
of growing up in Detroit

May 4, 1986

On the way to go swimming at Olsen's Beach in St. Clair Shores, we used to have to slow down for the big curve on Lake Shore in front of the Edsel Ford estate.

I would point to the gatehouse and tell whoever was in the car that I had been inside that place. That when I was very small — too small to remember — I played in the garden out back while my mother was having tea with the chauffeur's wife.

She and my mother had become friends when they shared a room at Cottage Hospital the time my brother Jimmy was born, and when the weather was nice we would take the bus and spend an afternoon there.

What I didn't tell my friends was that in later years I would imagine what might have happened if young Henry Ford II had stopped by the gatehouse one day and asked if he could play.

We would have become fast friends, I imagined, and I would get to do whatever it was that rich kids did. I had no precise idea then what that involved, but I was sure it included ponies, little cars with real motors, swimming pools and prodigious amounts of ice cream served in silver bowls by butlers in swallowtail coats.

An article in the spring issue of the Michigan Quarterly Review reinforced my regret that Henry never showed up at the gatehouse while I was there.

It is an excerpt from an interview with Henry Ford II by David Lewis, for a memoir to be published after Ford's death. In it, Ford talks about his childhood:

"Grandfather built a Santa Claus hut out in the middle of Fair Lane. He had Santa Claus there and filled the hut with toys. . . . He would have Santa Claus up on the roof dumping candies down the chimney, and, oh, it was a super existence for children."

The Review is published at the University of Michigan, and the spring issue, which confirms my best suspicions about the lives and times of rich kids, is titled "Detroit: An American City." It is the kind of literary tribute to this town that reminds me once again why I have so much affection for this place.

Available at bookstores for $8, it is a collection of essays, art, poetry and articles by Detroit writers — past and present — that seem to capture what is real about Detroit and the people who live here.

Writer Gloria Whelan, for example, remembers the Depression, living in her grandfather's four-family flat on E. Grand Blvd. near the Packard plant, and the circumstances that brought them there from the pretty suburban colonial home they had lived in until they had to move.

"Strange men with shuffling feet and an air of having to do a job against their will had come to the door of the colonial with official pieces of paper entitling them to carry off the nicest things in our house. My father was stoical until they took away his Purdey rifle, a rifle he was to search for in pawn shops the rest of his life, for with that gun, whose leather case carried the elegant legend 'By Appointment to His Majesty the King,' he had thought to close behind him, forever, the door to the farmhouse where each day he was beaten with his father's belt and where the china plates were thick and cracked."

Author Joyce Carol Oates lived with her husband in a house at the corner of Woodstock and Litchfield, in northwest Detroit. They live now in Princeton, N.J., and have not been back to Detroit, the place she calls "that fast-beating stubborn heart," since they left in 1978.

In the Review, she writes: "Those streets. Those years. Livernois. Gratiot. Grand River. John R. Outer Drive. Michigan. Cass. Second. Third. Woodward. Jefferson. Vernor. Fort. Jos. Campau. Dequindre. Warren. Hancock. Beaubien. Brush. Freud. Randolph. Ceaseless motion, the pulse of the city. The beat. The beat. A place of romance, the quintessential American city.

"We were so happy there. Why did we leave?"

It's a question a lot of us understand. ■

Memories of Betty Hutton
bring smiles at the Green Tree

Feb. 7, 1982

It would please me considerably to be able to report here that the institutions that were an influential part of my early years can be lumped into that desirable category called "cultural."

Nothing would make me happier than to put the Detroit Institute of Arts at the top of any list headed: "Name 10 Places That Made a Distinct Impression on Your Eager Young Mind During Your Formative Years."

But, alas, putting church and school off to one side, I end up with an embarrassingly long list of beer gardens on E. Jefferson between Lycaste and Montclair. Marty Mulligan's, Jock Davidson's, the Cave, Ted's Ten High, the Tiger Tavern, the Jefferson Inn, the Union Bar and the Green Tree.

My connection with all of them was more economic than it was alcoholic. Those were the places where it was always possible to make some loose change selling papers, shining shoes, doing odd jobs and, on Halloween night, the places where the patrons would drop coins into your sack after making you sing "God Bless America" or some contemporary favorite they were sure you could at least stumble through.

I learned some things about crime and punishment, since it was not possible to walk past many of those places without occasionally seeing a customer or two being heaved out the door for violating whatever minimum standards of conduct existed inside.

Those who landed on their faces ended up with an affliction my father used to call "pavement rash." It was some time before I found out that people with large painful patches of healing skin on their faces were not suffering, as I thought, from some epidermal ailment not of their own making.

Neighborhood bars in that part of town have gone to wherever neighborhood bars go. Victims of the economy, HUD and demographics.

There is, however, one survivor in that old neighborhood. The Green Tree still blooms on the southwest corner of St. Jean and Jefferson, not much different from when it opened in 1933, right after Prohibition was repealed.

Inside, one day last month, Warren Williamson is keeping busy even though he's tending only four customers at midday.

"It's a quiet place," he says, wary of questions from a stranger and doing his best to keep his answers simple and non-incriminatory.

"Are you from around this neighborhood?"

"Nope," he replies instantly. "From out of town. Ohio. But I live around here now."

"For how long?"

"Since 1939."

Sensing that my conversation with Warren is not going to improve dramatically, I direct the next question to the three beer drinkers halfway down the bar.

"Any of you guys ever hear of Betty Hutton?"

The response is remarkable. They all know about Betty, the singing comedy star of Hollywood in the 1940s and early 1950s and how she got her start in the '30s, singing and dancing for nickels and dimes at the Green Tree as a little girl.

"Betty Hutton made this place famous," says Bill Brooks, who, at 34, was several years away from being born when Betty Hutton was at the top of her career.

"Everybody around here knows that," he continues as bartender Williamson, warming a bit to the stranger, is now poking around behind the packages of beer nuts for a picture.

He finds it, and dusts the glass of the frame with his sleeve and smiles for the first time since the interview started. "Betty Hutton," he announces proudly.

It's an old studio still. Long gown, upswept hairdo, lots of lipstick. The autograph is an impersonal imprint over the name of her employer, Paramount Pictures. Now the small midday clientele is gathered around Brooks, who's talking about a friend who knows a guy who went to Foch Intermediate with her. "Don't think she ever finished Southeastern," he says. She didn't.

Williamson is now out from around the bar, leading everyone to a room behind a partition to a small stage where — in the days when people danced in bars — the band played and sometimes people sang.

Behind the cases of empty beer bottles, the dust is gathering on an old Kimball upright piano. A couple of antique microphones lie next to it. The place where a bright little blonde sang for small change, and 40 years later still doesn't like to talk about it much because memories of Detroit in the 1930s are not soft memories.

At the height of her career, Betty Hutton came back to the Green Tree, stood on the little stage, looked down at the floor and said: "It's the same carpet," and burst into tears.

But there are only smiles at the Green Tree this day. And the memories, based more on legend than recollection, are not harsh. ■

They're still grinding it out, but not with the same class

Dec. 19, 1982

As a person whose enthusiasm for civic improvement is virtually limitless, I have always drawn the line at tearing down burlesque theaters to make room for municipal structures.

For that reason, I have never been able to fully understand the decision to demolish the Avenue Theater on Woodward simply because they needed someplace to put the City-County Building.

Urbanologists may disagree, but I think that kind of indiscriminate destruction erodes part of a city's cultural richness. Which part, I'm sure, depends entirely on the cultural level one assigns to burlesque houses and one's historic relationship with institutions such as the Avenue and its sister establishments, the Empress, the Gayety and the National.

Since the Avenue Theater provided me with the first opportunity to wallow heedlessly in the fleshpots of the city, my affection for that wonderfully seedy place is substantial.

It was a Friday night. Fall 1948. To get to the University of Detroit football game, it was necessary to transfer to the Second Avenue bus on Woodward, just north of Jefferson. In front of the Avenue Theater, which beckoned seductively with promised delights.

Since neither the spirit nor the flesh was all that fascinated with the prospect of another Friday night of U-D football, the decision to join the crowd in the Avenue was quick and uncomplicated.

It was made in collaboration with a longtime neighborhood friend and U-D classmate whose interests — personal and professional — will not be served by being identified here. But that night, the Avenue Theater delivered on everything it promised.

There was music, there was song, there were beautiful dancers. Beautiful, at least, in keeping with the relaxed standards in effect then on the east side.

And there was, most of all, Scurvy Miller, the burlesque comic whose double takes, double entendres and predictable punch lines inspired as much enthusiasm from the audience as did the strippers.

It was a memorable encounter for both of us in spite of the nagging reality that we were probably in technical violation of at least one and maybe two commandments. A situation of the conscience we were able to reconcile satisfactorily after a few years of Jesuit training at U-D.

There were more trips to the Avenue, to laugh at Scurvy Miller, to applaud the dancers who always left more to the imagination than to the view, and to nudge each other knowingly as newcomers eagerly purchased boxes of candy from hawkers who promised "in each and every box" either a Swiss watch, a leather wallet or a pair of nylon stockings.

We felt no responsibility to warn these first-timers away from the candy or from the innocent photographs sold with the instruction to take them home, run a little warm water on them and watch them turn into something less innocent and absolutely too suggestive to discuss in public.

None of the hawkers mentioned disintegration, which is what actually happened when you ran warm water over the pictures.

All those places are gone now. Victims of what Scurvy Miller described in a 1967 Free Press interview as "tight-fisted theater managers and vulgarity."

It started when the pit bands gave way to records and tapes that hardly ever included "A Pretty Girl Is Like a Melody" or "Temptation."

The comics disappeared, so did the chorus line, and the house singer, all for the same reason the bands did — economics.

There are still places in the area where so-called exotics perform between showings of mechanically repetitious adult films.

In the interest of research, I stopped by one of these places a few weeks back, carefully choosing a part of town where I probably would not be recognized.

Three young women, one with a Penthouse cover to her credit and all with modest but limited talents, danced and removed a maximum of clothing in a minimum of time to rock music before a small but unenthusiastic audience.

The star attraction, the Penthouse cover, redressed after her act and offered to answer questions for an audience obviously not there for the Q & A opportunities.

When she insisted that someone ask a question, a voice in the darkness inquired: "Where are you from?"

"Kitchener, Ontario," she replied. End of questioning.

It was all kind of depressing. I was glad Scurvy Miller wasn't there. ∎

A neighborhood bar trades in patience and sympathy

July 3, 1983

There is something irresistibly seductive about the institution we have come to know as the neighborhood bar.

A safe harbor from the world's tempests. A smoky refuge where understanding abounds in kindred patience. Where the problems of life are diminished in quiet conversations. Where personal solace is found in statements which begin: "Heck, you ain't got it nearly as bad as my brother-in-law . . . "

Places where conversation is available for those who seek it and never forced on those who need to be left alone. Places with resident experts on government and politics, local sports, world religions, the weather, international affairs and introductory philosophy.

Hamtramck probably does not have any more neighborhood bars than other communities its size, but it certainly seems that way.

They are inviting places, most of them, often carrying the names of the people who run them, an added encouragement to drop in and see the folks whose names are on the window.

When I covered Hamtramck for the Free Press in the 1950s, I did as much journalistic business in bars as I ever did in City Hall. It was always where people wanted to meet and, truthfully, the bars seemed every bit as conducive to the pursuit of news as the mayor's office. Probably more so.

I was always able, for example, to get an inordinate amount of good information at a bar called Shy & Red's, on the corner of Evaline and Dequindre. Mostly because Shy, one of the owners, who was more formally known as Joe Piasecki, was a longtime member of the Hamtramck Board of Education.

Which brings me to the centerpiece of this discourse, Dr. Thaddeus J. (Ted) Wietrzykowski, whom I will call Ted, thereby saving 11 letters each time he is mentioned.

Ted lives in Grosse Pointe Park, practices medicine in Detroit and owns a neighborhood bar in Hamtramck.

His home may be in the suburbs, his professional life in his chiropractic office, but his heart is over on Yemans Street, five steps down into the subdued hospitality of his Polish Village Cafe.

This, of course, is a particularly subjective judgment on my part,

179

based on nothing more substantial than a long and pleasant conversation in that bar. But I am fairly good at subjective judgments, having worked at it with mixed success these many years.

Ted bought the Polish Village seven years ago but it had a part in his life going back beyond that.

"When I was a kid," he says, "I shined shoes in this place (the Polish Village) when it was called the Yemans Bar and I sold the Detroit Times in here. It never occurred to me 30 years ago that I would ever own it. In, fact, I don't ever remember even wanting to own it."

Ted grew up in Hamtramck, a few blocks from the Polish Village Cafe, which is at 2990 Yemans, just east of Jos. Campau.

His late father was a sanitation worker for the city of Hamtramck and his mother still lives in the neighborhood. His wife, the former Frances Stachurski, grew up in an upper flat on Yemans, a block from the Polish Village.

Ted went to St. Ladislaus School and then to Hamtramck High and spent his formative years picking up pocket money playing the accordion with a local musical organization known as the "Polka Kings."

"We played in a lot of bars in this neighborhood," but never the old Yemans Bar, he says. "But in the early '50s most every bar around here had a small dance floor and there was always live music."

At 46, Ted has been a chiropractor for 14 years, but acknowledges his interest in other things.

"Neighborhood bars are special places," he said at our lunch in the Polish Village, "and part of me will always be partial to places like this."

Much of the talk at the table that afternoon was talk about neighborhood bars. The Schuper Bar, on Chene. "You could be standing there having a beer with a judge and next to the judge is a guy who heisted a bank last week."

And talk of the people of the neighborhood bars. "You remember him. Left his wife and ran off with that barmaid and lived with her for two years until she shot him."

The Polish Village is unpretentious, in keeping with its genre. The food is Polish, which means the food is very good. It's also very inexpensive.

And on some days you can find Dr. Thaddeus J. Wietrzykowski there. He's the guy near the bar who smiles a lot. But you can call him Ted.

It's that kind of place. ∎

Paradise was lost,
but the 606 hung on

Aug. 10, 1986

"I guess you could call this a neighborhood business," Michael Pye was saying. "And then I-75 comes through and takes out Hastings Street and removes the neighborhood. Then one day we are a neighborhood business without a neighborhood."

Pye is talking about the 606 Horseshoe Lounge. What he modestly calls a neighborhood business could be described more accurately as a neighborhood institution.

A couple of weeks ago, the 606 celebrated 50 years of existence and quietly acknowledged its responsibility to urban history as the last survivor in a part of Detroit that was known as Paradise Valley.

There was a party one weekend and the regulars were there, and so were a lot of people who remembered.

Mayor Young was there, Pye said, "knockin' elbows with his old friends and buying a few rounds. He had a great time."

They talked about other days and the places that had been an important part of their lives.

The Club Plantation, the Choklate Bar, Club 666, the Turf Bar, Lee Lucky's, Sportree Jackson's, the Iroquois, the El Cino, Cookie's Place. All part of Paradise Valley and gone now, victims of a city doing its best to keep up with changing times.

That bright strip of night life, centered in the area around Adams and St. Antoine, was created as much by necessity as anything else. Black people lived in an area called Black Bottom, and it made sense that they would find their entertainment there, as well.

It made even more sense when you add the reality that there were places in Detroit — clubs, hotels, restaurants — where blacks were not welcome, even the most well-known black entertainers and sports figures.

So they came to Paradise Valley. Joe Louis and Sugar Ray Robinson. The Ink Spots, Count Basie, Duke Ellington, Billie Holiday, Cab Calloway and Dinah Washington.

Michael Pye said his grandfather, W.T. Johnson, opened the 606 in 1936 and operated it until his death in 1962. It is now owned by Pye's mother, Thelma Young, who is Johnson's daughter.

Pye, 40, who is also a junior high math teacher, manages the club, which took its name from its address on Adams. In 1968, the club moved to 1907 St. Antoine.

Pye said W.T. Johnson had been a waiter at the Detroit Athletic Club and for a while operated a private club for the city's black bartenders and waiters.

"Most people just called him W.T.," Beatrice Buck said, "and his personality just lit up the sky."

Buck, who is the telephone auditor for the Detroit Police Department and author of a play, "Paradise Valley Re-visited," said Johnson was, in those days, the black connection with the white political power structure.

"If someone needed a job or needed help with a (traffic) ticket, or if you were in trouble and needed someone to put in a good word for you with a judge, he could just pick up the phone and call downtown.

"He was an ambassador of goodwill and probably had more influence on the lives of people who lived and worked in the Valley than anybody else," Buck said.

Pye said the patrons these days are mostly regulars, plus some people who work nearby. They serve a good lunch, he said, and it's a place where people feel comfortable.

It's not the same place it was a few decades ago, but it's a survivor, and there's certainly something to be said for that.

On the street, under the sign that proclaims the place "The Oldest and Last Club in Paradise Valley," I asked Pye what caused the move from 606 Adams.

"Stroh's needed space for a parking lot," Pye said, "so they bought all the buildings on the block and tore them down."

We looked across the street for a moment, to the place where workers are finishing the demolition of the Stroh Brewery.

Michael Pye shrugged and mumbled something about progress and went back inside the 606. ■

A modern Mary and Joseph found room for a little boy

Dec. 22, 1985

This is a Christmas story.

It's about a husband and wife. Their names are Mary and Joseph.

It's also about a little boy. His name is Larry.

The first names are real. Last names aren't important to the story, so there will be none.

It began during the holiday season about 13 years ago, Joseph recalls.

"Mary got the fine idea that we should go to the St. Francis Home for Boys and bring one of the kids who lived there home for Thanksgiving dinner," he said. "She thought it might be nice to get to know a boy there so that he could visit during the holidays and special occasions."

So the night before Thanksgiving, Mary and Joseph went to the St. Francis Home on Fenkell near Linwood, to pick up their young dinner guest.

A nun brought Larry in to meet them. He was 12. He had a wide grin, Joseph remembers, and big ears. His hair was cut in bangs low on his forehead. He was carrying two Kroger grocery bags, one in each arm, packed with his belongings.

"The first clue I got that something was wrong," Joseph continued, "was when I saw his baseball glove on top of one of the bags and a baseball bat sticking out of the other bag. I knew we weren't going to be playing much baseball on Thanksgiving day."

Joseph said he was still looking down at the smiling youngster when the nun asked where they planned to send Larry to school. She had already made out the school transfer forms, she said, but did not include Larry's last name because she thought Mary and Joseph might like to use their own last name.

"By that time I was in a state of shock," Joseph said.

Joseph quickly tried to explain to the nun that it was their intention to limit the extent of their involvement with the boy to Thanksgiving dinner, but she interrupted him and said quietly: "He thinks you're going to keep him. I didn't have the heart to tell him you weren't."

Mary and Joseph took Larry home that night — and kept him.

Their oldest daughter was married, and they had a son a year older than Larry.

"He was a kid who needed a home," Joseph said, "and we had room.

183

And Mary is a very giving person, a person of great heart."

Larry was not an orphan. He was from a broken home, and the first 12 years of his life had not been particularly good ones.

When he moved in with Mary and Joseph he couldn't read, write or tell time. He also had serious behavioral problems.

"He was truly Saturday's Child," Joseph said. "He was in five schools in five years. None of the schools would take him back."

Although most of the trouble he managed to find was small trouble, he always seemed able to find more than his share.

"One Halloween night," Joseph recalled, "he came running into the house and shot upstairs to his room, which was unlike him. A few minutes later there was a very large policeman at our door."

He told Joseph that Larry had fired a BB through a neighbor's window. Joseph told the policeman he would fix the window.

"Then he told me the window was three stories high. It cost me $750 to have it repaired."

What Larry had, Joseph said, was an uncanny talent for antagonizing people. "He could have walked into the College of Cardinals and started a riot in 10 minutes."

When they took Larry to Lafayette Clinic to try to get a better understanding of his problems, the doctors there suggested he would do better in a male-dominated environment.

He was accepted at Boys Town, ran away once, and was taken back. They taught him welding there, Joseph said, and got him a job in Omaha.

"We used to hear from him, usually around Christmas," Joseph said, "but we haven't heard now for about three years. He was in St. Louis for a time, and we heard later that he was living on an Indian reservation in South Dakota.

"He is a very resourceful person. Street-smart. An aggressive, hard-working kid. He'll do all right."

Larry is 26 now, but to Mary and Joseph their strongest memory continues to be of a little boy on the night before Thanksgiving, his world crammed into two paper bags, smiling up at the people he believed had come to take him to live with them.

Two people with an abundance of love who could not find it in their hearts that night to say no to a little boy who needed all the love he could get.

Merry Christmas. ∎

Suppose there were no party but somebody came anyway

Jan. 22, 1984

The wonderful thing about strong personal convictions is the absence of any overwhelming need ever to test them.

We are usually so convinced of their correctness that we simply accept them as valid and let it go at that.

I have always believed, for example, that people who live in Detroit and Michigan are largely congenial and hospitable folks, willing to extend themselves for friend and stranger alike.

I believe also that, under the right circumstances, it is entirely possible for a stranger to blunder into the wrong house and still be received warmly by the people there. It is a conviction I have always accepted as an article of faith, nothing I have ever tested. Until Christmas week.

Even then, it was hardly a calculated test conducted under controlled conditions. My wife and I simply walked into the wrong house and made ourselves at home.

We had been invited to the Christmas party given each year by the Free Press' The Way We Live department.

It was at the home of Pat Anstett, assistant editor of the department. She and her husband, Tim Kiska, who is a city desk reporter here, live in a nice house in Grosse Pointe Woods.

We pulled up in front of a nice house in Grosse Pointe Woods, parked the car and headed for the front door.

We rang the bell, eager to get out of the cold and into the eggnog. The door was opened by a smiling woman.

I did not recognize the woman but assumed she was Pat Anstett's mother, Irene. I decided to establish a point of identification by harking back to Pat and Tim's wedding two years earlier, the first and last time I saw Mrs. Anstett.

"Merry Christmas," I said, adding: "The last time I saw you you were dancing."

It was a calculated risk, but my percentage of getting away with things like that is higher than the national average.

I didn't give the woman a chance to respond and brushed past her and into the house.

I took off my coat and handed it to her.

185

My wife removed her boots, then she, too, handed over her coat.

All of us were in the front room and the woman with our coats was strangely silent, but still smiling. My wife was looking around for some signs that there was a Christmas party anywhere close. In the meantime, small but important messages were starting to get through to me.

Messages like: If The Way We Live is having a party here, which was supposed to start an hour ago, where are all the people from The Way We Live? And, why is it that the only people in this house act like they live here?

I decided to confront the issue.

"You know what?" I asked. "We may be in the wrong house."

"I wouldn't be surprised," said the lady with the coats, starting to laugh.

Her husband walked into the room and introduced himself. He was dressed for mixing paint, not making merry. His wife was laughing harder now. I knew we were in the wrong house.

After some discussion it was determined that we were at the right address, but on the wrong street. Missed the Kiskas by two blocks.

The people who live there are Phyllis and Bill Beaudry. They were not having a party, but invited us to sit down and have a drink — as long as we had our coats off.

Bill is in charge of the advertising production department at J.L. Hudson and the other people in the house included their kids: Paul, 22, who had just graduated from Western Michigan University, and one of his friends; another son, Peter, 19, and daughter Jenny, 16. Jay, 14, was not home and missed all the fun.

I asked Phyllis Beaudry why she let me in.

"The doorbell rang," she said, "and here are these people coming through the door saying 'Merry Christmas.' I am thinking, 'Who are they?' and then I decide, 'Well, they know me so I must know them.'

"I figured they must be friends of Bill's and I am saying to myself, 'Where is he? I can't hold this together very much longer.' I am bad on faces, but if I stall long enough I can usually remember. But now I am thinking, 'Phyllis, this time you're not going to pull it off.' When I realized that you had the wrong house, all I could do was laugh."

We eventually took our leave of the Beaudrys and got to the party, but not before being invited back to their house for a Super Bowl party.

Like I was saying, this town is a place where people are naturally friendly.

You can test it yourself, if you like.   ■

The kindness of a stranger
saves a dog from the streets

July 22, 1984

This is a short, happy story about a dog.

A story that began sometime before last New Year's Eve, when a large, black dog ran away or was abandoned by its owners.

It was a pretty dog, with a dense, dull, black coat. A Newfoundland, with maybe a trace of Labrador somewhere in her bloodlines.

She was somebody's dog once. Loved and pampered, with a place to run, a place to sleep and maybe even a dish with her name on it.

How she ended up as one of the thousands of stray dogs that roam Detroit's streets may never be known.

What is known about the handsome black dog dates from the day Keith Muir saw her in a Shell station at E. Jefferson near Alter.

It was last Dec. 31, New Year's Eve, and he was making sure he had enough gas for the holiday weekend. It was a cold day. The temperature would go to zero that night.

"I had filled the tank," Muir said, "and I looked inside the station and saw her. A beautiful, black dog."

Keith said he assumed the dog belonged to the station owner. She did not.

"He told me she was a stray," Muir said. "She had been hanging around the station and he brought her inside with him after she nearly got killed in traffic."

Muir asked the station owner what he was going to do with the dog when he closed that night for the weekend. "He told me he was going to have to push her outside."

It's difficult to drive or walk in the city and not notice the dogs.

They move through the streets, alone or in packs, but with a quickness that leaves the impression that they are always on the way to someplace. That if there is nothing else on their schedule, there is at least a sense of destination.

They are invariably skinny, often frightened. Living off refuse and handouts, dodging traffic, trying to survive without help. Unwanted. Invisible.

When I see them, I often wonder if they were ever somebody's dog. If they can remember happier days and children who brushed them and scratched them and took them for walks. Who romped with them, fed them under the table at suppertime and who let them lick their faces.

Or are they simply incidental reminders of the harshness of city living, whelped in an empty building or vacant lot somewhere, existing the only way they know.

Dave Wills, executive director of the Michigan Humane Society, says the life span of a stray in Detroit is something under two years. Automobiles take a dreadful toll, he says; his organization picks up 25 to 35 injured stray dogs every day.

But on New Year's Eve, Keith Muir was not concerned with statistics.

"I knew the dog probably belonged to somebody," he said. "She had no license, but was wearing a choke chain. So I took her to the Grosse Pointe Park police station and they took her."

The police sent the dog to a nearby veterinary hospital, and the following Tuesday Muir, a Comerica Bank vice-president, called the vet to see if the dog had been claimed. She had not.

"I asked him what he was going to do with her," Muir said. "He told me he would put an ad in the Grosse Pointe News and if no one claimed her she'd be turned over to the Michigan Humane Society. If they couldn't find her a home they would put her to sleep."

When no one answered the ad, Muir — whose St. Bernard, "Maudie," had died a few weeks earlier — went to the vet and took the big dog home. "She was too beautiful to end up any other way," Muir said.

He ran more ads in the local paper and in the Free Press and News. No responses.

Then one day he took her out to Rochester, to Leader Dogs for the Blind. They accepted the big, black dog who had since been named "Tar" by Muir's 16-year-old son, Cameron.

On March 21, the Muirs heard from the folks at Leader Dogs. They were told that "Tar" had become the 6,606th dog to graduate from the special training school in Rochester.

"You can be justifiably proud of 'Tar,' " the letter went on, "for as you know, not more than 30 percent of all dogs accepted actually complete Leader Dog training. One more deserving blind person has been placed back in the mainstream of life — because of your generosity."

Charles G. Schepel Sr. of Grosse Pointe Woods is 81 and blind. His new leader dog is about two years old, but nobody really knows for sure.

Her name is "Tar," and she was found on New Year's Eve in a gas station in Detroit by a man who cared. ∎

A promise to Irish Nellie
for a stone with a Celtic cross

March 31, 1985

Nellie Sarver was 86 when she died on April 8, 1982.

They buried her in a corner of Mt. Elliott Cemetery, across the street from St. Bonaventure Monastery, a few miles from the apartment at Cass and Myrtle where she spent the last years of her life.

Her friends called her "Irish Nellie," and she represented, as well as anyone ever has, the strength of spirit of the people who live in that part of Detroit we call the Cass Corridor.

They are the ones for whom getting through each day is often a personal challenge — and for whom the only reward for dealing with that challenge successfully is trying to do it all again tomorrow.

No one remembers exactly when they made their promise to Nellie. The promise that when she died, they'd see to it that her resting place would be marked by a fine stone topped with a Celtic cross.

But she died that Holy Thursday, content in the understanding that the promise had been made and that her friends would see to it that it was honored.

She bought the plot, close to her beloved Capuchin monks, after seeing it advertised for sale in a newspaper classified ad. All she needed, she thought, was her own piece of ground. The stone would come later. Her friends had promised to take care of it.

But promises to the dead have a way of being set aside for the more pressing considerations of the living. Nellie's grave is still unmarked, and the lack of an appropriate memorial is apparently troubling her.

The Rev. Russell Kohler seems a little bit uncomfortable talking about it, but says: "I have been hearing from people who knew her, and they tell me they keep dreaming about her and the marker. One person called from Newport (near Monroe) to tell of being awakened in the wee hours with a clear visit from Nellie asking when she's going to get her Irish tombstone."

Father Kohler is director of the Pope John XXIII Hospitality House at Second and Alexandrine, a facility for cancer outpatients and their families. It is a place that Nellie Sarver took to her heart.

"She took an active interest in the welfare of the cancer patients here," Father Kohler says. "She would buy things for them, go shopping for them. She'd save what she could from her Social Security and bring

189

us things that we needed. Just before she died, she gave us a leather-bound Bible with giant type. She said it would be her last gift to us. Like she was getting things in order.

"I have to admit that when I was getting ready to decorate the house for St. Patrick's Day, my train of thought kept being interrupted by thoughts of Nellie and our promise to get her a stone. Maybe it's because one of the things she did every year was get the house ready for St. Patrick's Day."

Nellie's story is probably not a lot different from her Cass Corridor neighbors', only Nellie wrote it all down one August day in 1980. Her life in 10 pages, handwritten in ballpoint pen on both sides of five lined sheets of notepaper.

It talks about her Irish-born grandparents. About her parents' divorce when she was two, about her childhood years in St. Anne's Foundling Home in Washington, D.C., and later at the St. Vincent's Orphan Home and the Good Shepherd Convent in Baltimore.

No bitterness, no self-pity, no tears for things that might have been possible. Just her memories.

"I often think of those days at Christmas time," she wrote. "We had so much, and we learned so much Latin. I loved to sing the high mass. Oh, my heart was broken when I had to leave St. Vincent's. That was my heaven on earth. I could sing tenor, soprano, alto, contralto. Years ago I had a chance for movies, but my father said no. He was terrible about everything I had a chance for. I could write a book, but no one would believe it."

She came to Detroit in 1922. She cleaned houses for a living, and later worked in small manufacturing plants. In her last years she was a familiar figure in the neighborhood, walking with one crutch because of arthritis. In 1979, she told a Free Press reporter: "People ask me how I keep on going. I tell 'em it don't do no good to cry."

Father Kohler said she was "the spirit of the Cass Corridor." He said her friends are going to recognize that spirit by getting her the grave marker they promised.

Everybody who knew her feels that Nellie should not be required to spend any of her time in eternity pressing her friends for something already promised. ∎

His poetry always returns
to the streets of Detroit

March 2, 1986

The Daniels family lived right across from the church, which may have put them in comfortable proximity to God, but which also deprived them of any reasonable excuse for being late for mass.

Jack Daniels was in my room and died when we were in the 10th grade. I'm not sure now, after 40 years, just what it was he died of. Appendicitis, maybe. But in a school as small as ours, the death of a classmate was a major tragedy, and understanding specifics of the cause of death never seemed important.

When Jack's older brother, Ray, graduated from St. Rose and got out of the Army, he married a girl from Annunciation and they moved into a flat on Harding.

Ray later moved to Warren, where he and his wife, Mary, raised four boys and a girl.

I don't know how many years Mr. and Mrs. Daniels continued to live in their house across from the church, but it seemed that every time I drove down Beniteau it was clear they were still there.

While other houses seemed to reflect the harder times that slowly overtook that block, the Daniels' house, always brown and yellow, looked as I had always remembered it.

Along with the church across the street, it was an encouraging constant in a neighborhood that was finding it increasingly difficult to be encouraged about anything.

The church is gone now, and so are the Danielses. Ray and the kids came over one day and moved them out to Warren.

One of Ray's boys, Jim, is an assistant professor in the English department at Carnegie-Mellon University in Pittsburgh. He teaches poetry, and he also writes it, most of it about Detroit.

It was in a new book of Jim Daniels' poetry that I found out the circumstances of the move from Beniteau. He calls it: "Moving My Grandfather."

> He wouldn't move
> after fifty years in the same house.
> He put a burglar alarm sign on his door
> a chewed-up shoe in his yard
> a baseball bat by the door

191

though he had no alarm, dog, strength.
He didn't carry a wallet.
Pinned money to his shirt
but had no sign for that.
He got jumped often
for change not worth
kicking an old man's ass for.
Last time they cracked his skull
blood in his white hair.
He came out of the hospital
lobotomized by fear
sitting in his front room
listening to the street.
We packed up his belongings
three broken TVs
a stringless harp from the burned out
church across the street.
My father cried its music
up and down the stairs.
We loaded up fast, in daylight
one truckload. No one could figure out
how to free the rocking chair
chained to the porch so we left it
creaking in the heavy air.

There is a lot of the pain and hardness of Detroit in Jim Daniels' poetry, even though he is only 29 and has lived in Pittsburgh for the last five years. He writes about the city's frustrations and the hopes that linger just beneath the toughness of the people who live here. About its factories and its supermarkets. Its snowstorms and unemployment lines.

His grandfather worked for Packard for 50 years. His father, Ray, is a cost analyst for the Ford Motor Co., where he has worked for 32 years.

The auto worker in his poetry is called "Digger," but he is every person who ever built a transmission or turned a bolt on an assembly line.

Daniels' book is called "Places/Everyone," and it costs $7.95. You can buy it at Maximus & Co. in Birmingham, i Browse in West Bloomfield, Marwil Book Store on Cass near Wayne State, and the bookstore at the University of Detroit.

I like Jim Daniels' poetry because Detroit is a place poets should care about. And he does. He writes about the places and the people we all know. Places like the house where his grandfather used to live. It's still there, across from the lot where the church stood.

It could use a few coats of brown and yellow paint. ∎

8. Characters I have known

The job paid chicken feed, but Rupert didn't mind

June 1, 1986

In the beginning they were a team: Rupert and Zenobia.

Rupert played the piano, Zenobia did a little dancing. Nothing fancy, mind you, but the audience never failed to respond warmly.

"Rupert was a real showman who loved every minute he was on stage," Joe B. Sullivan says. "Even when he was sick, the minute he came on stage he was full of pep.

"But Zenobia never really liked to perform. I don't think she liked people. Besides that, she was mean."

So somewhere along the way, Joe and Rupert decided that show business was not really for Zenobia and dropped her from the act. From that point on, Rupert worked alone.

Joe handled the bookings, and Rupert continued to delight crowds in several states doing four or five shows a day.

What ever happened to Zenobia?

"I don't really remember," Sullivan says now, "I think she probably ended up in somebody's stew."

It was not a surprising fate for such an unfriendly chicken.

Rupert, a personable rooster, continued his career in show business until he died.

Sullivan decided that a career in law probably offered a more substantial future than stage-managing performing poultry. He finished law school at the University of Detroit. He is now a judge on the Michigan Court of Appeals.

How he ended up in a traveling show with a couple of chickens is, actually, a reasonably uncomplicated story.

"I was just out of the Army, recently married, going to U-D at night," he says, "and I was looking for work."

He took a job in sales promotion in 1947 with the Larrowe division of General Mills. Among its other products, Larrowe made chicken feed.

It was just another job until the head office in Minneapolis heard of a researcher at the University of Minnesota, Keller Breland, who was teaching animals to do things not normally expected of animals.

Sullivan says Breland had taught pigs to play the piano, an instruction that ended when the pigs grew and 300-pound piano-playing pigs became hard to handle.

General Mills decided to use a couple of Breland's trained chickens —
Rupert and Zenobia — in sales promotion. When the act went on the
road, Sullivan, by then the company's sales manager, was sent along.

At trade shows, fairs and conventions, Rupert drew the crowds and
Larrowe's sales force sold the feed.

"Rupert played poker," Sullivan says, "played a little three-card
monte, did his own version of the shell game and answered arithmetic
questions."

He also played the piano, with the help of wires, for Zenobia's
unenthusiastic dance routines, but card-playing was his passion.

"He never lost a poker game in his life," Sullivan says, "because we always played with a marked deck."

Sullivan would deal the cards face-down from a 15-card deck to
Rupert and two designated members of the audience.

"Rupert would get first pick," Sullivan says, "and he'd pace up and
down, studying the cards like he was thinking it over, even though he
knew which cards he was going to choose."

The mark was a tiny black dot in the wheel hub of the bicycle design
on the back of the deck. It was too small for the audience to notice, but
Rupert pecked unerringly at the marked cards.

"He'd always end up with four aces or a straight flush or a full house,"
Sullivan says.

He played the shell game with a marked shell, and rang a bell in answer to arithmetic questions. He would continue ringing until Sullivan
triggered a device that fed Rupert a kernel of corn.

"All I had to do was wait until he had come up with the right total on
the bell and then slip him the corn."

Rupert died in 1952, after two seasons on the road with Sullivan.
Sullivan, who by then had his law degree, left General Mills a short time
later.

He speaks of his old friend Rupert with convincing affection and
genuine fondness.

"I had a real soft spot in my heart for that chicken," he says. ■

They lead serious lives now, but it wasn't always that way

Jan. 31, 1982

I have no intention of turning this weekly effort into a gossip column.

Gossip is information with only a minimal foundation in truth, trafficked in by people with no regard for quality of material.

What I have here is information that is elevated from common gossip status by virtue of its firm footing in fact. In other words, I know a bunch of good stuff about some people, it's all true, and I'm willing to share.

There are a number of people around town whose importance to the social, political and industrial success of the area is unquestioned. Also unquestioned, fortunately for them, are a number of eminently questionable episodes in their backgrounds that do not appear in their official biographies.

Cases in point:

• State Court of Appeals Judge Vincent J. Brennan is central casting's perfect jurist. White hair for wisdom, deep blue eyes for compassion, square jaw for justice evenly and fairly administered. Not the kind of guy you'd suspect of messing with people's religious dietary laws.

But in 1949, Judge Brennan and his accomplice, James McCormick, currently a leading bond broker in Detroit, went into the corned beef business at the State Fair to help pay their tuition at the University of Detroit.

But their sign, attesting to the kosherness of their product, was questioned by other State Fair entrepreneurs, and it was not long before a representative of a local Jewish organization dropped by.

"Is this really kosher corned beef?" he asked.

"Strictly," Brennan replied.

"Made under rabbinical supervision?"

"Absolutely," said Brennan.

Unconvinced, the man told them to change the misleading sign to read "Kosher Style," or he would pursue the question with State Fair officials. A complaint was filed, but not in time to keep the two from moving an awful lot of not-very-kosher corned beef that had been carefully prepared at home by their mothers.

Under rabbinical supervision?

"No," says the judge, "but only because we didn't have a rabbi on our block."

197

• Anthony O. Weiss and Bernard J. Mullins are important public relations executives, Weiss with Anthony M. Franco Inc. and Mullins with Chrysler Corp. They are successes in their field, admired by their colleagues, respected by the media.

One December night in 1956, Mr. Weiss and Mr. Mullins, in those days known simply as Tony and Moon, entered the Stone Burlesk on Woodward and ordered the houselights up. Then they ordered the patrons up and began a series of interrogations and identity checks, while a nervous stripper waited on stage for the audience to sit down and the music to start.

After 20 minutes or so, Tony and Moon thanked the patrons for their co-operation, bade the show go on, and left.

At the time, Mullins and Weiss were reporters for the old Detroit Times. They looked enough like cops to guarantee that none of the patrons in the Stone that night was inclined to do anything foolish like ask to see a badge.

• Herbert D. Levitt is an administrator of the state Supreme Court, an important and serious pursuit in the judicial scheme of things in Michigan. His good friend is Joseph N. Hartmann, deputy managing director of the Wayne County Road Commission.

They have teamed up on a number of projects over the years, perhaps the most intriguing being the Good Friday afternoon in the late 1950s when they sheared the neckties off a couple of dozen unwary people in the pressroom in the old Recorder's Court.

They summoned the unwary victims — judges, lawyers, bailiffs, clerks, newsmen — to the pressroom, pounced on them and lopped off their ties with a pair of shears.

The remnants of the ties were taped to the wall (where they remained on display for a number of years) and the victims then became participants, eagerly awaiting the arrival of fresh cravats.

In the interest of even-handedness, I will admit to minor participation in the events outlined above, with the exception of the shameless dietary deception by Brennan and McCormick. I was in those days — as my mother will attest — easily led.

And the fact that the people involved in these doings, again with the exception of Brennan and McCormick, were newspapermen at the time, should in no way reflect negatively on that profession anymore than it should reflect badly on the professions in which these individuals subsequently took refuge.

All now lead serious lives, full of reflective content in keeping with their station. I just thought you'd like to know what they were like when they were operating out of an entirely different station. ■

For Flash and his neighbors, the feeling was parimutuel

March 20, 1983

Ask Flash Thomas why he's still part of a neighborhood that stopped being part of him years ago and he'll tell you: "I like it here. I'm loyal. You can call me the Coleman Young for this part of town."

Flash has been part of the lower east side neighborhood since the day he and his wife and their two-year-old son moved into the lower flat on the northeast corner of E. Jefferson and Lycaste in 1932. The Shine family moved in upstairs six years later.

The paradox of Flash Thomas in those years — the 1930s and 1940s — was that when he dressed for work he dressed better than anybody else in the neighborhood. But then he never got any farther than the firehouse on the corner of Jefferson and Hart. And we knew he wasn't a fireman.

His day would be spent on the corners, under the marquee of the Hudson Hotel, at the soda fountain in Jacqueline's Sweet Shop, on the top step of the Union Bar and just inside the big, green folding doors of Engine Co. 32.

It became clear at some point that what Flash was doing was providing a vital service to the residents of our working-class neighborhood. Serving as a conduit for people too busy to leave their homes or their jobs to visit the nearest thoroughbred racing facility to participate in the parimutuel opportunities available there.

Flash was simply on hand to accommodate whatever modest wagers his neighbors were inclined to make, providing quick, reliable service while keeping a minimum of records.

There was never a negative stigma attached by others in the neighborhood to the kind of work Flash Thomas did. He was a provider of service as much as any other neighborhood merchant.

We lunched together in Kopitzke's, over on Mack, a couple of weeks ago. Flash was elegant in his brown, three-piece tweed. A silk, polka-dot kerchief that matched his tie drooped with contrived casualness from his coat pocket. He won't talk about his age, which I put at somewhere beyond the mid-70s. He talks instead of his prowess as a disco dancer. He says his footwork is legendary at such diverse institutions as Pinkey's Boulevard Club, Little Harry's and the Monday night singles gathering at the Polish Century Club.

There's a trace of toughness in his voice that reflects the character of the sometimes mean streets of the east side that have been so much a part of his life. But the face, with deep, soft lines, is friendly, even gentle.

"I have no plans to retire," he offers. "I'll start thinking about retirement when I die."

So he's still a regular in the neighborhood he moved into more than 50 years ago, and he has no immediate plans to change any of that, even though the neighborhood isn't what it was in the years before World War II.

"I don't want to move anywhere else. Don't want to live anywhere else. I've been down here a long time and I like it. The only thing I worry about is what I've always worried about. Getting hit on a big bet."

In what amounted to a bit of informal social commentary, Flash did allow as how the police, with more important things to be concerned with these days, pay less attention to incidental violations of the gaming statutes than they once did.

"One time I got convicted and all I had in my pocket was a scrap of paper with the name of a horse written on it," he says. "Another time I get picked up and I've got a grocery list my wife gave me before I left the house. The police think it's code, and they keep me half a day while they're trying to figure out what the list really means."

Policemen from the nearby Jefferson Station keep an eye on Flash now to make sure nothing happens to him. "He's pretty much a part of this neighborhood," one said, "and we want to be sure that he's all right."

Flash came to Detroit in 1923 from Pittsburgh where, he says, he was invited to leave by the sheriff. "I used to get in a lot of fights," he says, "and the sheriff wanted me gone."

He did not feel he was leaving much since his last Pittsburgh job was with Westinghouse at nine cents an hour.

His wife, Lillian, died several years ago, and his son, Jim, who has two children, lives in California where he has his own business.

The Thomases moved off Lycaste in the mid-1940s to another house on Detroit's east side. He has been there ever since.

There's nothing in our conversation that day which hints of any impending change in his life.

"I have been," Flash says with a smile that would convince you a five-horse train is a cinch bet, "a bookie all my life." It's a statement that implies his intention to keep things that way. ∎

It was a desirable address for the living and the not so

May 16, 1982

The code words were conceived not so much in a spirit of subterfuge as they were to protect command officers from any undue alarm, which might have occurred had they detected the presence of an unusual number of police cars in Elmwood Cemetery.

Besides, only a small number of policemen understood the cryptic references over the police radio to a place called, alternately, "Bill Barclay's" or "Barclay Square."

No. 1 Cruiser would arrange to meet No. 7 Cruiser at Barclay Square, or a scout car would simply inquire on the radio if there were "any cars making Bill Barclay's." There were always a number of affirmative responses.

Barclay Square was actually a quiet spot in the middle of Elmwood Cemetery, recorded officially in the cemetery office as Lot 168, Section Q. It has been, since the 1800s, the final resting place of the William Barclay family.

In later years, it became a temporary resting place for a handful of Detroit police officers who found in that place a quiet respite from the often mean streets of Detroit. A place where it was possible to take some comfort in the proximity of people who were beyond violence and whose peace was eternal.

Elmwood is probably the city's most distinguished cemetery. A place where Detroit has buried its prominent citizens since 1846 in a manner fully compatible with their stations in life. A place where the architecture of the dead rivals that of the living. A place with names rich with the history of Detroit — Alger, Cass, Blain, Stroh, Hendrie, Standish, Trowbridge, Newberry, Bethune, McMillan, Duffield.

Add to that illustrious roster the name of Ricktor (Ace) Gutowsky, Detroit policeman. Permanent resident of Barclay Square, courtesy of his friends who felt a promise was a debt owed.

Gutowsky was assigned to the Seventh (Mack) Precinct and was one of those who spent what quiet moments they could at Barclay Square.

He claimed lineal kinship with Detroit Lions running back (1934-38) Leroy (Ace) Gutowsky. Ricktor Ace never bothered to reconcile the obvious conflict that the family of Leroy Ace was from Oklahoma and his family was from Detroit. But his friends never asked him to. They called him Ace anyway.

Sgt. Carl Apfel, now with the police Special Events Section, and Patrolman Don Wandzel, of the Harbormaster Bureau, had both worked as partners with Gutowsky.

Wandzel gave Gutowsky the highest accolade one policeman can give another. He said he was a good cop. "He saved my life once," Wandzel said. "Got a guy off me who was cutting me with a knife. Saved my life."

Apfel recalls Gutowsky as a person with an enthusiasm for living. "He was a real character. Full of the devil." Both recall Gutowsky's fondness for that gentle spot in Elmwood they all called Barclay Square.

They remember when Gutowsky made them promise that if anything happened to him, they would see to it that he was buried in Elmwood. In Barclay Square, so he'd always be near his friends.

Gutowsky was 28 when he died. He was killed Aug. 15, 1968, when his scout car hit a bus while he was chasing a traffic offender. He left a wife and three children, including a daughter 13 days old.

His Barclay Square friends remembered their promise. The cemetery agreed to let his friends and family bury him in an unplatted portion of the place that had come to be known as Barclay Square.

They got him a nice bronze marker, at a good price, from a monument maker at Mt. Elliott and Farnsworth. It lies flush with the ground, a few yards from William L. Barclay's impressive block of granite.

It reads: "Ricktor Ace Gutowsky. Husband-Father. 1939-1968. He Loved People & Laughter."

If there's any conversation on the police radio about Barclay Square anymore, nobody's talking about it.

"Every now and then," one retired sergeant said, "you'll see a scout car there with some guy, usually an old-timer, sitting on the hood eating a sandwich. But it's not like before."

One day this spring, Barclay Square belonged only to the Barclays and to Ace Gutowsky. Last fall's leaves scraped across the empty road and wisps of children's shouts carried on the April breeze from Duffield Elementary School. Sounds of life in a dead place.

Barclay Square was as peaceful as it ever was. And kind of lonely.■

Rose Bowl or bust, on a thumb and a prayer

Dec. 29, 1985

The University of Michigan is not going to the Rose Bowl this season, but then neither is Ed Breslin.

The last time Breslin went, he did it the hard way, because his editors at the Detroit Times — who believed reporters should do everything the hard way — thought it would make good reading. Which it did.

Breslin was one of that wild crew of Times reporters of the '40s and '50s who are remembered as much for their personal antics as for the stories they wrote.

Edward T. Breslin was among the most irrepressible of that questionable collection of journalists who made the Times, which closed in 1960, one of the liveliest dailies in the country.

Breslin is now 59, retired from General Motors public relations and living in Dearborn Heights.

But in 1947 he was 21 and fresh from the copyboy ranks when his city editor, John MacLellan, called him in and told him he was going to the Rose Bowl. In 1948, it was to be Michigan against Southern California.

"I couldn't believe it," Breslin recalls. "I was planning to take vacation time to drive out there with my friends anyway; now I was going to get to go first-class. On the train with the team, or maybe even fly out there. And the paper was going to pay for it."

That was not what MacLellan had in mind.

"He told me that I was going to hitchhike to California," Breslin said, "and after I got there I'd have to figure out a way to get into the game for nothing. He told me to take $50, and if I got there without spending it all and got into the game, the Times would reimburse me. Otherwise I was out the $50."

The plan was for Breslin to write daily accounts for the Times of his adventures on the road to Pasadena. And the paper was betting him $50 that he wouldn't make it.

One public relations problem popped up the day after the first story about Breslin's trip appeared in the Times.

"The people at Taylor's Market at Allendale and Grand River, in my neighborhood, took a sausage jar, punched a slot in the lid so you could drop coins in it, and put up a sign saying something like, 'Help Ed Breslin get to California because the Times is too cheap to pay his way.'"

Breslin said the Times got the market to drop its fund-raiser after explaining that he had agreed to the deal.

Breslin got the assignment on the morning of Dec. 10, 1947 and was on the road that afternoon.

"MacLellan asked me if I could get a gun," Breslin remembers. "When I told him I could, he said it might be a good idea to take one along for protection."

Breslin had already decided against going armed when another Times reporter, Jack Crellin, warned him that if he took a gun, MacLellan was going to call the police and tip them off about a gun-toting hitchhiker.

"He figured it would start things out on an interesting note," Breslin said.

Another restriction imposed by the kindly editors of the Times was that none of Breslin's rides could exceed 100 miles.

"They said that if the first driver who picked me up was going all the way to LA, it wouldn't be much of a story.

"A lot of drivers thought it was strange when they stopped and asked me how far I was going and I'd tell them just to let me out after we had gone 100 miles."

In his stories, datelined Chicago, St. Louis, Kansas City, Tulsa, Dallas, Tucson and points west, Breslin spoke of his rides, kept readers informed on his financial condition, and told how he cadged free meals or lodging from friends in various towns.

Breslin got to Los Angeles on Christmas Eve with $27.34 remaining of his original $50. He had nine days to figure out how to get into the game.

He called actress Betty Hutton, a former Detroiter, at home. "She said she didn't have a ticket and would have stood in line to get me one, but she was eight months pregnant."

He decided to sneak into the Rose Bowl four days early and hide until game time. "I got caught and chased out the first day."

The day before the game he was able to convince a local DeSoto dealer, who provided the cars that would carry the U-M team into the stadium, to let him drive one.

On Jan. 1, 1948, after 2,700 miles and nearly 50 rides, Breslin drove a maize-and-blue DeSoto into the Rose Bowl and watched from the Michigan bench as the Wolverines won, 49-0. He had $8.58 left.

"They (the Times) were good sports about paying off," Breslin said.

"But I don't think MacLellan ever forgave me for turning in 99 hours of overtime."

It's called the last laugh.   ∎

'You should be a reporter' was advice he took to heart

March 7, 1982

Mitch Kehetian's news instincts were sharpened in the early 1950s at a very basic level. The Detroit Times paid him a dollar every time he called in a news tip that Times editors deemed newsy enough to be worthy of at least minimum recompense. A fire here, a traffic accident there. It wasn't the big time, but it was a beginning.

Then there was the time they carried the guy out of the First and Last Stop Bar on a stretcher and covered with a sheet. The bar came by its name as a result of its proximity to Woodmere Cemetery.

"I was pumping gas at my brother's station across the street, and when I saw them haul this guy out, the first thing I thought of was to call the Times," Kehetian recalls. "The editor I talked to loved it. Carting a stiff out of the First and Last Stop Bar. It was perfect."

The editor loved it enough to tell Kehetian, "You should be a reporter, kid."

When Kehetian found out later that the man he assumed was dead had merely passed out, he was crestfallen.

"I had to call the Times back the next morning and tell them I was wrong," he says. The editor was no less impressed."You should still be a reporter," he told Kehetian. "I've got a lot of reporters here that would never call me and admit they were wrong."

Kehetian grew up in Delray, and after a couple of years in the DeSoto plant, he upgraded to a job in his brother's service station and continued to flood the Times with tips.

Kehetian decided that life behind a gas pump held little allure. He wanted to work on a newspaper, and one day he put on his suit — the one he bought for his wedding — took a collection of stories he had written as a reporter for his Armenian Youth Club, caught the Lafayette-Green bus and headed downtown.

"I was on the bus trying to decide which paper I wanted to visit first," he says, "and I picked the Times because I liked William Randolph Hearst." Kehetian's affection for Hearst carried little weight with the crusty editors of the Times. They were unimpressed with his education (a 1948 diploma from Southwestern High), his professional experience (DeSoto and the gas station) and his writing samples (a collection of club notes from his Armenian youth group).

The editors told him to go to college, get some experience on a small paper and come back in a few years.

"On the way out of the newsroom, I passed the office of the managing editor," Kehetian says. "He looked like a nice old guy, so I walked in and told him how much I wanted to be a reporter at the Times."

Managing editors are, traditionally, softies and pushovers, and the Times' managing editor was no different. He hired Kehetian as a copyboy.

Kehetian said he was struck in those early months by the practiced cynicism of the reporting staff.

"There was a city desk editor on midnights who would get these terrible coughing spells, and the reporters would sit there watching him, saying things like, 'Choke, you bastard!'

"Once he got so sick that word came in that he was not going to make it," Kehetian says. "The reporters immediately started a pool on when he was going to die."

They also decided that it was only fair to let the editor himself participate. Kehetian was told to call him in the hospital and make the offer.

"He sounded pretty bad, but he was pleased when I told him the boys were having a pool and thought he might like in on it. He said to put him in and to thank the guys for their thoughtfulness. Then he asked what the pool was for. 'It's for when you're going to die,' I told him. He dropped the phone, and I hung up."

The editor recovered, but he never saw the humor in the situation.

Kehetian became a reporter, survived the collapse of the Times in 1960, worked in public relations until his doctor told him his skin rash was caused by his job and is now managing editor of the Macomb Daily.

His elaborate mustache and gray hair make him look more like the head man of an Armenian village than a newspaper editor, a marked contrast to the fresh-faced copyboy a soft-hearted editor hired in 1953.

When I asked him for a vintage picture of himself, he sent along his 1956 Detroit Times press card with a note:

"Everyone said I would never get a press card. So when I fooled 'em, I vowed to keep it for life and bury it with me with some soil from Armenia, and a picture of my wife . . . Damn, I wish I was 25 again and at Times Square and Cass." ∎

He thumbed his nose at protocol and blew his nose on evidence

Nov. 25, 1984

Probably because he understood the imperfections of the newspaper process better than most people, Joe Umek decided it was risky to assume that when he died, his former colleagues would handle news of his passing with dispatch and precision.

So I was saddened, but not surprised, when I was called one afternoon in late October by a woman who wanted to know where to send the obituary information on Joe Umek.

"I'm sorry to hear that he died," I said.

"He's not dead," she responded. "But he's very sick and he wanted to prepare this himself and asked me to call you with it."

The friend put the obituary in the mail, and Joe Umek died that same week in Harper Hospital. He was 69.

Umek's most recent profession was lawyer, but his close friends always considered him a newspaperman who happened to take up law.

Joe Umek was from Calumet and came to Detroit with his parents as a child.

In the obituary he prepared, Umek said of himself: "He left home at an early age and was hired as an office boy at the now-defunct Detroit Times newspaper."

The obit does not tell how he walked into the Times newsroom that day in the mid-1920s and asked city editor Henry Montgomery for a job as a copyboy.

Montgomery, busy with the work of the day, looked up at him and told him to come back later. Five minutes later Umek was back at Montgomery's desk. "Is this late enough?" he asked. He was hired.

John Montgomery, the son of the city editor, remembers another element in that hiring.

John, also a former Times reporter and currently a public relations executive in Detroit, recalls: "Three weeks after my father hired Joe Umek, he called him into his office and was furious with him. 'You're only 12 years old!' my father shouted at him. I could go to prison for hiring someone your age. You lied to me. Why didn't you tell me you were only 12?' Joe looked at him as if it was the dumbest question he'd ever heard: 'If I didn't lie, you wouldn't have hired me.' "

But, adds John Montgomery, "I don't know anybody that didn't like

Joe Umek."

The Times eventually made Umek a reporter. Another Times reporter, Bob Madigan, remembers him as a man with a skepticism for all things official.

"I remember him coming up to me when I was a 19-year-old reporter and telling me: 'Kid, always remember that nothing's on the level, not even bass fishing.' "

During World War II Umek joined the U.S. Maritime Service and saw action in the Atlantic and Pacific war zones.

"When he got back here after the war," Madigan says, "he came back with a lot of money, some kind of torpedo zone pay. He moved into the Statler Hotel, which was a pretty fancy place for a reporter in those days. He liked good food and the horses, so his prosperity lasted several months and he was soon reduced to the same poverty level as the rest of us."

Umek's colleagues were always impressed with his drive to educate himself. He finished high school while he worked as a copyboy, and after the war got his law degree from the Detroit College of Law.

As a reporter, he was assigned for many years to coverage of the police and courts.

While working the police beat, Umek was involved in an incident that people still remember and laugh about.

He had come late one day to the room in which a police trial board was being held. An officer had been accused of theft while investigating a suspected burglary at a jewelry store.

The only material evidence was a piece of tissue found in the policeman's possession, which had been identified by the store owner as the same paper he used to wrap his merchandise.

Umek, suffering a bad case of the sniffles, sat down next to the main table and rooted in his pockets for a handkerchief. Finding none, he reached over the table, picked up the piece of tissue, wiped his nose with it and dropped it in the wastebasket.

Corporation Counsel Nathaniel Goldstick interrupted the proceedings to announce that they would be unable to proceed with the case because "the gentleman from the Times has just blown his nose in Exhibit A."

The folks from the Times gather this month at the Press Club to mark the 24th anniversary of the closing of that newspaper.

They will take time, I'm sure, to talk of Joe Umek, and of how much he will be missed. ∎

Mixing glamor with garbage and trashing a grand jury

Feb. 5, 1984

It sometimes troubles me that today's newspaper reporters might not be having as much fun doing their job as they should.

There's no empirical evidence I can provide to substantiate this concern. It's just a feeling I have, and I trust my feelings. Not because of their remarkable reputation for validity, but because I have so many of them. Besides, Tony Weiss feels the same way.

I understand that daily journalism puts tremendous pressures on the people who do it for a living and that reporters take their work seriously, as they should. Those who don't usually drift into something that demands less of them.

But none of this means that the work cannot be enjoyable from time to time and, in the odd instance, even a lot of fun.

When I was trying to convince the Free Press in 1955 to elevate me from copyboy to reporter, I was required to take a series of tests from our newly acquired personnel director.

There were IQ tests, a psychological evaluation, and some kind of occupational preference test that plainly showed that I should be either a teacher or social worker. The personnel man urged me to find a nice school somewhere and go teach in it.

The next thing he said panicked me.

"I believe," he said, "that you are blinded by the glamor of this profession and that's why you want to be a reporter."

"My God," I thought. "He knows!"

That was exactly the case, and I thought I had managed well during my copyboy years not to let it show.

A six-month tryout as a reporter was offered and things just went along from there.

I was a reporter for seven years; I have been an editor for 21 years. Being an editor is nice. Being a reporter was fun.

Which brings us to Tony Weiss.

Tony was a reporter for the Detroit Times with an acknowledged reputation as a cutup. He stopped being a reporter in 1960, when the Times stopped being a newspaper.

We covered Macomb County for our newspapers in the late 1950s. When we get together we never talk about how good we were as reporters, but about how much fun we had.

Like the time we were covering a one-man grand jury investigation into corruption in Macomb County. Grand jury coverage is tedious and boring and information is hard to come by. To pass the time, the reporters, including Weiss and Stewart Didzun of the Detroit News, started a Hearts game in the corridor outside the grand jury chambers.

County officials decided that a non-stop card game added little to the decorum of the hallway. So they built a cubicle in the corridor to house the press and keep the card game out of sight.

Witnesses arriving to give testimony immediately assumed the cubicle was an information booth and would approach it seeking further instruction. Our jobs suddenly became much easier.

What the witnesses got were several questions concerning the thrust of their testimony and their involvement in the investigations.

An angry assistant state attorney general would emerge from the grand jury chambers periodically, warn us about the secrecy provisions of the proceedings, and tape a hand-lettered "PRESS" sign on the cubicle. A sign that always ended up taped to the door of the rest room.

Then, Weiss remembers, there was the day the witness walked out of the chambers and asked for a favor.

"He was ashen-faced and perspiring and told me about all his records being in the trash at home. Then he gave me a number and asked me to call and tell his wife to burn the garbage.

"You want me to tell her do burn the garbage or don't burn the garbage, I asked him. He said, 'Do burn the garbage.'"

Weiss reported the request to the grand juror, Judge Timothy Quinn, of Caro.

"The State Police and the assistant attorney general went to the guy's house and picked up the garbage," Weiss remembers, "and brought it back to the judge's chambers. They spread it all over the place and there was absolutely nothing there but garbage."

The judge thought it was funny. The witness said it was all a misunderstanding. The assistant attorney general was convinced that Weiss had conspired with the rest of us to make him look foolish. The corridor smelled awful for two weeks.

I'm going to lunch with Tony Weiss next week. We'll talk about how much fun it all was and how we miss it.

I might even admit to him after all these years that I really was blinded by the glamor of the profession.

And I still am.   ∎

Where is Bullet? A mystery of the highest caliber

June 5, 1983

It is the most puzzling mystery to survive the administration of the late mayor Jerome P. Cavanagh and it continues to perplex serious students of urban politics.

What ever happened to Bullet?

It is a question that the people involved are unwilling to discuss in any forthright way. They are quick to minimize their connection with the mystery, referring questioners instead to others "who know more about it than I do."

Bullet was — and perhaps still is — a dog. A black and white springer spaniel.

It was the Cavanagh family dog, although it really was the pet of young David Cavanagh, who was 12 when he got the dog as a pup in 1967. He was nearly 14 when Bullet disappeared without a trace.

The dog lived in the Manoogian Mansion, the mayor's residence, where the responsibility for his care shifted quickly to the mayor's police detail. It was, it can be said safely, a responsibility greeted with less that gracious acceptance.

"For openers," one former member of the police detail said, "Bullet didn't like living in the mansion and was unco-operative in our efforts to make our relationship with him a mutually rewarding experience." The officer, who asked for anonymity to protect his pension rights, described how the arrival of Bullet changed the routine of the police detail.

"There was always a lot to do anyway," he said, "but now it was our job to feed Bullet, walk Bullet, take Bullet to the groomer, take Bullet to the vet, let Bullet out, let Bullet in, clean up after Bullet and go out and find Bullet every time he ran away. Every morning the day detail would be told by the shift they were relieving not to forget to 'raise the flag and feed Bullet.' "

He said the officers were generally unhappy that handpicked members of the mayor's security detail carried the additional burden of caring for Bullet. He said also that though the officers were scrupulous in caring for Bullet, they often directed remarks toward the dog not altogether fit for the ears of a puppy.

"We called him Bullet," David Cavanagh recalls, "because he could run so fast. The cops would chase him, but they never could catch him."

211

"I was driving down Dwight on my way to the mansion one morning," the former security officer said, "and I saw Bullet heading up the street like a rocket with Ken Hady (now commander of the Seventh (Mack) Precinct) right behind him, waving his gun and shouting for the dog to halt."

Free Press reporter Brian Flanigan talks to policemen better than most reporters. I asked him to talk to former members of the security detail — most of whom have progressed well in the ranks of the department — about what might have become of Bullet.

Cmdr. Hady: "I really think Bullet, who was such a wonderful animal and loved by all of us, fell in love and ran away with his bride to sunnier climes."

Inspector Isaiah McKinnon: "Whatever happened to old Bullet? Frankly, I really don't know, but it was always my understanding that love took him. He began keeping late hours and one morning he just didn't come home. But as the junior member of the team, my main jobs were to raise the flag and feed Bullet."

Inspector Gerald Solai: "I have no independent knowledge of the animal. I think he left when he reached the age of 21, which legally made him an adult."

Cmdr. William Dwyer: "I don't know what happened to Bullet. All I know is that one afternoon either Hady or Solai took him to the manicurist and that's the last I saw of him."

Inspector David Patterson: "I never touched that dog! Listen, I was only there for nine months. Shine was there for years. Ask him."

Sgt. William Shine (retired from the Police Department, and related to me as younger brother): "The last time I saw Bullet he was getting into the limousine with Hady. Hady came back and Bullet didn't."

David Cavanagh, a junior planner with the city, remembers only that "we let him out one night and he never came back."

How did the police detail react? They didn't react much at all, a former member of that group says. "It was just that one morning we showed up for work and the shift we were replacing said don't forget to raise the flag. That was all."

One police department source, not widely celebrated for his reliability, says that Bullet was taken to Canada by person or persons unknown, given a new identity and placed with a family there.

But nobody really knows for sure.

If they keep case files on missing dogs, the case of old Bullet, the speedy springer, is still open. ∎

9. Reflections

A neighbor's watchful eye
kept order from the porch

Sept. 12, 1982

It may not be a generally accepted principle among specialists in urban affairs, but it still made a lot of sense to me.

This theory maintains that the decline of the American neighborhood can be traced directly to the disappearance of the front porch.

It was proposed to me one day at lunch by Patti Knox, an assistant vice-president of Boblo who knows more about cities than she does about boats or roller coasters.

"Think about it for a minute," she said. "Porches were where the people spent most of their time, and they knew everything that was going on in the block. Let a stranger walk up to a door of somebody's house and the lady on the next porch would call out to him: 'She's gone to the store. Be back in half an hour. You can wait on the steps or come back.' You'd need 38,000 cops to even start to provide that kind of protection, and it still wouldn't be half as effective."

Ms. Knox pointed out that porch sitters were the original Neighborhood Watch, and among those being watched were the kids.

"It was impossible to get away with anything because the people on the porches were watching. They'd either make you stop or tell your parents. Neighbors on porches were a major deterrent to juvenile delinquency.

"And when you'd come home from school and the door was locked because your mother wasn't home yet, there was always one neighbor on her porch who would be waiting for you and she'd feed you milk and crackers in her kitchen until your mother showed up."

The replacement of the American front porch by concrete slabs suitable only for pots of geraniums and doormats is not suffered gladly by Patti Knox. "You can walk or drive down most streets now and not see anybody. They're either inside watching TV or out in the yard cooking. At one time, we used to go to the bathroom outside and eat inside. Now we've reversed the entire process."

It's not exactly true that the front porch has disappeared totally as an architectural appendage to all the houses in Detroit and the suburbs. I made a limited tour of some Detroit and suburban neighborhoods and found that although there are still lots of houses with substantial front porches — mostly in Detroit — they are being underutilized. Lots of porches, not many people sitting on them.

I didn't see one porch swing. You know, the kind with the chains that were hung from hooks that screwed into the porch ceiling and squeaked so comfortably. I didn't hear the tinkle of wind chimes or music from a single radio playing softly in a window.

There was, however, one glider, on a porch on Pallister in the New Center Commons development. It was, unfortunately, draped with a green plastic cover even though it didn't look like rain. The lack of serious porch furniture on many of the other lovely old porches in that area concerns me. Is it possible for an old neighborhood to make a comeback if the porches aren't an important part of the revival?

Reflecting on Patti Knox's theory, I was surprised at how many fond memories I had that involved porches.

Busy time on the porches was from suppertime until bedtime. Acceptable dress in a working-class neighborhood was work pants and undershirts for the men, cotton housedresses for the women. Acceptable topics for conversation: What a good job FDR was doing and why Wendell Willkie didn't have a snowball's chance; whether or not we could stay out of war if England got in; politics, religion, the auto industry and trade unionism.

Lawns were watered by the head of the household wielding the hose from a sitting position on the top step. Drinks of water were also available from the hose and the brassy sensation of the nozzle on the tongue and the rubbery taste of the water added to the delight.

Our next-door neighbor surveyed the entire block from the seat of her wicker rocker. She was known to all of us as the eyes and ears of the world and we were sure she never blinked for fear of missing something.

Porches were, importantly, sanctuary from the depredations of the neighborhood bullies. Sovereign territory upon which trespass was forbidden. Reach the safety of the porch one step ahead of the pursuer and you were free to stand behind the railing and express your disdain for his behavior — keeping in mind, of course, that tomorrow you would probably have to leave the safety of the porch for school and the dangers of the playground.

You make a lot of sense, Patti Knox. This weekend I'm going to spend some time sitting on my porch. I might even slip into an old undershirt and water the lawn. ∎

For my first writing efforts, the canal was the best critic

April 17, 1983

Strange stuff, this writing business.

I have been doing it now, in one form or another, for nearly 40 years.

Since 1956, the Free Press has rewarded me generously for providing journalistic prose for its news columns. Everything from homicides to heartwringers. And, for the past 18 months, for this weekly effort.

The problem is, I am feeling a bit guilty about not spending more time appreciating the opportunity I have been afforded. My literary conscience was rustled a few weeks ago when I had lunch with a friend who is a talented and successful advertising executive.

He has planned and created successful ad campaigns. He is admired by his colleagues, respected by his clients, appreciated by the people who own the agency. And he is very good at what he does.

But what he really wants to do is write. I got the unmistakable impression that afternoon that he would give up all this advertising stuff if somebody would pay him just to write.

He had written some sample columns and brought them to the lunch. They were very good. He said he was looking for some way to get them syndicated.

He didn't come right out and say it, but the subliminal message that afternoon was that I was a singularly fortunate human being because I was doing what made me happiest. I was writing.

Maybe the reason I don't spend as much time appreciating this opportunity is because I have been doing it for such a long time. In fact, I do not remember a time in my life when I was not writing something, either for myself or for somebody else.

My earliest literary excursions were secret ones.

The neighborhood in which I grew up was not one which was particularly supportive of the arts. It was a place where the more practical considerations in life dominated contemporary thought.

When he found me in the back room of his butcher shop writing stories on wrapping paper instead of spreading the sawdust he was paying me 35 cents an hour to spread, old John Sullivan warned me: "This writin's fine for your school days, but you'd best learn something that'll make you a living."

So most of my non-academic writing was done furtively and out of

217

sight of other people.

I would take my spiral notebook to the most desolate expanse of landscape in the neighborhood. The deserted fields along the canals in the shadow of Detroit Edison's seven great smokestacks. The place we called "the dumps."

There, with no one to ask what I was doing, I would write. Essays, short stories and — God save me from the kids on the playground — poetry.

Since it was risky to my physical well-being to have this material available permanently on paper, I would tear up the results of my musings each day and solemnly commit the scraps to the forgiving waters of the canal.

Don't misunderstand, there was some critical appreciation of my writing then. Sister Clarissa, my eighth-grade teacher, told me she thought the composition I did for her entitled "Christmas on Tarawa," was thoughtful, sensitive and creative.

Actually, it was overwritten and poorly constructed, with one sappy analogy piled on another. I thought it was wonderful.

Then came my only writing encounter with the Detroit News.

The News devoted a page each week to what it called the Young Writers' Club. It was presided over by a person known in print only as Aunt Kaye. It carried writing — and drawings — submitted by kids.

I was 13 when I sent my first manuscript to Aunt Kaye. A poem.

I worried that Aunt Kaye might not like it. That she might laugh at its ragged meter and forced rhyming. That she would show it to her helpers and they, too, would laugh.

So, in the perverse logic of childhood, I submitted it under an assumed name. If they laughed, I reasoned, then they wouldn't be laughing at me.

Then one Saturday, there it was. In the News. My poem. And the made-up name. I seriously considered joining my earlier literary works in the canal.

It did not seem to me like an auspicious beginning to a writing career.

I put my real name on everything I write now, good or bad, and I have dropped none of my work in the canal since 1944.

And, since the lunch with my advertising friend, I have resolved to devote some time each week to being thankful that I'm doing what makes me happiest. ∎

In an alley or under lights, it has all the right stuff

May 30, 1982

There is a reason my heart is always a little lighter every year at this time.

It has little to do with the solstice or the sound of the robin being heard in the yard or the re-emergence of leaves on the trees and green in the grass.

It has everything to do with the emergence from athletic hibernation of little kids who play baseball.

I am, truth be told, a pushover for kids' baseball. Show me a bunch of kids under 18 playing ball and I'll show you a game I want to watch.

For 10 years I was commissioner of a Babe Ruth baseball league in my neighborhood and am still referred to in some circles by the courtesy title of "commissioner." I think it has a nice ring to it.

I took that job not because I enjoyed drawing up schedules, supervising tryouts and drafts, arranging for field time, rescheduling rainouts and cutting the infield grass. I took it because it gave me the perfect excuse — under the guise of community involvement — to spend much of the summer watching kids play ball.

There are those, of course, who argue that kids' sports today are over-organized and that the competitive pressure on the young athletes by peers and parents is less than good for their social and emotional development. And that it was a lot better when kids got together and played a pickup game among themselves.

I will concede readily that some adults take some of the fun out of the game for some of the kids these days. I am not ready to agree that playing in the alley between Hillger and Lycaste with a ball that buzzed when it sailed through the air because it was trailing a piece of frayed electrician's tape was really any more fun than playing on a team with uniforms, a schedule, regular opponents and trophies for the winners.

In fact, I think the opposite is true.

After years of alley ball, my first experience with organized baseball came when I was about 13 years old. I joined the Billy Rogell League, which was operated on our side of town out of the St. Clair Recreation playground.

There must have been 40 teams formed that first day and, even though I ended up on a team called the Parrots (all the good animal and bird names had already been picked by teams that got to choose ahead of us), I was delighted. It was hands-down better than any combination of all of the scrub games in all the vacant lots I had ever played.

So when I watch these kid games these days, I see the same enthusiasm for competing that I saw in the alley games. Even the fleeting tragedies of childhood games are relatively unchanged.

Last season I watched a four-foot center fielder circle a fly ball that eventually dropped through the fingers of his glove and bounced off the top of his head.

The tearful fielder picked up the ball and started running with it toward the infield. He ran through the infield, still clutching the ball and still crying, oblivious to the shouts of his teammates and to the runners from the other side frantically circling the bases.

He ran off the field, into the stands and the arms of his mother, someone every ball player needs at one time or another in his career.

He was back next game, catching more than he missed, yesterday's disasters just part of baseball history.

If kid baseball is, as some claim, hard on the kids, it doesn't do a whole lot for mothers, either. Especially mothers of pitchers. I have seen mothers of pitchers — including the one to whom I am married — live and die with every pitch.

At a game in Midland earlier this season I saw a mother, who had driven from Detroit to watch her son pitch, get up suddenly in mid-contest and leave.

She said her son always did better when she was not around, so she went back home.

If there was a prayer for mothers of pitchers, it would probably sound something like this:

O, Lord, You who asked that the little children be allowed to come to You, look with special kindness on this little pitcher. Keep his arm strong, his eye sharp. In Your infinite wisdom, let him understand that winning isn't always better than losing and help him learn to accept both graciously. And, Lord, if You can help him keep the ball down and away from time to time, I know he'd appreciate it. I know that in the grand scheme of things, it's not a major consideration, but it's awfully important to him. He's a good little boy, Lord, and he always looks so lonely out there. ■

Get the kids off the streets and back into the alleys

June 3, 1984

In light of the recent events surrounding the 1984 Summer Olympics, I believe the time has come to reclaim our athletic heritage and return it to its rightful place. The alleys.

In good faith, we turned America's games over to people who we believed would manage them in a way that would reflect favorably not only on the humble origins of these games, but on their humble originators.

These people convinced us that contests of skill belonged in the sports arenas of the world and not in the alleys of urban America. We believed all this — and we were wrong.

We turned our backs on alley games and things have never been the same.

There was a time when we resisted substantial pressure to move the games from the alley to the playground.

Even then we understood that there are games developed with the alley in mind. Games designed for playing areas 18 feet wide.

Activities tailored for those kinds of specifications were not transferred easily to the wide-open spaces of a playground.

Besides, access to the playgrounds was a sometimes thing, because of the likelihood of being run off in the middle of a game by toughs who decided they wanted the space you were using.

There was never that kind of problem in the welcome confines of the alley. If the playgrounds belonged to the bullies, the alleys belonged to the people.

I often wonder what kind of games baseball and basketball would be today if Abner Doubleday or James Naismith had grown up in a two-family flat in Detroit with a reasonably unobstructed view of the alley.

The unnatural hazards alone precluded any standardization of rules and had to be incorporated in any game plan before the event could take place.

If a telephone pole was in the way of your scrub baseball game, you made it first base. Any ball that disappeared into Mr. Phelan's ash pile was a ground-rule double. When the ash pile was taken away, so was the rule.

Harry Lencione, who was known as "Junior" in the neighborhood around Olympia Stadium where he grew up, is an advertising account executive at the Free Press. We were talking about all this the other day and decided that if we would have had an annual athletic contest in the alleys, it might have become the standard for cities everywhere.

The Detroit Alley Olympics. The west side versus the east side.

Home alleys would alternate each year and be chosen by a panel of the Alley Olympic Committee (AOC).

Neighborhood committees would propose alleys for consideration and submit their bids to the AOC.

The committee would take into consideration such things as how many people whose yards abutted the proposed alleys owned chow dogs, and the alleys' overall reputation for having residents who returned any balls inadvertently batted or thrown into their yards.

Recognizing that the social and cultural differences that divided the east side from the west side would be reflected in the kinds of games played and the way they were played, the AOC would have responsibility for standardizing the competition, as much as that would be possible.

In the Duck-on-a-Rock competition, for example, the AOC would have to decide whether to make the small Carnation Milk can or the small Pet Milk can the official Duck-on-a-Rock can of the Alley Olympics.

There would be no sponsors. We would accept no free empty cans from the condensed milk interests, opting instead to get them from the traditional source, the garbage cans.

At the opening ceremonies, competitors from both sides of the city would march together. The Duck-on-a-Rock and the Kick-the-Can teams; the Red Rover Teams; the Red Light teams; the Pom-Pom Pullaway teams; the Release the Prisoner teams; the Hopscotch and Tag teams.

There would be a float with the Statue teams, frozen in their most artistic poses, while the spectators applauded from garage roofs along both sides of the route.

Then would come the teams who would race scooters made from two-by-fours with roller-skate wheels, and the two-person cart teams (one driver, one pusher) in their vehicles with tomato basket hoods and baby-buggy wheels.

The Olympic torch would be carried by a team of runners with tin cans wrapped around their shoes.

It would have been wonderful. We could have written a whole new chapter in east-west relations. ■

One man's junk may be another child's jalopy

Oct. 27, 1985

People who have clean garages are devoid of any substantial sense of the past.

Garages are the repositories of contemporary history. People's museums.

If they had had garages in Pompeii, we would have even a greater knowledge of Pompeiian culture than we got from the paltry reminders people there left behind on the day Mt. Vesuvius surprised them.

Garages are the places where the days of our lives are measured by the artifacts stacked in the back, stored in the loft or hanging from the walls. The role of the garage as shelter for the car is secondary to its importance as keeper of our memories.

In my garage, for example, there is a collection of a dozen old bicycles in various stages of inoperability.

But each has its own story, each triggers its own memories of wide-eyed Christmas mornings, the excitement of birthdays, training wheels, scraped knees, children's tears.

Old bikes, no longer shiny, left behind by children no longer children, who have gone their own ways to build memories in garages of their own.

So it was with some genuine concern recently that I examined the impressive pile of goods that had been placed at my curb to await the arrival of the trash collectors.

It was, my wife told me, the inevitable by-product of a long-overdue garage-cleaning effort.

To her credit, she understands my inexplicable fascination with things nostalgic and carefully avoids tampering with anything to which I profess sentimental attachment. But she recognizes the existence of a clear distinction between sentimentality and what she calls useless junk.

So what was piled at the curb a few weeks ago qualified, by her definition, as belonging to the latter category.

I was willing, however grudgingly, to concede that the junk label could probably be modified to include the two old lawn mowers — a reel mower that has not run since the mid-1960s and an electric rotary mower that has not been used since I ran it over the cord a few years ago.

Nor was I prepared to argue in behalf of the perfectly good trailer hitch, the broken electric lawn edger, two aluminum storm doors, a plastic scuttle for charcoal, a rusty one-gallon gasoline can, the fertilizer spreader or the two mattresses.

But when I saw the scooter sitting there, I could not overcome the feeling that a little bit of my past was waiting for the DPW.

It was your classic homemade model — a couple of used two-by-fours, a piece of broomstick for the handle and wheels from an old roller skate. Easy as that, the perfect scooter.

I lifted it from the pile and took it for a test run up and down the block.

Two neighbors, Fred and Gloria Gieseking, stopped on their evening walk to see if I could ride the scooter up the driveway without falling. I didn't fall. There are some things you never forget.

We talked some about its basic craftsmanship, and I offered to give it to Fred, lest it fall into the hands of an uncaring junkman.

I think he was interested, but I could detect no enthusiasm from Gloria. They continued their walk without the scooter.

By this time, a crowd of neighborhood kids was looking on, attracted by the spectacle of this older person wheeling up and down the street on a strange contraption.

I immediately saw an opportunity for a generational breakthrough. Why should these children spend their lives never knowing the wonder of a toy that has not been mass-produced?

"Who wants a good scooter?" I asked.

Silence.

"Free," I continued my pitch. "A genuine, Depression-era antique. Made by hand. Not available in stores. One of a kind. Will never be advertised on TV or sold by Toys 'R' Us."

Chris Holley, who is 10 and lives on the corner, stepped forward. "I'll take it," he said. His friends giggled.

Before he wheeled it home, I explained that the scooter lacked a few adornments. Get an old coffee can and nail it on the front for a headlight, I told him, and find an old license plate to put on the back. For trim, try nailing a few pop-bottle caps to the sides.

I heard subsequently that the rear wheels were judged to be in bad shape and that Salena Przepiora, also 10, told Chris she had an old pair of skates he could have to replace the bad wheels. A very encouraging sign.

Now, if I can find four old baby-buggy wheels and a tomato basket, I'll bet I could teach these kids how to make a cart.

Happy days! ■

Sorting out my thoughts
on the route not taken

Nov. 14, 1982

I watched Charlie Gallagher deliver mail the other day, still trying to figure out what there was about the United States Post Office that my father found so intriguing.

Though he insisted that his three sons get a college education, Patrick Shine had this uncommon affection for the Civil Service.

He always seemed willing to let us decide our own career paths, but whenever I talked newspaper business, he talked Post Office. He didn't know a lot about the economics of publishing, but he found it hard to see much of a future for a business that sold its product for three cents a copy. A man, he said, especially a family man (something he assumed I would eventually become) needed something he could count on.

Something like the Post Office.

The government, he reasoned, would always be able to meet payroll, would always pay its pensioners — in full and on time. Even in hard times.

I think "hard times" might have been the key to it. He was proud that he never missed a day of work during the Depression. A circumstance he attributed to the ultimate dependability of his employer, the City of Detroit.

He retired in 1951 after 37 years as a streetcar conductor for the Department of Street Railways and its privately owned predecessor, the DUR. He died in 1969, still blessedly content that his theory of governmental solvency would prevail forever.

He would have been terribly disappointed.

But still, after 32 years at the Free Press, I think often about the Post Office. Especially in times of work-connected aggravation when a quiet mail route in a friendly neighborhood has immense appeal.

I must, however, confess that I have never been particularly taken with the snow, rain, heat and gloom of night stuff. Any one of those elements could very likely have stayed me from the swift completion of my appointed rounds.

Carrying the mail always had been an accepted and honored profession in our neighborhood. Some of the best did it, are still doing it or have retired from it. Dick Fleming, Don Lalonde, Charlie Conover, Ray Mackin, John and Bill Skipper, Dan Boone, Wally Hatcher, Harry

225

Galen, Bud Ross. And Charlie Gallagher.

It's been 30 years and 15 dog bites since Charlie started carrying mail on the east side, a job he took after being laid off at Hudson Motor Car Co.

I called Charlie to ask if I could spend some time with him on his mail route and maybe discover the mystique of the letter carrier that had somehow eluded me all these years. He was happy to oblige.

"What time are we starting?" I asked.

"Seven a.m.," he replied.

Since I was thinking more in terms of my established life-style, I made arrangements to meet him at the Grosse Pointe Branch Post Office at 9:30 a.m., after he had sorted his mail and before he started on his route.

Charlie is nothing if not brisk and businesslike as he moves from house to house, avoiding lawns and sticking to front walks that appear to have been purposely designed to make sure they do not provide the shortest route to the mailbox.

I ask him about his job as we walk along Huntington, a quiet street in Harper Woods.

"I liked this work when I started and I still like it," he says. "You have to like what you do and I like what I do. I like being outdoors, even in winter. I think I might even like winter best."

I worry when I find people who might be happier in their jobs than I am. Mostly because I think that's terribly important and because I want to be at least equally happy with the happiest .

"Must be healthy," I observe, "all this walking and the fresh air. How's your health?"

"Pretty good since the heart attack," he tells me. I find myself feeling better already.

That was two years ago, when he was 50. He was active then, he says, in the letter carriers' union and probably under too much stress.

Charlie lives in Richmond with his wife of 24 years and their four children. He's on the school board, involved in Boy Scouts and active in kids' sports.

We're about one-third of the way through the route and I tell Charlie I've got to get back to the office. I don't tell him my feet hurt and I'm starting to get cold.

I decide on the way back downtown that I'm happy that Charlie's happy and that we both probably made the right career choice.

I also decide that it's easier writing about all that walking than doing it. And just the thought of not having to be at work at 7 a.m. is enough to keep me happy indefinitely. ∎

An ointment for the ages
that your nose is sure to know

Feb. 10, 1985

It's a nice house. It sits on a bluff about three miles north of Lexington, with a big picture window that looks out on a bird feeder doing a steady business this time of year. Just beyond the feeder is the wintry expanse of Lake Huron.

It is the home of James T. Liddell. It is also the world headquarters of the Wonderful Dream Salve Corp.

Some of you may have vivid recollections of that amazing ointment with the strong, tarry smell and the unusual name. It has been a popular medicament around these parts since Hannah D. McDonald started dispensing it in Detroit in 1849.

Not many of my school days passed without one or another of my classmates arriving liberally lathered with Wonderful Dream Salve and as aromatic as a refugee from a road-tarring crew.

It was the day of the over-the-counter cure. When the local druggist was all the HMO you needed.

Patent medicine was a lot more popular — and a lot cheaper — than prescription medicine, and if you were able to find one with proven success for a broad range of ailments, you went with it.

So for bug bites, bee stings, rashes, minor burns, scalds, cold sores, cuts, scrapes, scratches, slivers, bruises, abrasions, infections, hemorrhoids, eczema and affiliated afflictions, Dream Salve, at 30 cents a tin, was the answer to a mother's prayer.

For all intents and purposes, Jim Liddell is the Wonderful Dream Salve Corp. He owns it and runs it out of his home near Lexington. He packs the flat red and white tins and ships them to individual customers and wholesale distributors.

And he answers the mail. People who use Wonderful Dream Salve are the kind of people who write chatty, friendly letters to the company.

Liddell is a retired Detroit pharmacist. He bought the Wonderful Dream Salve Corp. in 1962.

"I am only the fifth owner in 136 years," he says, "and I bought it because at the time I owned four drugstores in the Detroit area and life was getting a little hectic."

He made a few minor changes after he bought the company. "We took Hannah's picture off the can," he says, "and got a lot of mail complaining about it."

Actually, Hannah McDonald's glowering visage could hardly be considered an asset to attractive packaging. I always thought she was there to give visual impact to the warning that appeared on the tin, just over her likeness: "Beware of Imitations."

I asked Liddell what happened to the message that used to appear on the rim of the container, proclaiming the contents fit "For Man or Beast."

"The Food and Drug Administration asked us to take that off," Liddell says, "but in our literature we still say that it is good for the treatment of household pets."

Actually, it was while I was watching my dog getting Dream Salve applied to her inflamed forepaws by my wife that I decided to call Mr. Liddell and drive up one morning to corporate headquarters and talk about salve.

Liddell is 75 and his knees are giving him trouble. But he still runs the business himself, driving the 18 miles every day to the Post Office in Croswell to pick up the mail and then packing the orders in time for pick-up by the UPS driver.

He says he sells about 10,000 tins of the salve, mostly in Michigan and surrounding states. At $2.75 for a 34-gram tin (1.199 ounces), "It's not a lucrative business," he says. "But it's one of the best moves I ever made and it keeps me from getting into trouble."

A company in Roseville mixes the formula and packs the tins. The ingredients, which have not changed substantially since 1849, include oil of tar, turpentine oil and resin, olive oil, linseed oil, rosin, burgundy pitch, camphor, beeswax and mutton tallow.

Liddell allows that every now and then it is necessary to "root around a little" to locate mutton tallow and beeswax.

About the strong, tarry odor, he says: "Some people like it, others don't, so I'm going to leave it alone."

About the unusual name? "Legend is that when Hannah McDonald was a young girl in Detroit she got a terrible infection in her leg. The doctors said they would have to amputate it. One night she had a dream in which all these ingredients came to her. The next morning, she asked her folks to put them together and put it on her leg. It saved her leg and she later went into business selling the salve. I don't know if it's true or not. Probably just folklore."

True or not, it is probably the most interesting story that's ever been told about salve. ■

A devotee of the babushka look in a couture clash with maillots

Sept. 16, 1984

Days before the event, I had the sinking feeling that it was going to be the ill-starred matchup of the year.

Neal Shine and high fashion.

I had agreed, when the nice people at St. John Hospital called me, to say a few words at their fashion show fund-raiser.

It seemed like a good enough idea at the time. After all, it would be a perfect opportunity to speak to 1,100 women and say a few nice things about the expanded fashion coverage the Free Press had been planning.

Then I discovered, to my absolute panic, that they expected me to commentate the fashion show — to describe each outfit as the models spun down the long runway.

I tried to explain to the promoters of this event that my comments on women's fashions had been limited up to this point to unenlightened comments like, "Is that a new dress, or are you losing weight?"

"Just be yourself," they reassured me. I was not reassured.

I called Linnea Lannon, the fashion editor of the Free Press, and told her what I had been asked to do. Her response was direct. "What do you know about fashion?" Truth is not always a comfort.

At the Dawood Boutique, which was providing the fashions for the show, Toni Dawood was polite and helpful and tolerant of my dumb questions.

"We'll be opening the show with a nice collection of maillots," she said. "How nice," I replied.

I called Linnea again. "A maillot is a one-piece bathing suit," she explained. My state of mind was not improving.

Time was running out, and I decided that I had to fall back on a speaker's version of what old writers always tell new writers: "Write about the things you know about."

Did I know about fashion? No. Did I know about clothes? Yes.

All the people in my old neighborhood wore them, but the operative phrase was "serviceable" rather than "stylish."

It is reasonable to assume that my indifference to the purveyors of fancy clothing is directly related to my east-side origins.

In our neighborhood, for example, the peasant look was universally accepted. It said a lot for the social and economic status of the area.

Anyway, it was mostly what people were wearing when they got here, and they probably figured that if it was good enough for the boat, it was good enough for the east side.

High-fashion loungewear in that neighborhood meant a chenille robe that did not have a pocket ripped off.

One of the "looks" I learned about during my brief interlude in the glamorous precincts of high fashion was called Bohemian Black. I remember when that look meant that somebody's husband had died.

When I was in high school, all the girls wore their fathers' clothes, and it drove their parents — and the nuns — crazy. Now they call it "the Annie Hall look" and they have to buy the hand-me-downs new.

The three-quarter-length sleeve was also popular among girls then. But what it meant was that your arms were three-quarters longer than the older sister for whom the dress was bought.

"Accessorizing" meant deciding whether or not to wear a babushka.

I found out, too, during my research for this assignment, that people are spending money to be "color analyzed," to find out what their most flattering colors are.

We had a couple of simple rules about color. If it's a color not found in nature, it will probably make a nice sports jacket; blue and green should never be seen, and white socks will go with anything.

In the local clothing stores, items were called "classics" when they were left over from last year. Or maybe the year before.

Anyway, I managed to bumble my way through the event and came away impressed with how interested people seemed to be in high fashion. So I asked Linnea why.

"I often think clothes are like cars," she said. "When I listen to men talk about the cars of 25 years ago, they rave about those cars, describing exact details as if the car was in front of them. Generally, they were too young or too poor to own the cars they talk about, but they remember them as being fabulous."

Linnea says she is convinced that people like to look at clothes, even if they can't have them. "They're beautiful. They're exciting. They're different. They're an escape."

I couldn't agree more. I haven't felt the same about fashion since my first escape — in a gray gabardine overcoat and oxblood cordovans from Flagg Bros. ∎

Clothes may make the man, but underwear makes him worry

Oct. 21, 1984

It is my sincere belief that for generations of American children, life at home involved an endless series of maternal precepts.

"Eat your broccoli. Children are starving in (the location varied according to world economic conditions at the time) and would love to have that food." Or "Don't put that in your mouth, you don't know where it's been." Or "You are not leaving this table until your plate is clean." "Don't ever swallow chewing gum because it will stick to your insides." I could go on, but you get the general idea.

But of all the admonitions rained down on generations of young heads by their concerned mothers, the one that seems to have had the most lasting effect is: "Put on clean underwear. How would it look if you got in an accident and had to go to the hospital wearing those old things?"

We have, to our credit, managed to overcome most of these childhood instructions. We are not against swallowing gum when there is no other convenient way to dispose of it. We don't eat the broccoli or parsnips if we don't want, and we can leave food uneaten on a plate with no more than the usual amount of guilt. Underwear is a different story.

When my brother Jim got hit by a car while we were crossing Jefferson on our way to school, I remember hoping as they took him away in the police ambulance that he had put on clean underwear that morning. His injuries were minor. I never asked about the underwear.

I have always believed that if my mother were put in charge of medical operations for any kind of regional disaster, she would triage patients according to the condition of their underwear.

Admittedly, I had not given this subject much thought over the years until I went to Henry Ford Hospital one day to have a dermatologist, Dr. Clarence Livingood, examine some worrisome spots on my scalp.

When his nurse learned that this was my first appointment with the doctor, she told me: "Go in that room and strip down to your shorts."

"I just want him to look at the top of my head," I protested. But she insisted, and as she was leaving the room she smiled and said to me: "See. You should have listened to your mother." I was stunned. I was not wearing my best shorts and she knew it.

I feel that we've been friends long enough for me to discuss this with you.

You see, my boxer shorts fall into two general categories. A recent style in subtle, tasteful pastel shades with piping on the seams, which makes them look more like bathing trunks than underwear. And an older collection of white shorts, worn but serviceable. And a bit long in the leg, making them resemble the running shorts worn by the U.S. track team in the 1936 Olympics.

Neither the doctor nor his nurse commented on the Jesse Owens look of my underwear that day, but I found myself worrying more about that than about the diagnosis.

Since then, I have engaged in a little emergency room research and found that my concerns did not make me unique.

Among patients whose injuries are not terribly serious or life-threatening, says Yvonne Lesniak, an emergency room nurse at Detroit Receiving Hospital, "It starts as soon as they get here. The condition of their underwear seems to be a major concern."

Her co-worker, nurse Iris Pita, says: "There are always lots of apologies for the condition of their underwear. Sometimes I think it's the first thing they think of when we're undressing them. Men seem to worry more about it than women."

But Pita says she understands the concern. "My mother always told me the same thing, and I have told it to my own child."

Dr. Ronald Krome, who is head of emergency medicine at William Beaumont Hospital, Royal Oak, said my suspicion about the lasting effects of the underwear warning is "100 percent correct."

"I have never heard anyone apologize for their outer clothes not being up to par, but people really feel bad if they're not wearing good underwear," he said.

"A fellow came in here the other day, a construction worker. Some equipment had fallen on him. He told me he was sorry that he was a little dirty, but he had not planned to be here. I told him not to worry, because you can't stay clean working construction. Then he told me he was talking about his underwear."

When I finish this, I think I'll check the underwear drawer and consign some of the older stuff to the rag bag.

You never know when you might get in an accident. ■

Old grudges never die, but maybe they should

Oct. 17, 1982

After almost 34 years, I have made my peace with Jack Shook.

It was a decision not lightly arrived at, since I have a genetic tendency for simmering resentment.

But it seemed, somehow, the right time to set things straight and drop Mr. Shook from my selective roster of active grudges.

Grudges that are dated can distract you from the very serious business of dealing with contemporary resentments, so it is probably a good idea to purge the list from time to time.

It is not easy to sit here and admit to what might appear to some as a major character flaw. But I feel an obligation to expose a few minor truths about myself every now and then and keep the major character flaws a secret. I wish I felt worse about being an accomplished grudge-holder. The truth is, I have always felt that a good grudge can be a wonderful thing if you maintain a reasonable perspective.

A grudge that is bitter, corrosive or all-consuming is a grudge that has gotten out of hand.

A workable grudge is one you can call up on quiet winter evenings to fan the embers that have been cooled by the intervening years and bask in its warmth as you recall all the delicious details of the transgression. Control is vital.

In the 1920s a man sold my father shares of a worthless stock for $200. Whenever the memory of that unhappy transaction would begin to fade, my father would take out the worthless stock certificate and study it until the fraud was once again fresh in his mind.

When the man who sold him the stock died in the 1950s, my father studied the newspaper death notice for a while and then said: "I hope that when he gets to heaven, God asks him about the stock." He never mentioned the incident again.

Which brings us back to Jack Shook.

In 1948 Jack was a student assistant to the dean of men at Dowling Hall, then the downtown campus of the University of Detroit where I was a freshman.

His various duties included collecting rent on the hall lockers — 50 cents a semester.

For a reason that now eludes me, I failed to pay my half-buck on time and went home for semester break. When I returned, the lock on my locker had been removed. So had my books, my notes and everything else.

My textbooks had been sent to the bookstore to be sold second-hand. My notes, the diligent work of an entire semester, had been thrown in the trash. It was, it seemed then, a calamity of monstrous proportions.

I retrieved what books were still unsold from the bookstore — the notes were gone forever — and then went looking for Jack Shook.

I found him in the dean's office and he explained to me that rules were rules. No rent, no locker. The rules were on his side, but time was on mine.

For the last 34 years the memory of that incident has not ceased to rankle and I have bored countless people with the story.

A few weeks ago, in a chance conversation, his sister-in-law assured me that despite my academic disaster, Jack was really a nice fellow. His brother Bill, another friend of mine, told me several times that Jack was a good person and my years-old grudge was badly misplaced. So a few days ago I drove out to Royal Oak where Jack Shook sells Chevrolets for Matthews-Hargreaves. I told him why I was there. About the locker and the books and the notes and how it had been on my mind all these years.

He didn't remember any of it, of course, and seemed embarrassed by my vivid recollections.

"I sure don't remember doing any cruel things like that," he said.

It was my turn to be embarrassed. Here I was summoning up an insignificant incident 34 years old, and the more I talked about it, the dumber it sounded. I found myself apologizing to Jack Shook for the stupidity of it all.

He was, indeed, a nice guy. He has seven children and a lovely wife and a good job (for the past 16 years he has sold more used cars than any Chevy salesman in the Detroit zone) and seemed as pleasant as anyone I have ever known. I realized early in our conversation that I had wasted at least 34 years of creative brooding when I should have settled it at the time, on the spot, with one magnificent outburst.

On the way back to the paper that day I was amazed at how good I felt. I decided that I would reassess my grudge list and seriously consider a thorough, but selective, disposition of some of them. The thought of all that pleased me more than I would have imagined.

Maybe there's more to this forgive and forget stuff than I realize.■